Fashion Knitting

Fashion Knitting

Glamorous Ideas for all the Family

Edited by Pam Dawson

Orbis · London

Acknowledgments
Camera Press 7,34,35,37,38,50,52,54,58,62,68,
70,78,80,101,113,114,117

First published in Great Britain
by Orbis Publishing Limited, London 1984

© Eaglemoss Publications Limited 1983, 1984

This material previously appeared in the
partwork *SuperStitch*

Printed in Italy

ISBN 0 85613 638 7

Contents

Introduction

The exciting variety of yarns with their enormous range of colours and textures has brought knitting to the forefront of fashion. This collection of patterns for all the family gives new ideas for both traditional designs as well as patterns which are right up to date. You can choose from cool cottons, lightweight mohair and chunky yarns depending on the season.

Knitting for children is quick to do and saves money. There is a delightful layette for a new baby and young children will love the colourful fun motifs added to their jumpers.

The simpler styles with the minimum of shaping are ideal for the beginner while those with more detailed stitch patterns are rewarding to knit and repay the time and trouble taken.

Bear in mind that patterns often rely on colour or texture for effect so experiment with different colourways, especially on striped or Fair Isle patterns, or mix and match the cardigans and tops for a more co-ordinated look.

The patterns give both metric and imperial measurements but it is important you decide at the start which one to follow as they are not interchangeable. Standard abbreviations are used throughout and a complete list is given at the end of the book. If you are unable to find the recommended yarn, consult the yarn data on page 126 for spinners addresses and mail order stockists.

Always knit up a tension square before starting on the garment. Unless you obtain the correct tension it will end up too small or too large and the texture will also be altered. Cast on and knit four extra stitches and four extra rows than the tension recommended so that you can check the sample accurately. If it is larger than the recommended size you are working too loosely — change to a size smaller needles and work another sample. If it measures less — change to a size larger. The width tension is the most important — length can be adjusted by working more or less rows.

Use the pattern pieces charts to check the measurements. Block and press the pieces according to the instructions given on the ball band and always consult the manufacturer's instructions before washing or dry cleaning a garment. A useful guide to aftercare symbols is given on page 127.

Cool cotton jersey

This jersey with its pretty, full sleeves is worthy of a place in any leisure-wear wardrobe.

The clusters of grapes 'growing' up and over the right shoulder and down the right sleeve are knitted in to the fabric of the garment. The leaves are embroidered on afterwards . . . here they have been worked in three contrasting colours of embroidery silk but could be worked in one only, if you prefer.

Crocheted picot edging at the neckline adds a crisp finishing flourish.

Below: Knitted in cool cotton this jersey is a fairly simple shape. The picot edge can be omitted if you prefer.

Sizes

To fit 86 [91:97]cm/34 [36:38]in bust
Length to shoulder, 60 [61:62]cm/
23½ [24:24½]in
Sleeve seam, 30cm/11¾in
The figures in [] refer to 91/36 and
97cm/38in sizes respectively

You will need

8 [9:9]×50g balls of DMC Pearl
  Coton No 4 (100% cotton), in main
  colour A
2 skeins each of embroidery silk or
  cotton in each of 3 contrast
  colours, B, C and D for leaves
One pair 3mm/No 11 needles
One pair 3¾mm/No 9 needles
One 3.00mm/No 10 crochet hook

Tension

24 sts and 32 rows to 10cm/4in over
st st worked on 3¾mm/No 9 needles

Back

With 3mm/No 11 needles and A cast
on 102 [106:114] sts.
1st row (Rs) K2, *P2, K2, rep from *
to end.
2nd row P2, *K2, P2, rep from * to end.
Rep these 2 rows for 6cm/2¼in,
ending with a Rs row.
Next row (inc row) Rib 6 [5:7] sts,
*M1, rib 9 [8:10] sts, rep from *
9 [11:9] times more, M1, rib 6 [5:7]
sts. 113 [119:125] sts. **

Change to 3¾mm/No 9 needles.
Beg with a K row cont in st st until
work measures 40cm/15¾in from
beg, ending with a P row.

Shape armholes

Cast off at beg of next and every
row 4 sts twice, 3 sts twice and 2 sts
4 times. Dec one st at each end of
next and every alt row until
85 [89:93] sts rem. Cont without
shaping until armholes measure
20 [21:22]cm/7¾ [8¼:8¾]in from
beg, ending with a P row.

Shape shoulders

Cast off at beg of next and every
row 8 sts 4 times and 8 [9:10] sts
twice.
Leave rem 37 [39:41] sts on holder
for centre back neck.

Front

Work as given for back to **.
Change to 3¾mm/No 9 needles.
Commence bunch of grapes bobble
patt.
1st row (Rs) K30 [33:36] sts, make
bobble by K into front, back, front,
back and front of next st, making
5 sts, (turn, P5, turn, K5) twice, lift
2nd, 3rd, 4th and 5th sts over first st
and off needle – **called MB**, K to
end.
Beg with a P row work 3 rows st st.

5th row K28 [31:34] sts, MB, K3,
MB, K to end.
Beg with a P row work 3 rows st st.
9th row K30 [33:36] sts, MB, K3,
MB, K to end.
Beg with a P row work 3 rows st st.
13th row K28 [31:34] sts, MB, (K3,
MB) twice, K to end.
Beg with a P row work 3 rows st st.
17th row K26 [29:32] sts, MB, (K3,
MB) 3 times, K to end.
Beg with a P row work 3 rows st st.
21st row K24 [27:30] sts, MB, (K3,
MB) 4 times, K to end.
Beg with a P row work 3 rows st st.
25th row K22 [25:28] sts, MB, (K3,
MB) 5 times, K to end.
Beg with a P row work 3 rows st st.
29th row K20 [23:26] sts, MB, (K3,
MB) 6 times, K to end.
Beg with a P row work 3 rows st st.
33rd row K26 [29:32] sts, MB, (K3,
MB) 4 times, K to end.
Beg with a P row work 3 rows st st.
37th row K28 [31:34] sts, MB, (K3,
MB) 4 times, K to end.
Beg with a P row work 3 rows st st.
41st row As 33rd.
Beg with a P row work 3 rows st st.
45th row K28 [31:34] sts, MB, (K3,
MB) twice, K15, beg 2nd bunch of
grapes with MB, K to end.
Beg with a P row work 3 rows st st.
49th row K30 [33:36] sts, MB, K3,
MB, K15, for 2nd bunch of grapes
MB, K3, MB, K to end.
Beg with a P row work 3 rows st st.
53rd row K52 [55:58] sts noting that
first bunch of grapes has been
completed, MB, K3, MB for 2nd
bunch of grapes, K to end.
Beg with a P row work 3 rows st st.
Cont working 2nd bunch of grapes
to match first bunch, beg bobble
patt with 13th row and working
3 rows st st between each bobble
patt row until 41st bobble patt row
has been completed. Cont working
3 rows st st between each bobble
patt row.
89th row K50 [53:56] sts, MB, (K3,
MB) twice, K15, beg 3rd bunch of
grapes with MB, K to end.
93rd row K52 [55:58] sts, MB, K3,
MB, K15, for 3rd bunch of grapes
MB, K3, MB, K to end.
2nd bunch of grapes has now been
completed. Cont working 3rd
bunch of grapes to match first
bunch, beg bobble patt with 9th
row, *at the same time* shape armholes
when work measures 40cm/15¾in
from beg, ending with a Ws row.

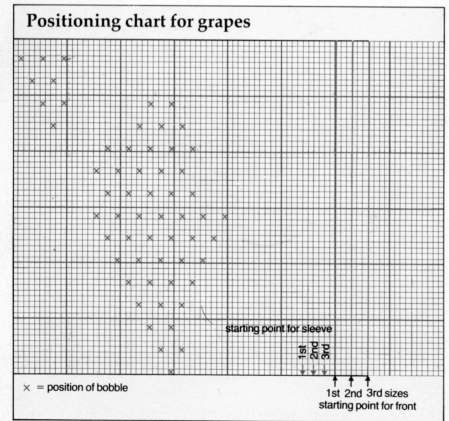

Positioning chart for grapes

starting point for sleeve

1st 2nd 3rd sizes

x = position of bobble

1st 2nd 3rd sizes
starting point for front

Shape armholes

Keeping patt correct throughout, cast off at beg of next and every row 4 sts twice, 3 sts twice and 2 sts 4 times. Dec one st at each end of next and every alt row until 85 [89:93] sts rem. When 3rd bunch of grapes has been completed, cont without shaping until armholes measure 12 [13:14]cm/4¾ [5:5½]in from beg, ending with a Ws row.

Shape neck

Next row K34 [35:36] sts, turn and leave rem sts on holder.
Complete left shoulder first. Cast off at beg of next and every alt row 3 sts once, 2 sts twice and one st 3 times. 24 [25:26] sts.
Cont without shaping until armhole measures same as back to shoulder, ending with a Ws row.

Shape shoulder

Cast off at beg of next and every alt row 8 sts twice and 8 [9:10] sts once.
With Rs of work facing, leave first 17 [19:21] sts on holder for centre front neck, rejoin yarn to rem sts and K to end. P one row.
Complete to match first side, reversing all shapings.

Right sleeve

With 3mm/No 11 needles and A cast on 66 [66:70] sts. Work 6cm/2¼in rib as for back, ending on a Rs row.
Next row (inc row) Rib 1 [8:10] sts, *M1, rib 3 [2:2] sts, rep from * 20 [24:24] times, M1, rib 2 [8:10] sts. 88 [92:96] sts.
Change to 3¾mm/No 9 needles. Beg

Right: Close up view of the grape motif showing the positioning and shape of the leaves for embroidery.

with a K row work 2 rows st st. **
Commence bunch of grapes bobble patt.
1st row K24 [26:28] sts, MB, K to end.
Beg with a P row work 3 rows st st.
5th row K22 [24:26] sts, MB, K3, MB, K to end.
Beg with a P row work 3 rows st st.
Cont to work first bunch of grapes as given for front, beg bobble patt with 9th row and working 3 rows st st between each bobble patt row until 44th row has been completed.
45th row K22 [24:26] sts, MB, (K3, MB) twice, K15, beg 2nd bunch of grapes with MB, K to end.
Beg with a P row work 3 rows st st.
49th row K24 [26:28] sts, MB, K3, MB, K15, for 2nd bunch of grapes MB, K3, MB, K to end.
Beg with a P row work 3 rows st st.
53rd row K46 [48:50] sts noting that first bunch of grapes has been completed, MB, K3, MB for 2nd bunch of grapes, K to end.
Beg with a P row work 3 rows st st.
Cont working 2nd bunch of grapes to match first bunch, beg bobble patt with 13th row and working 3 rows st st between each bobble patt row, *at the same time* shape top when sleeve measures 30cm/11¾in from beg, ending with a Ws row.

Shape top

Cast off at beg of next and every row 2 sts 14 times, one st 18 [20:22]

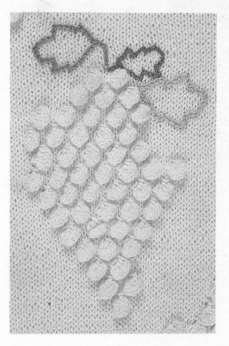

times, 2 sts 6 times, 3 sts 4 times, 4 sts twice and 10 [12:14] sts once.

Left sleeve

Work as given for right sleeve to **
Cont in st st only and complete as given for right sleeve.

Neckband

Join right shoulder seam. With Rs of work facing, 3mm/No 11 needles and A pick up and K18 sts down left front neck, K across front neck sts on holder, pick up and K18 sts up right front neck then K across back neck sts on holder. 90 [94:98] sts.
Beg with a 2nd row work 2.5cm/1in rib as given for back. Cast off loosely in rib.

To make up

Press each piece lightly under a damp cloth with a warm iron, taking care not to flatten bobble patt.
Embroider leaves at top of each bunch of grapes in three colours and chain st, as illustrated.
Join left shoulder and neckband seam. Sew in sleeves.
Neck edging With Rs of work facing and 3.00mm/No 10 hook work one round of dc all round neck edge. Join with a ss to first dc.
Next round 2ch to count as first dc, miss first dc, 1dc into next dc, *3ch, 1dc into first of these 3ch, 1dc into next dc, rep from * to end. Join with a ss to 2nd of first 2ch. Fasten off. Press seams.

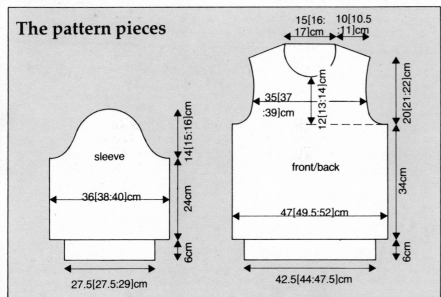

The pattern pieces

sleeve

14[15:16]cm

36[38:40]cm

24cm

6cm

27.5[27.5:29]cm

15[16:17]cm   10[10.5:11]cm

35[37:39]cm

12[13:14]cm

20[21:22]cm

front/back

34cm

6cm

47[49.5:52]cm

42.5[44:47.5]cm

Chunky designer sweater

Knit yourself this stunning sweater in 100% pure wool and you'll have a designer original worth a small fortune. It has wide sleeves cleverly set into framing panels of the main colour and a flattering turned-back neckline finished with a bright tassel.

Sizes

To fit 86 [91:97]cm/34 [36:38]in bust
Length to shoulder, 53 [58:63]cm/ 20¾ [22¾:24¾]in
Sleeve seam 42cm/16½in
The figures in [] refer to 91/36 and 97cm/38in sizes respectively

You will need

9 [9:9] x 50g balls of Sirdar Pullman Chunky 100% wool in main colour A
6 [7:9] balls of contrast colour B
1 ball of contrast colour C
One pair 5mm/No 6 needles
One pair 6½mm/No 3 needles

Tension

13 sts and 20 rows to 10cm/4in over st st worked on 6½mm/No 3 needles

Left: Notice the flaps on the shoulder line which can be worn raised or folded down towards the back of the sweater.

Note

Do not twist yarns at back of work when changing colours in st st patt: do twist yarns at back of work when changing colours between st st and g st side panels

Back

** With 5mm/No 6 needles and A cast on 65 [71:77] sts.
1st row (Rs) K1, *P1, K1, rep from * to end.
2nd row P1, *K1, P1, rep from * to end.
Rep these 2 rows 6 times more then 1st row once more. Change to 6½mm/No 3 needles. Commence patt.
1st row (Rs) Using A, K10 sts for side panel, using B, K25 [28:31] sts, using separate ball of A, K20 [23:26] sts and K10 sts for side panel.
2nd row Using A, K9 sts for side panel, using same ball of A, P22 [25:28] sts, using B, P25 [28:31] sts, using separate ball of A, K9 sts for side panel.
3rd row Using A, K10 sts for side panel, using B, K23 [26:29] sts, using separate ball of A, K22 [25:28] sts and K10 sts for side panel.

4th row Using A, K9 sts for side panel, using same ball of A, P24 [27:30] sts, using B, P23 [26:29] sts, using separate ball of A, K9 sts for side panel.
Cont in patt as now set until 40 rows of chart have been completed. Keep 9 sts at each side in g st throughout, noting that extra sts in st st are worked inside g st panels at each side on medium and large sizes.
Next row K10 A, K45 [51:57] B, using separate ball, K10 A.
Next row K9 A, P47 [53:59] B, K9 A.
Rep these 2 rows 4 [9:14] times more.
Next row K10 A, using same ball, K25 [28:31] A, K20 [23:26] B, K10 A.
Next row K9 A, P22 [25:28] B, P25 [28:31] A, using same ball, K9 A.
Cont in patt from chart again as now set until 12 rows have been completed, beg with 3rd row. Note that colours have been reversed on st st panel and that 10th st from right-hand edge will be in A on all rows and 10th st from left-hand edge will be in A on Rs rows and B on Ws rows. **
Cont in patt from chart until 40 rows have been completed. Break off B and 2nd ball of A.

Back neck and shoulders

Using A throughout work 10 rows g st across all sts. Cast off loosely.

Front

Work as given for back from ** to **
Next row K10 A, using same ball, K21 [24:27] A, K13 B, using separate ball, K2 A, using separate ball, K9 [12:15] B, using separate ball, K10 A.
Next row K9 A, P11 [14:17] B, P2 A, P14 B, P20 [23:26] A, K9 A.
Next row K10 A, K17 [20:23] A, K15 B, K4 A, K9 [12:15] B, K10 A.

Divide for neck

1st row (Ws) K9 A, P11 [14:17] B and leave these sts on a holder, join in C, K1 C noting that yarn is not twisted round next change of colour, P3 A, P16 B, P16 [19:22] A, K9 A.
Complete left side first on last 45 [48:51] sts.
2nd row K10 A, K13 [16:19] A, K17 B, K3 A, noting that yarn is not twisted round change of colour, K2 C.
3rd row K3 C, P3 A, P18 B, P12

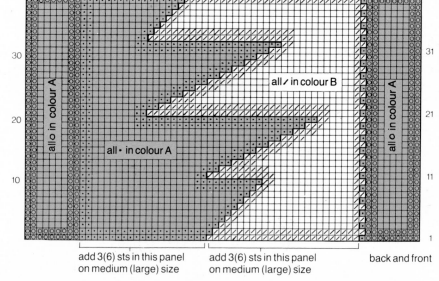

all o in colour A

all ∕ in colour B

all · in colour A

all o in colour A

add 3(6) sts in this panel on medium (large) size

add 3(6) sts in this panel on medium (large) size

back and front

o = garter st in colour A   • = st st in colour A   ∕ = st st in colour B   sleeves

11

[15:18] A, K9 A.
4th row K10 A, K9 [12:15] A, K19 B, K3 A, K4 C.
5th row K5 C, P3 A, P20 B, P8 [11:14] A, K9 A.
6th row K10 A, K15 [18:21] A, K11 B, K3 A, K6 C.
7th row K7 C, P3 A, P11 B, P15 [18:21] A, K9 A.
8th row K10 A, K13 [16:19] A, K11 B, K3 A, K8 C.
9th row K9 C, P3 A, P11 B, P13 [16:19] A, K9 A.
10th row K10 A, K11 [14:17] A, K11 B, K3 A, K10 C.
11th row K11 C, P3 A, P11 B, P11 [14:17] A, K9 A.
12th row K10 A, K9 [12:15] A, K11 B, K3 A, K12 C.
13th row K13 C, P3 A, P11 B, P9 [12:15] A, K9 A.
14th row K10 A, K7 [10:13] A, K11 B, K3 A, K14 C.
15th row K15 C, P3 A, P11 B, P7 [10:13] A, K9 A.
16th row K10 A, K5 [8:11] A, K11 B, K3 A, K16 C.
17th row K17 C, P3 A, P11 B, P5 [8:11] A, K9 A.
18th row K10 A, K3 [6:9] A, K11 B, K3 A, K18 C.
19th row K19 C, P3 A, P11 B, P3 [6:9] A, K9 A.
20th row K10 A, K1 [4:7] A, K11 B, K3 A, K20 C.
21st row K21 C, P3 A, P12 [11:11] B, P0 [4:7] A, K9 A.
22nd row K10 A, K0 [2:5] A, K10

Above: A back view showing the shoulder flaps and side panels framing the design.

[11:11] B, K3 A, K22 C.
23rd row K23 C, P3 A, P10 [11:11] B, P0 [2:5] A, K9 A.
24th row K10 A, K0 [0:3] A, K8 [11:11] B, K3 A, K24 C.
25th row K25 C, P3 A, P8 [11:11] B, P0 [0:3] A, K9 A.
Keeping colours correct cast off in patt.
With Rs of work facing, rejoin yarn as required and complete right side of neck.

2nd row Using C, cast on 6 sts, K6 C, K10 [13:16] B, K10 A.
3rd row K9 A, P12 [15:18] B, K5 C.
Rep last 2 rows 11 times more.
Keeping colours correct cast off in patt.

Sleeves

With 5mm/No 6 needles and A cast on 39 sts for all sizes. Work 15 rows K1, P1 rib as for back, inc one st at end of last row. 40 sts.
Change to 6½mm/No 3 needles.
Commence patt, noting that sleeve has a centre panel of 8 sts in g st.
1st row K15 B, K10 A, K15 B.
2nd row P16 B, K8 A, P16 B.
Rep these 2 rows 4 times more. Inc one st on the 4th st in from each end on next and every alt row 15 times in all. 70 sts.
40th row P31 B, K8 A, P31 B.
41st row K30 B, K10 A, K30 B.
Rep last 2 rows 4 times more.
50th row P26 B, P1 A, P4 B, K8 A, P4 B, P1 A, P26 B.
51st row K25 B, K3 A, K2 B, K10 A, K2 B, K3 A, K25 B.
Cont in patt from chart as now set until 64th row has been completed.
65th row K28 A, K2 B, K10 A, K2 B, K28 A.
66th row P27 A, P4 B, K8 A, P4 B, P27 A.
Rep last 2 rows until sleeve measures 49cm/19¼in from beg, or 7cm/2¾in more than required length. Cast off.

Bobbles

Using C, work bobbles at random in st st areas in B on body and sleeves.
To work bobbles, insert needle from Rs under the loop of a st and out again to Rs, (K1, P1, K1) into this loop, turn and K3, turn and K3 tog. Fasten off. Pull ends through to Ws and knot tog.

To make up

Press st st areas lightly under a damp cloth with a warm iron. Join shoulder seams including 6 sts in C at each side of neck, level with the first of the 10 rows of g st on back, allowing this g st section to stand up along back neck and shoulders.
Sew in sleeves beneath g st panels at each side of body. Join ribbing of body and sleeves seams on Ws. Join g st seams of body on Rs. Cut 7 lengths of A about 10cm/4in long. Make into a small tassel and fasten off with C. Sew to end of collar.

The pattern pieces

31cm | 8cm | 34cm | 7cm | 54cm | 49cm
sleeve | sleeve

15 [17:19] cm | 15 [17:19] cm
14cm
53 [58:63] cm | 39 [44:49] cm | front | 45 [50:55] cm
50 [54.5:59] cm

4cm
7cm | back | 53 [58:63] cm
8cm
50 [54.5:59] cm

Knitted two-piece in pastel stripes

Slender bands of colour lend a distinctive touch to this lively duo. The stylish batwing sleeves of the easy-fitting top are knitted as one with the back and front sections, which means there's very little making up to be done.

The skirt is knitted from the waist downwards, so it can be whatever length you prefer – simply stop the striped pattern sequence when the desired length is reached and work the hem. A short-skirted version is perfect for the teenager who loves to go disco dancing, while a longer length takes on a sophisticated look.

Sizes

Top to fit 81 [86:91]cm/32 [34:36]in bust
Length to shoulder,
56.5 [57.5:58.5]cm 22¼ [22¾:23]in
Length from cuff to cuff,
147 [149.5:152]cm/58 [59:60]in
Skirt to fit 86 [91:97]cm/34 [36:38]in hips
Length of skirt, 46cm/18in for short version, 61cm/24in for longer version
The figures in [] refer to 86/34 and 91cm/36in bust sizes respectively

You will need

Top 8 [9:10]×50g balls of Twilley's Stalite (100% cotton) in main shade A
1 [2:2] balls each of 7 contrasts B, C, D, E, F, G and H
Skirt 5 [6:7]×50g balls in main shade A for short version, 6 [7:8] balls for the longer version
1 [1:1] ball each of 7 contrasts B, C, D, E, F, G and H for short version, 1 [2:2] balls for longer version
Waist length of elastic
One pair 3mm/No 11 needles
One 3mm/No 11 circular needle, 80cm/32in long
One pair 2¾mm/No 12 needles

Tension

26 sts and 40 rows to 10cm/4in over patt worked on 3mm/No 11 needles

Top back

With 2¾mm/No 12 needles and A cast on 98 [104:110] sts. Work 6cm/2¼in in K1, P1 rib ending with a Rs row.
Next row (inc row) Rib 11 [14:17], (inc in next st, rib 14) 5 times, inc in next st, rib 11 [14:17].
104 [110:116] sts.
Change to 3mm/No 11 needles.
1st row With A, K.
2nd row With A, P.
3rd row With B, K.
4th row With B, K.
5th and 6th rows As 1st and 2nd.
7th and 8th rows With C, K.
9th and 10th rows As 1st and 2nd.
11th and 12th rows With D, K.
13th and 14th rows As 1st and 2nd.

Left: The striped batwing top is worn here with a short skirt.

15th and 16th rows With E, K.
17th and 18th rows As 1st and 2nd.
19th and 20th rows With F, K.
21st and 22nd rows As 1st and 2nd.
23rd and 24th rows With G, K.
25th and 26th rows As 1st and 2nd.
27th and 28th rows With H, K.
These 28 rows form patt. Cont in patt as set inc one st each end of next and every foll 4th row until there are 108 [114:120] sts. Work 3 rows without shaping.
Inc one st at each end of next and every foll alt row until there are 188 [194:200] sts. Work one row. **

Shape sleeves
Change to 3mm/No 11 circular needle and work to and fro in rows.
Cast on at beg of every row 9 sts 16 times and 9 [10:11] sts twice. 350 [358:366] sts.
Mark both ends of last row for beg of cuff edge.
Cont in patt without shaping until cuff edge measures 17 [18:19]cm, 6¾ [7:7½]in ending with a Ws row. Cast off loosely.

Front
Work as for back to **.

Divide for neck
Next row Keeping patt correct throughout, cast on 9 sts, K across these 9 sts then K94 [97:100], turn. Complete left side first.
Dec one st at beg of next and every foll alt row 3 times, then every foll 4th row 19 [20:21] times, *at the same time* cast on at beg of every Rs row for sleeve 9 sts 7 times and 9 [10:11] sts once.
Cont neck shaping and keep cuff

edge straight until work measures same as back to shoulder. 153 [156:159] sts. Cast off loosely. With Rs of work facing rejoin yarn and work right side to match left side, reversing all shaping.

Neckband
Join right shoulder and upper arm seam. With Rs facing, 2¾mm/No 12 needles and A, pick up and K66 [70:74] sts down left neck edge, one st from centre front 'V', (mark this st), 65 [69:73] sts up right neck edge, 44 [46:48] sts from back neck. 176 [186:196] sts.
Working marked st as a K on Rs rows and P on Ws rows, work 8 rows in K1, P1 rib, dec one st each side of marked st on every row. Cast off in rib.

Cuffs
Join left shoulder and upper arm seam.
With Rs facing, 2¾mm/No 12 needles and A, pick up and K72 [76:80] sts evenly along cuff edge. Work 6cm/2¼in K1, P1 rib. Cast off in rib.

Skirt back
With 2¾mm/No 12 needles and A, cast on 98 [104:110] sts beg at waist. Work in K1, P1 rib for 4cm/1½in ending with a Rs row.
Next row (inc row) Rib 11 [14:17], (inc in next st, rib 14) 5 times, inc in next st, rib 11 [14:17].
104 [110:116] sts. Change to 3mm/No 11 needles. Commence patt.
Work in striped patt as for top, with colour sequence in reverse by beg with 2 rows st st in A, 2 rows g st in H, 2 rows st st in A, 2 rows g st in G

and so on, ending with 27th and 28th rows g st with B, *at the same time* work the first 10 rows without shaping.

Shape skirt
Next row (inc row) K6, M1, *K10, M1*, rep from * to * twice more, K to last 36 sts, M1, rep from * to * 3 times, K6. 112 [118:124] sts.
Work 11 rows without shaping.
Rep these 12 rows 3 times more. 136 [142:148] sts.
Cont working in patt rep the inc row when work measures 24/9½, 29/11½, 37/14½ and 44cm/17¼in from beg. 168 [174:180] sts.
Cont without shaping until skirt measures 46cm/18in for the shorter version or 61cm/24in for the longer version, ending after a 2nd g st row. Change to 2¾mm/No 12 needles and A. Beg with a K row, work 3cm/1¼in st st. Cast off loosely.

Skirt front
Work as given for back.

To make up
Press all pieces with a warm iron under a damp cloth taking care not to flatten the g st ridges.
Top Join side and underarm seams.
Skirt Join side seams. Fold hem to wrong side at ridge formed by last patt row and sl st into place. Join waist elastic into a circle and attach to Ws of waist rib with herringbone casing.

Right: Knit just the top to wear with trousers or a skirt. The yarn requirements for the skirt and top have been given separately in the pattern.

The pattern pieces

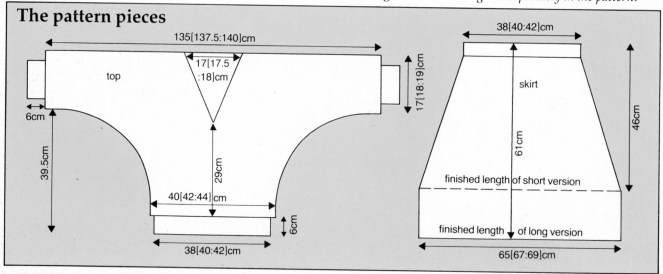

Bobble and bead jersey

The bobble pattern on these jerseys can be highlighted for evening wear with clusters of beads threaded on the wool. Silver or gold looks particularly elegant on black. Instructions overleaf give an easy method of threading beads on to wool.

Knit the jersey with short or long sleeves – with or without beads.

Sizes

To fit 86 [94]cm/34 [37]in bust
Length to shoulder, 56 [58]cm/ 22 [22¾]in
Short sleeve seam, 15cm/6in
Long sleeve seam, 46cm/18in
The figures in [] refer to the 94cm/ 37in size only

You will need

Short-sleeved jersey 7[8]×50g balls of Sirdar Majestic 4 ply, 100% wool
Long-sleeved jersey 9[10] balls of same
One pair 2¾mm/No 12 needles
One pair 3¼mm/No 10 needles
Pearl beads 3mm/⅛in, optional.

Tension

28 sts and 36 rows to 10cm/4in over st st worked on 3¼mm/No 10 needles

Short-sleeved jersey back

With 2¾mm/No 12 needles cast on 129[139] sts. Commence rib.
1st row K1, *P1, K1, rep from * to end.
2nd row P1, *K1, P1, rep from * to end.
Rep these 2 rows for 7cm/2¾in, end on a 2nd row. Change to 3¼mm/ No 10 needles. Beg with a K row work 2 rows st st. Commence bobble patt.
1st row (Rs) K9, *(K1, P1) twice into next st, turn and K4, turn and K4 tog – **called MB**, K9, rep from * to end.
2nd and every alt row P to end. **
3rd row K to end.
5th row K7, *MB, K3, MB, K5, rep from * to last 2 sts, K2.
7th row K to end.
9th row As 1st.
11th and 13th rows K to end.
15th row K4, MB, *K9, MB, rep from

Left: Bobbles and beads are features that give a jersey an expensive look. They give a simple style a touch of class.

* to last 4 sts, K4.
17th row K to end.
19th row K2, *MB, K3, MB, K5, rep from * to last 7 sts, MB, K3, MB, K2.
21st row K to end.
23rd row As 15th.
25th and 27th rows K to end.
28th row P to end.
These 28 rows form the patt. Rep them 4 times more.

Shape armholes

Keeping patt correct throughout, cast off 4[5] sts at beg of next 2 rows. Dec one st at each end of next and every alt row until 107[111] sts rem. Cont without shaping until work measures 56 [58]cm/22 [22¾]in from beg, ending with a P row.

Shape shoulders

Cast off at beg of next and every row 10 sts 4 times and 10[11] sts twice. Cast off rem 47[49] sts.

Short-sleeved jersey front

Work as given for back until front measures 47 [48]cm/18½ [19]in from beg, ending with a P row.

Shape neck

Next row Patt 41[42] ts, turn and leave rem sts on holder.
Complete left side first. Dec one st at neck edge on next 6 rows, then on every alt row until 30[31] sts rem. Cont without shaping until work measures same as back to shoulder, ending with a P row.

Shape shoulder

Cast off at beg of next and every alt row 10 sts twice and 10[11] sts once. With Rs of work facing rejoin yarn to rem sts, cast off 25[27] sts for neck, patt to end.
Complete to match first side, reversing shaping.

Short sleeves

With 2¾mm/No 12 needles cast on 69 [73] sts. Work 4cm/1½in rib as given for back, ending with a 2nd row and inc 10 [16] sts evenly in last row. 79 [89] sts.
Change to 3¼mm/No 10 needles. Beg with a K row work 2 rows st st. Cont in bobble patt as for back, inc one st at each end of 5th and every foll 4th row until there are 89 [99] sts, then cont without shaping until sleeve measures 15cm/6in from beg, ending with a P row.

Shape top

Cast off 4[5] sts at beg of next 2 rows. Dec one st at each end of next and every alt row until 43[47] sts rem, then at each end of every row until 23 sts rem. Cast off.

Long-sleeved jersey back

Using yarn without beads threaded on to it, work as given for short sleeved jersey back to **. Join in yarn with beads. Commence bobble and bead patt.
3rd row K8, *P1, sl 2 beads up yarn to front of work, sl 1 purlwise – **called B1**, P1, K7, rep from * to last st, K1.
5th row K7, *MB, P1, B1, P1, MB, K5, rep from * to last 2 sts, K2.
7th row As 3rd.

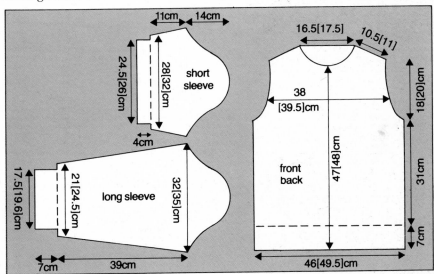

17

Left: The bobble and bead jerseys are a flattering shape and feature a neat little Peter Pan collar.

Collar (both versions)

With 3¼mm/No 10 needles cast on 105 [109] sts. Beg with a K row work 2 rows st st. Cont in st st, inc one st at each end of next and every alt row until there are 121[125] sts, ending with a P row. Dec one st at each end of next and every alt row until 113[117] sts rem, ending with a P row. Break off yarn.

Edging

Next row With Rs of work facing, pick up and K18 sts along side edge of collar, K across 113[117] sts on needle, then pick up and K18 sts along other edge of collar. 149[153] sts.
Next row P to end.
Next row K9[11], *MB, K9, rep from * to last 0[2] sts, K0[2].
Beg with a P row work 3 rows st st.
Next row (picot holes) K1, *yfwd, K2 tog, rep from * to end.
Beg with a P row work 3 rows st st.
Cast off loosely.

To make up (both versions)

Press each piece very lightly under a damp cloth with a warm iron, taking care not to flatten patt. Join shoulder seams. Sew in sleeves. Join side and sleeve seams. Turn in hem on collar to Ws at row of picot holes and sl st in place. Sew collar round neck edge, leaving about 2cm/¾in free at centre front. Press seams lightly.

9th row As 1st.
11th and 13th rows K to end.
15th row K4, MB, *K9, MB, rep from * to last 4 sts, K4.
17th row K3, *P1, B1, P1, K7, rep from * to last 6 sts, P1, B1, P1, K3.
19th row K2, *MB, P1, B1, P1, MB, K5, rep from * to last 7 sts, MB, P1, B1, P1, MB, K2.
21st row As 17th.
23rd row As 15th.
25th and 27th rows K to end.
28th row P to end.
Working in patt as given above, complete as given for short-sleeved jersey back.

Long-sleeved jersey front

Working bobble and bead patt as given for long sleeved jersey back, work as given for short-sleeved jersey front.

Long sleeves

With 2¾mm/No 12 needles and yarn without beads cast on 49 [55] sts. Work 7cm/2¾in rib as given for back, ending with a 2nd row and inc 10 [14] sts evenly in last row. 59 [69] sts. Change to 3¼mm/No 10 needles. Beg with K row work 2

rows st st. Join in yarn with beads. Cont in bobble and bead patt as given for back, inc one st at each end of 9th and every foll 8th row until there are 89[99] sts. Cont without shaping until sleeve measures 46cm/18in from beg, ending with a P row.

Shape top

As given for short sleeves.

Note on knitting with beads

The short and long-sleeved versions can be worked in bobble pattern or in bobble and bead pattern.
The total quantity of beads required for the short-sleeved version is about 2450[2550] and for the long-sleeved version, 3050[3150]. Thread about 400 beads on to each of several balls of yarn, keeping one or two balls without beads for the welt and cuffs. Further beads can be threaded on to the remaining balls as required.

To thread beads on to yarn

Take a 15cm/6in length of sewing cotton and thread both cut ends

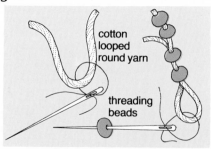

into a fine sewing needle from opposite sides, making a loop of cotton. Put 15cm/6in of the yarn to be used through the cotton loop and slide the beads down the needle, over the cotton and on to the yarn.

Yoked jersey

Frills at neck, wrist and round the deep yoke make this jersey look special.

Sizes

To fit 86 [91:97]cm/34 [36:38]in bust
Length to shoulder, 56 [57:58]cm/ 22 [22½:22¾]in. Sleeve seam, 46cm/ 18in from beg of frill
The figures in [] refer to 91/36 and 97cm/38in sizes respectively

You will need

8 [8:9] × 40g balls of Argyll Starlite Double knitting (80% Courtelle, 20% nylon) in main colour A
1 ball of same in contrast colour B
One pair of 3¼mm/No 10 needles
One pair 4mm/No 8 needles
One pair 4½mm/No 7 needles

Tension

22 sts and 30 rows to 10cm/4in over st st worked on 4mm/No 8 needles

Front

With 3¼mm/No 10 needles and A cast on 93 [97:105] sts.
1st row (Rs) K1, *P1, K1, rep from * to end.
2nd row P1, *K1, P1, rep from * to end.
Rep these 2 rows for 5cm/2in, ending with a 1st row.
Next row (inc) Rib 5 [6:7] sts, (M1, rib 12 [12:13] sts) 7 times, M1, rib to end. 101 [105:113] sts.
Change to 4mm/No 8 needles.
Beg with a K row cont in st st until work measures 32cm/12½in from beg, ending with a P row.

Yoke

1st row With A, K44 [46:50] sts, P1, K3, P2, with B, (P1, K1, P1, K1, P1) all into next st, lift 2nd, 3rd, 4th and 5th sts over first st – **called MB**, with A, P2, K3, P1, K to end.
When working bobble patt row, join in B and carry it loosely across back of work, breaking off at end of row.
2nd row P44 [46:50] sts, K1, P3, K2, P1, K2, P3, K1, P to end.
3rd row K43 [45:49] sts, P2, K3, P2,

Overleaf: The yoke frill is knitted separately and sewn on.

K1, P2, K3, P2, K to end.
4th row P43 [45:49] sts, K2, P3, K2, P1, K2, P3, K2, P to end.
5th row With A, K42 [44:48] sts, with B, MB, with A, P2, K3, P2, with B, MB, with A, P2, K3, P2, with B, MB, with A, K to end.
6th row P42 [44:48] sts, P1, K2, P3, K2, P1, K2, P3, K2, P1, P to end.
7th row K41 [43:47] sts, P1, K1, P2, K3, P2, K1, P2, K3, P2, K1, P1, K to end.
8th row P41 [43:47] sts, K1, P1, K2, P3, K2, P1, K2, P3, K2, P1, K1, P to end.

Shape armholes

Beg with 9th row of chart, cont in patt as now set and cast off 5 [5:7] sts at beg of next 2 rows.
Dec one st at each end of next 5 [7:7] rows, then at each end of every alt row until 75 [77:79] sts rem.
Cont without shaping until 48th [50th:52nd] row of chart has been completed.

Shape neck

Next row Patt 29 [30:30] sts, turn and leave rem sts on holder.
Complete this side first. Keeping armhole edge straight, dec one st at neck edge on next and every row 4 times in all, then on every alt row until 20 sts rem.
Cont without shaping until 66th [68th:70th] row of chart has been completed.

Shape shoulder

Cast off at beg of next and every alt row 7 sts twice and 6 sts once.
With Rs of work facing, rejoin yarn to rem sts, cast off first 17 [17:19] sts loosely, patt to end.
Complete to match first side, reversing shaping.

Back

Work as given for front, omitting yoke patt and neck shaping, until back measures same as front to shoulders, ending with a Ws row.

Shape shoulders

Cast off at beg of next and every row 7 sts 4 times and 6 sts twice.
Leave rem 35 [37:39] sts on holder for centre back neck.

Sleeves

With 4½mm/No 7 needles and B cast on 67 sts for all sizes. Work 2 rows g st. Break off B. Join in A.
Commence lace patt
**1st row (Rs) K3, *yfwd, K2, sl 1, K1, psso, K2 tog, K2, yfwd, K1, rep from * to last st, K1.
2nd row P to end.
3rd row K2, *yfwd, K2, sl 1, K1, psso, K2 tog, K2, yfwd, K1, rep from * to last 2 sts, K2.
4th row P to end.
Rep last 4 rows once more.****
Next row K1 [1:2] sts, (K2 tog) 10 times, K0 [2:3] sts, (K2 tog) 12 [10:8] times, K1 [2:3] sts, (K2 tog) 10 times,

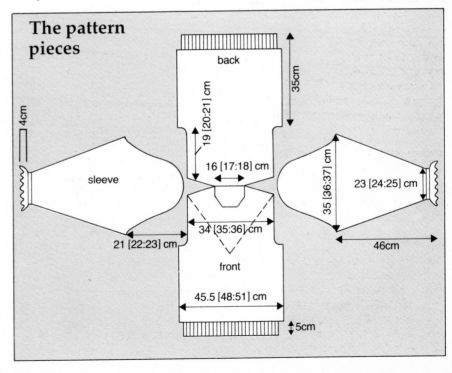

The pattern pieces

back

35cm

4cm

sleeve

19 [20:21] cm

16 [17:18] cm

35 [36:37] cm

23 [24:25] cm

21 [22:23] cm

34 [35:36] cm

46cm

front

45.5 [48:51] cm

5cm

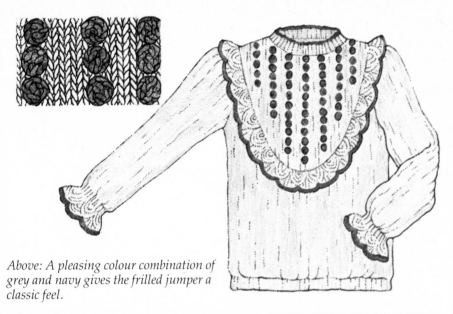

Above: A pleasing colour combination of grey and navy gives the frilled jumper a classic feel.

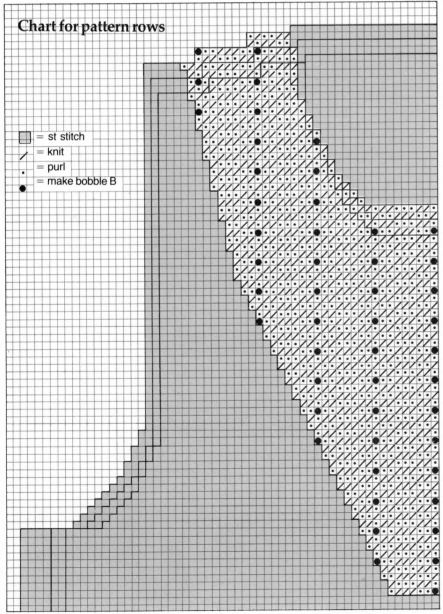

Chart for pattern rows

▨ = st stitch
╱ = knit
• = purl
● = make bobble B

K1 [2:3] sts. 35 [37:39] sts. Change to 3¼mm/No 10 needles. Work 6 rows rib as given for front.

Next row (inc) (Rib 2, M1) 7 [6:6] times, (rib 3, M1) 2 [3:4] times, (rib 2, M1) 7 [7:6] times, rib 1 [2:3]. 51 [53:55] sts.

Change to 4mm/No 8 needles. Beg with K row cont in st st, inc one st each end of 7th and every foll 8th row 4 times in all, then at each end of every foll 6th row until there are 77 [79:81] sts.

Cont without shaping until sleeve measures 46cm/18in from beg, ending with a P row.

Shape top

Cast off 5 [5:7] sts at beg of next 2 rows.

Dec one st at each end of next and every foll 4th row 12 [12:14] times in all. Dec one st at each end of every alt row until 35 sts rem, then at each end of every row until 17 sts rem. Cast off.

Yoke frill

With 4½mm/No 7 needles and B cast on 202 [211:211] sts. Work 2 rows g st. Break off B. Join in A. Work in lace patt as given for sleeves from ** to **.

Next row (dec) K0 [1:1] st, (K2 tog) to end.

Next row P to end.

Next row With length of yarn in B, K into each st to end, s1 each st on to another spare length of yarn long enough to go round edge of yoke.

To make up

Do not press. With Rs facing sew frill neatly around edge of yoke, matching st for st in back st seam and undoing last row in spare yarn as each st is sewn down.

Join right shoulder seam.

Neckband

With 3¼mm/No 10 needles, A and Rs of work facing, K up 59 sts evenly around front neck, then K across back neck sts on holder, dec 3 sts evenly. 91 [93:95] sts. K one row to define neckline. Work 8 rows rib as given for front. Break off A. Join in B.

Next row K twice into each st to end of row.

Cast off.

Join left shoulder and neckband. Join side and sleeve seams. Set in sleeves, gathering fullness into top.

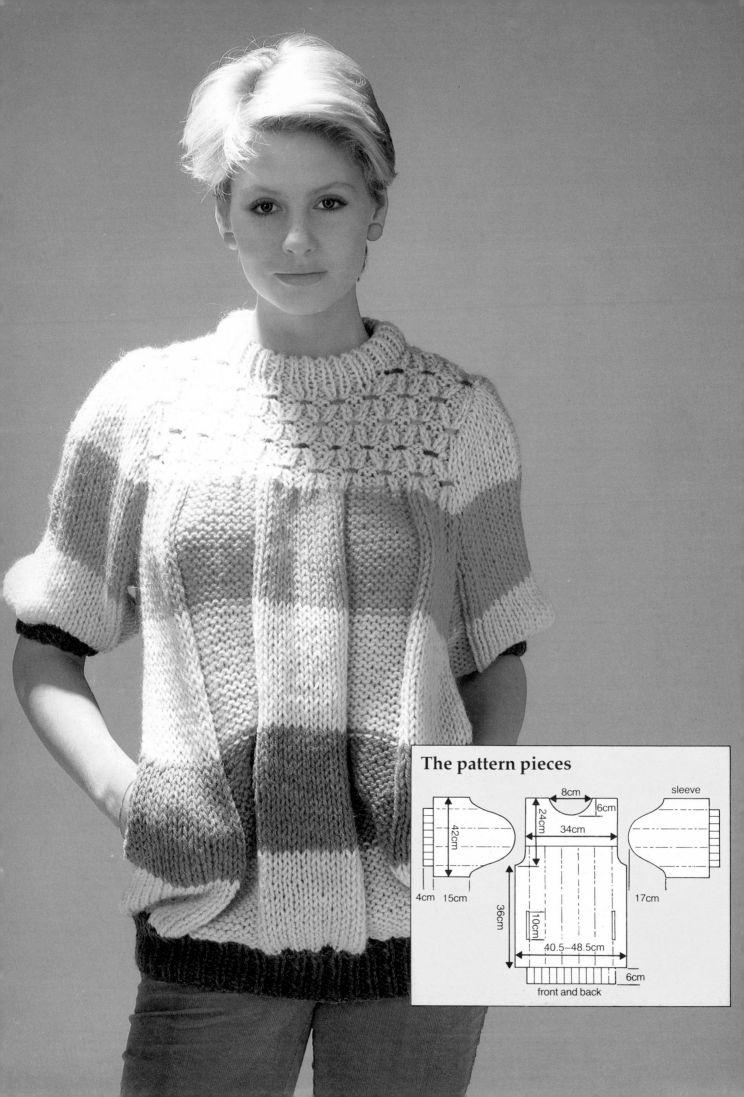

The pattern pieces

sleeve

42cm

4cm 15cm

8cm

24cm

6cm

34cm

36cm

10cm

40.5–48.5cm

6cm

17cm

front and back

Smock jersey

Size

To fit 81-97cm/32-38in bust
Length to shoulder, 66cm/26in
Sleeve seam, 19cm/7½in

You will need

6×40g balls of Argyll Ferndale
  Chunky (85% Courtelle, 15%
  wool) in colour A
3 balls of contrast B
2 balls of contrasts C and D
One pair 6½mm/No 3 needles
One pair 7½mm/No 1 needles
One pair 9mm/No 00 needles
One cable needle

Tension

11 sts and 15 rows to 10cm/4in over
st st worked on 9mm/No 00 needles

Back

**With 6½mm/No 3 needles and D
cast on 57 sts.
1st row (Rs) K1, *P1, K1, rep from *
to end.
2nd row P1, *K1, P1, rep from * to
end.
Rep last 2 rows for 6cm/2¼in
ending with a 1st row.
Next row (inc row) Rib 3, (M1, rib 2)
4 times, (M1, rib 3) 12 times, (M1,
rib 2) 4 times, rib 2. 77 sts. Change
to 9mm/No 00 needles and A, K one
row. Commence patt.
1st row (Ws) K7, (P13, K12) twice,
P13, K7.
2nd row P7, (K13, P12) twice, K13,
P7.
Work 13 more rows in patt. **
Break off A. Join in C and work 16
rows in patt.
Break off C.
Join in A and work 16 rows in patt.
Break off A. Join in B and work 6
rows in patt.

Shape armholes

Keeping patt correct and working in
B, cast off 4 sts at beg of next 2 rows.
Dec one st at each end of every row
4 times. 61 sts.
Work 2 rows patt in B, dec one st at
centre of last row, ending with a Ws
row. Break off B. 60 sts.

Change to 7½mm/No 1 needles.
Join in A and work one row in patt.
Commence smocked yoke patt.

1st row (Ws) K1, *P1, K2, rep from *
to last 2 sts, P1, K1.
2nd row P1, *K1, P2, rep from * to
last 2 sts, K1, P1.
3rd row As 1st.
4th row P1, *slip next 4 sts on to
cable needle, wrap C around these
4 sts from left to right *twice*, then
using A (K1, P2, K1) from cable
needle – **called smock 4**, P2, rep
from * to last 5 sts, smock 4, P1.
5th row As 1st.
6th row As 2nd.
7th row As 1st.
8th row P1, K1, P2, *smock 4 with
D, P2, rep from * to last 2 sts, K1, P1.
Cont in patt as set, changing to B
then C, D and B for smocking
thread until armhole measures
24cm/9½in from beg ending with a
Ws row.

Shape shoulders

Cast off 13 sts at beg of next 2 rows.
Leave rem 34 sts on a holder.

Front

Work as for back from ** to **.

Divide for pockets

Break off A. Join in C.
Next row P7, turn and leave rem sts
on a holder.
Next row Cast on 13 sts for pocket
lining, P these 13 sts, K7. 20 sts.
Work 13 rows in patt.
Next row Cast off 13 sts of lining,
slip rem 7 sts on to a holder.
With Rs of work facing rejoin yarn to
rem sts on holder, patt across 63 st,
turn and leave rem sts on holder.
Cont in patt on these 63 sts for 14
rows. Leave sts on a holder.
With Rs of work facing rejoin yarn
to inner edge of rem 7 sts, cast on
13 sts for pocket lining, K these
13 sts, P to end.
Work 13 rows in patt.
Next row Cast off 13 sts of pocket
lining, P7.
Next row K7 from first needle, patt
across 63 sts from centre, K rem
7 sts. 77 sts.
Break off C. Join in A. Cont in patt
as for back until work measures
18cm/7in from beg of armhole
shaping ending with 1st row of patt.

Shape neck

Next row Patt 20, turn and leave
rem sts on a holder.
Keeping armhole edge straight dec
one st at neck edge on every row

until 13 sts rem. If necessary work a
few rows straight until front
matches back to shoulder. Cast off.
With Rs facing slip centre 20 sts on
to a holder, rejoin yarn to rem sts
and complete to match first side.

Sleeves

With 6½mm/No 3 needles and D
cast on 26 sts.
Work in K1, P1 rib for 4cm/1½in
ending with a Ws row.
Next row (inc row) K1, inc in every
st to end. 51 sts.
Change to 9mm/No 00 needles.
Break off D. Join in A. K one row.
Commence patt.
1st row (Ws) K7, P12, K13, P12, K7.
2nd row P7, K12, P13, K12, P7.
Cont in patt for 13 more rows. Break
off A. Join in B. Work in patt for 6
rows.

Shape top

Cast off 4 sts at the beg of next 2
rows. Dec 1 st at each end of next
and every foll 3rd row 7 times in all,
ending with a Ws row. 29 sts.
Cast off 4 sts at beg of next 4 rows.
Cast off rem 13 sts.

Pocket tops

With Rs of work facing, 6½mm/
No 3 needles and C, pick up and
K17 sts along edge of pocket.
Work 3 rows rib as given at beg of
back. Cast off.

Neckband

Join right shoulder seam.
With Rs facing, 6½mm/No 3
needles and B, pick up and K12 sts
down left side of neck, work across
20 sts from front neck holder (P2
tog, K1) 6 times, P2 tog, pick up and
K12 sts up right side of neck, work
across 34 sts from back neck holder
(K1, P2 tog) 11 times, inc in last st.
61 sts.
Next row K1, *P1, K1, rep from * to
end.
Next row P1, *K1, P1, rep from * to
end.
Rep these 2 rows for 6cm/2¼in.
Cast off loosely in rib.

To make up

Join left shoulder and neckband.
Fold neckband in half to Ws and
sew in position. Sew pocket linings
in place on Ws. Sew down pocket
tops on Rs. Join side and sleeve
seams. Set in sleeves.

Batwing jersey

This simple batwing jersey looks equally attractive worn with an open-necked shirt, a roll neck jersey or on its own, and despite its good looks, even a beginner can knit it with confidence.

Sizes

To fit 86-91cm/34-36in bust loosely
Length to shoulder, 56cm/22in

You will need

9 × 25g balls of Jaeger Mohair Spun (67% mohair, 28% wool, 5% nylon) in main colour A
4 × 25g balls of Jaeger Mohair Spun with Glitter (67% mohair, 21% wool, 7% metallised, 5% nylon) in contrast colour B
One pair 5½mm/No 5 needles
One pair 4½mm/No 7 needles

Tension

16 sts and 20 rows to 10cm/4in over st st worked on 5½mm/No 5 needles

Back

With 5½mm/No 5 needles and A cast on 68 sts firmly and beg at sleeve edge.
Beg with a K row work 12 rows st st. Break off A. Join in B. Beg with a K row work 12 rows st st. Break off B. Join in A.
These 24 rows form striped patt. Cont in patt until 13 stripes in all have been completed. Cast off firmly.

Front

Work as given for back.

Ribbed welt

With 4½mm/No 7 needles and A cast on 70 sts. Work 20 rows K1, P1 rib. Cast off loosely.
Make another piece in same way.

Left: The batwing jersey is shown here without the crochet neckline. The elbow length sleeves make it ideal to wear on its own in warmer weather or over a shirt when it is cooler.
Right: If preferred, add a crochet edging to neaten the neckline.

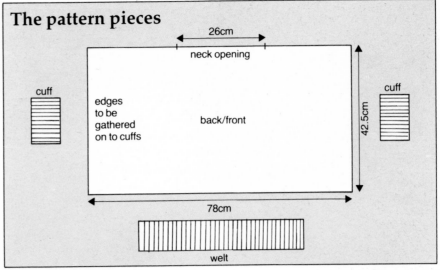

The pattern pieces

26cm
neck opening
cuff
edges to be gathered on to cuffs
back/front
cuff
42.5cm
78cm
welt

Ribbed cuffs

With 4½mm/No 7 needles and A cast on 60 sts. Work 16 rows K1, P1 rib. Cast off loosely.
Make another piece in same way.

To make up

Do not press. With Rs of back and front tog, join shoulder seams along edges without any colour changes, matching stripes and leaving about 26cm/10¼in open in centre for neck. Sew ribbed welts to lower edge of back and front, beg in centre of 4th stripe and ending in centre of 10th stripe.

Gather up sleeve edges with running sts to measure about 32cm/12½in. Join cast off edge of ribbed cuffs to gathered edge of sleeve. Join sides of ribbed welt and underarm seams.

Neatening neckline

Work a crochet neckline if required. Using a 4.50mm/No 7 crochet hook join the yarn to one side of neck at the shoulder seam. Work 2ch, then working in dc work right round neck edge working about 8dc along each stripe, ss to 2nd of 2ch. Fasten off.

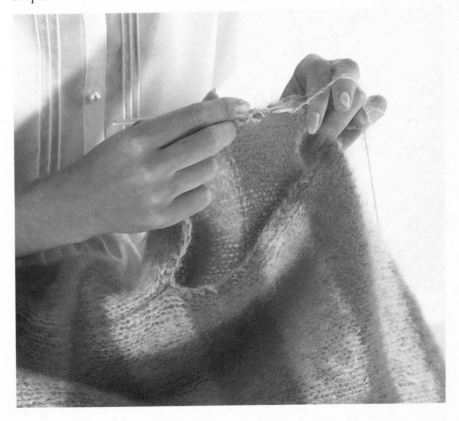

Lace front mohair jersey

The lacy pattern is only worked on the front, the rest is in stocking stitch.

Sizes

To fit 86 [91:97]cm/34 [36:38]in bust
Length to shoulder, 56 [57:58]cm/
22 [22½:23]in
Sleeve seam, 44cm/17½in

The figures in [] refer to the 91/36 and 97cm/38in sizes respectively

You will need

15 [15:16]×25g balls of Sirdar
  Nocturn (77% mohair, 13% wool,
  10% Bri-nylon)
One pair 4½mm/No 7 needles
One pair 5½mm/No 5 needles

Tension

16 sts and 21 rows to 10cm/4in over
st st worked on 5½mm/No 5 needles

Back

With 4½mm/No 7 needles cast on

Above: Extra care is needed when you knit this lacy pattern as the number of stitches changes on every row.
Inset: Detail of plain sleeve head.

62 [68:74] sts. Work 6cm/2¼in K1,
P1 rib.
Next row (inc row) Rib 7 sts, *pick up loop lying between needles and K tbl – **called M1**, rib 8 [9:10] sts, rep from * 5 times more, M1, rib 7 sts.
69 [75:81] sts.**
Change to 5½mm/No 5 needles.
Beg with a K row cont in st st until work measures 35cm/13¾in from beg, ending with a P row.

Shape armholes

Cast off 3 sts at beg of next 2 rows.
Dec one st at each end of next and
every alt row until 53 [55:57] sts rem.
Cont without shaping until
armholes measures 21 [22:23]cm/
8¼ [8¾:9]in from beg, ending with
a P row.

Shape shoulders

Cast off at beg of next and every
row 5 sts 4 times and 4 sts twice.
Leave rem 25 [27:29] sts on holder
for centre back neck.

Front

Work as given for back to **
Change to 5½mm/No 5 needles.
Commence lace patt.
1st row (Rs) K0 [3:6] sts, *sl 1, K1,
psso, yfwd, sl 2, K1, p2sso, yfwd,
K1 tbl, yfwd, sl 1, K1, psso, K7, K2
tog, yfwd, K1 tbl, yfwd, sl 2, K1,
p2sso, yfwd, K2 tog, rep from *
twice more, K0 [3:6] sts.
63 [69:75] sts.
2nd and every alt row P to end.
3rd row K0 [3:6] sts, *sl 1, K1, psso,
yfwd, K1, yfwd, K3, yfwd, sl 1, K1,
psso, K5, K2 tog, yfwd, K3, yfwd,
K1, yfwd, K2 tog, rep from * twice
more, K0 [3:6] sts. 69 [75:81] sts.
5th row K0 [3:6] sts, *K1, (yfwd, sl
2, K1, p2sso) twice, yfwd, k1 tbl,
yfwd, sl 1, K1, psso, K3, K2 tog,
yfwd, K1 tbl, (yfwd, sl 2, K1, p2sso)
twice, yfwd, K1, rep from * twice
more, K0 [3:6] sts. 63 [69:75] sts.
7th row K0 [3:6] sts, *(K1, yfwd, K3,
yfwd) twice, sl 1, K1, psso, K1, K2
tog, (yfwd, K3, yfwd, K1) twice,
rep from * twice more, K0 [3:6] sts.
81 [87:93] sts.
9th row K0 [3:6] sts, *sl 1, K1, psso,
(yfwd, sl 2, K1, p2sso) 3 times,
yfwd, K1 tbl, yfwd, sl 1, K2 tog,
psso, yfwd, K1 tbl, (yfwd, sl 2, K1,
p2sso) 3 times, yfwd, K2 tog, rep
from * twice more, K0 [3:6] sts.
63 [69:75] sts.
11th row K0 [3:6] sts, *sl 1, K1, psso,
yfwd, K1, yfwd, K2, K2 tog, yfwd,
K3, yfwd, K1, yfwd, K3, yfwd, sl 1,
K1, psso, K2, yfwd, K1, yfwd, K2
tog, rep from * twice more, K0
[3:6] sts. 75 [81:87] sts.
13th row K0 [3:6] sts, *K1, (yfwd, sl
2, K1, p2sso) twice, yfwd, K2 tog,
K3, yfwd, K1, yfwd, K3, sl 1, K1,
psso, (yfwd, sl 2, K1, p2sso) twice,
yfwd, K1, rep from * twice more, K0
[3:6] sts. 69 [75:81] sts.
15th row K0 [3:6] sts, *K1, yfwd, K2,

K2 tog, yfwd, K2 tog, K9, sl 1, K1,
psso, yfwd, sl 1, K1, psso, K2,
yfwd, K1, rep from * twice more, K0
[3:6] sts. 69 [75:81] sts.
16th row As 2nd.
These 16 rows form the patt. Cont
in patt until front measures same as
back to armholes, ending with a Ws
row.

Shape armholes

Keeping patt correct throughout,
cast off 3 sts at beg of next 2 rows.
Dec one st at each end of next and
every alt row 5 [7:9] times in all.
Cont without shaping until
armholes are 12 rows less than back
to shoulders, ending with a Ws row.

Shape neck

Next row Patt 20 [21:22] sts, turn
and leave rem sts on holder.
Complete left shoulder first.
Dec one st at neck edge on next and
every row until 14 sts rem.
Cont without shaping until work
measures same as back to shoulder,
ending at armhole edge.

Shape shoulder

Cast off at beg of next and every alt
row 5 sts twice and 4 sts once.
With Rs of work facing, sl first 13 sts
on to a separate length of yarn for
centre front neck, rejoin yarn to rem
sts and patt to end.
Complete to match first side
reversing shapings.

Sleeves

With 4½mm/No 7 needles cast on
30 [32:34] sts. Work 6cm/2¼in K1,
P1 rib.
Next row (inc row) Rib 4 [4:5] sts,
*M1, rib 7 [8:8] sts, rep from * twice,
M1, rib 5 [4:5] sts. 34 [36:38] sts.

Change to 5½mm/No 5 needles.
Beg with a K row cont in st st, inc
one st at each end of 5th and every
foll 6th row until there are
60 [62:64] sts.
Cont without shaping until sleeve
measures 44cm/17¼in from beg,
ending with a P row.

Shape top (for gathered sleeve head)

Cast off 3 sts at beg of next 2 rows.
Dec one st at each end of next and
every foll 6th row until 42 [44:46] sts
rem. Work 5 [7:9] rows without
shaping.
Cast off at beg of next and every foll
row 5 sts 6 times and 12 [14:16] sts
once.

Shape top (for plain sleeve head)

Cast off 3 sts at beg of next 2 rows.
Dec one st at each end of next and
every foll alt row until 24 [26:28] sts
rem. Work one row.
Cast off at beg of next and every foll
row 3 sts 4 times and 12 [14:16] sts
once.

Neckband

Join right shoulder seam. With Rs of
work facing and 4½mm/No 7
needles, pick up and K12 [14:16] sts
down left side of front neck, K13 sts
of front neck, pick up and K12
[14:16] sts up right side of front neck
and K across 25 [27:29] sts of back
neck. 62 [68:74] sts.
Work 4 rows K1, P1 rib. Cast off
loosely in rib.

To make up

Do not press. Join left shoulder,
side and sleeve seams. Set in
sleeves, gathering the sleeve head
to fit of the gathered sleeve version.

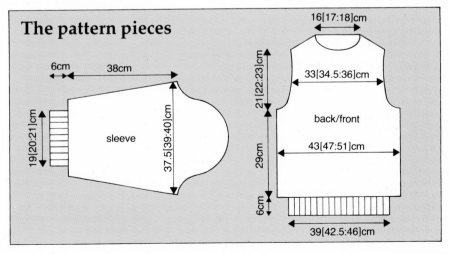

The pattern pieces

6cm · 38cm · 37.5[39:40]cm · sleeve · 19[20:21]cm

16[17:18]cm · 21[22:23]cm · 33[34.5:36]cm · back/front · 43[47:51]cm · 29cm · 6cm · 39[42.5:46]cm

27

Striped jersey

This jersey is easy to make in reversed stocking stitch and rib and there is very little shaping with the straight rib neckline.

Sizes

To fit 81[86:91:97]cm/32[34:36:38]in bust
Length to shoulder, 67[68:69:70]cm/26½[26¾: 27¼:27½]in
Sleeve seam, 48cm/19in
The figures in [] refer to the 86/34, 91/36 and 97cm/38in sizes respectively

You will need

7[8:8:9]×40g balls of Sirdar Wash 'n' Wear Double Crepe (55% Bri-Nylon, 45% acrylic) in main colour A
2[2:3:3] balls each of same in contrast colours B and C
One pair 3mm/No 11 needles
One pair 3¾mm/No 9 needles

Tension

24 sts and 32 rows to 10cm/4in over st st worked on 3¾mm/No 9 needles

Back

With 3mm/No 11 needles and A cast on 96[102:108:114] sts.
Work in K1, P1 rib for 9cm/3½in.
Next row (inc row) K2[4:8:10] sts, (inc in next st, K3) 23 times, inc in next st, K1[5:7:11].
120[126:132:138] sts.
Change to 3¾mm/No 9 needles.
Beg with a P row work in reverse st st in a stripe sequence of 2 rows B, 2 rows A, 2 rows C; 4 rows A.
Cont in patt without shaping until work measures 47cm/18½in from beg, ending with a Ws row.

Shape armholes

Cast off 12 sts at beg of next 2 rows.
96[102:108:114] sts.
Cont in patt without shaping until armholes measure 14[15:16:17]cm/5[5½:6:6½]in from beg, ending with 2 rows in B or C. Break off B and C.
Next row (Rs) P one row in A.
Next row (inc row) P3[6:9:12], (inc in next st, P5) 15 times, inc in next st, P2[5:8:11]. 112[118:124:130] sts.

Left: The loose fitting sleeves of this jersey are created by increasing into every stitch at the cuff.

alternative colourways

Yoke

Change to 3mm/No 11 needles.
Work 6cm/2¼in K1, P1 rib.
Cast off in rib.

Front

Work as given for back.

Sleeves

With 3mm/No 11 needles and A cast on 46[48:50:52] sts.
Work 9cm/3½in in K1, P1 rib.
Next row (inc row) Inc in each st to end of row. 92[96:100:104] sts.
Change to 3¾mm/No 9 needles.
Beg with a P row work in reverse st st in stripes as given for back until sleeve measures 48cm/19in from beg. Place a marker at both ends of last row.

Cont in st st until work measures 53cm/20¾in from beg.
Cast off loosely.

To make up

Press pieces with a warm iron over a damp cloth, omitting ribbing. Join shoulder seams for 5cm/2in. Set in sleeves. Join side and sleeve seams. Press seams.

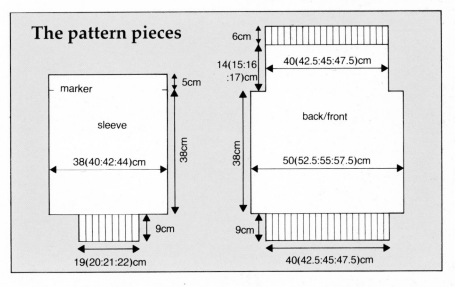

The pattern pieces

marker

sleeve

38(40:42:44)cm

5cm

38cm

9cm

19(20:21:22)cm

6cm

40(42.5:45:47.5)cm

14(15:16:17)cm

back/front

38cm

50(52.5:55:57.5)cm

9cm

40(42.5:45:47.5)cm

Yoked cable jersey

This attractive sweater gives the appearance of being a very complicated one to knit, and yet it is made up of simple shapes for the back, front and sleeves, with a straight strip of cable stitched in around the edge of a plain stocking stitch yoke. Cleverly, the neck edge of the yoke is allowed to just roll over to form the neckband, which eliminates the need for stitches to be picked up. You can make the bobbles in two sizes.

Sizes

To fit 86 [91:97]cm/34 [36:38]in bust
Length to shoulder, 60 [61:62]cm/ 23½ [24:24½]in
Sleeve seam, 42 [43:44]cm/ 16½ [17:17¼]in
The figures in [] refer to the 91/36 and 97cm/38in sizes respectively

You will need

7 [7:8]×50g balls of Pingouin Poudreuse (80% acrylic, 10% wool, 10% mohair)
One pair 3¾mm/No 9 needles
One pair 5mm/No 6 needles
One 4½mm/No 7 circular needle, 60cm/24in long

Tension

20 sts and 26 rows to 10cm/4in over st st worked on 4½mm/No 7 needles

Back

With 3¾mm/No 9 needles cast on 97 [101:105] sts.
1st row (Rs) K1, *P1, K1, rep from * to end.
2nd row P1, *K1, P1, rep from * end.
Rep these 2 rows until work measures 8cm/3¼in from beg, ending with a Rs row.
Next row (inc row) Rib 10 [12:14] sts, *inc in next st, rib 18, rep from * 3 times more, inc in next st, rib 10 [12:14] sts. 102 [106:110] sts.
Change to 5mm/No 6 needles.
1st row (Rs) K5[7:9] sts, P2, (K10, K2 tog, yfwd, K1 making 13 sts for first lace panel), K1, P2, (K12 for cable panel), P2, (K11, K2 tog, yfwd, K2, yfwd, sl 1, K1, psso, K11 making 28 sts for centre panel), P2, (K12 for cable panel), P2, K1, (K1, yfwd, sl 1,

K1, psso, K10 making 13 sts for last lace panel), P2, K5[7:9] sts.
2nd and every alt row P5[7:9], K2, (P13), P1, K2, (P12), K2, (P28 noting that on subsequent alt rows this should read P27), K2, (P12), K2, P1, (P13), K2, P5[7:9].
3rd row K5[7:9], P2, K9, K2 tog, yfwd, K3, P2, K12, P2, K10, (K2 tog, yfwd) twice, sl 1, K1, psso, yfwd, sl 1, K1, psso, K10, P2, K12, P2, K3, yfwd, sl 1, K1, psso, K9, P2, K5[7:9]. 101[105:109] sts.
5th row K5[7:9], P2, K8, (K2 tog, yfwd) twice, K2, P2, sl next 6 sts on to cable needle and hold at front of work, K6 from left-hand needle then K6 from cable needle – **called C6F**, P2, K9, (K2 tog, yfwd) twice, K1, yfwd, sl 1, K1, psso, yfwd, sl 1, K1, psso, K10 making 13 sts for last lace panel), P2, K5[7:9] sts.

K1, psso, K9, P2, C6F, P2, K2, (yfwd, sl 1, K1, psso) twice, K8, P2, K5[7:9].
7th row K5[7:9], P2, K7, (K2 tog, yfwd) twice, K3, P2, K12, P2, K8, (K2 tog, yfwd) twice, K3, (yfwd, sl 1, K1, psso) twice, K8, P2, K12, P2, K3, (yfwd, sl 1, K1, psso) twice, K7, P2, K5[7:9].
9th row K5[7:9], P2, K6, (K2 tog, yfwd) twice, K4, P2, K12, P2, K7, (K2 tog, yfwd) twice, K5, (yfwd, sl 1, K1, psso) twice, K7, P2, K12, P2, K4, (yfwd, sl 1, K1, psso) twice, K6, P2, K5[7:9].
11th row K5[7:9], P2, K5, (K2 tog, yfwd) twice, K5, P2, K12, P2, K6, (K2 tog, yfwd) twice, K7, (yfwd, sl 1, K1, psso) twice, K6, P2, K12, P2, K5, (yfwd, sl 1, K1, psso) twice, K5, P2, K5[7:9].

Below: A bobbled sweater always has an exclusive look. The sweater is shown with larger bobbles for a dramatic effect.

13th row K5[7:9], P2, K4, (K2 tog, yfwd) twice, K6, P2, K12, P2, K5, (K2 tog, yfwd) twice, K9, (yfwd, sl 1, K1, psso) twice, K5, P2, K12, P2, K6, (yfwd, sl 1, K1, psso) twice, K4, P2, K5[7:9].

Note: There are two sizes of bobbles given, for the smaller one work as given here, for the larger one follow the 15th row (large bobbles).

15th row (small bobbles) K5[7:9], P2, K3, (K2 tog, yfwd) twice, K3, (P1, K1, P1, K1, P1) all into next st, turn and K5, turn and P5, lift 2nd, 3rd, 4th and 5th sts over first st and off needle – **called MB**, K3, P2, K12, P2, K4, (K2 tog, yfwd) twice, K5, MB, K5, (yfwd, sl 1, K1, psso) twice, K4, P2, K12, P2, K3, MB, K3, (yfwd, sl 1, K1, psso) twice, K3, P2, K5[7:9].

15th row (large bobbles) K5[7:9], P2, K3, (K2 tog, yfwd) twice, K3, (K1, yfwd, K1, yfwd, K1, yfwd, K1) all into next st, turn and P7, turn and K7, lift 2nd, 3rd, 4th, 5th and 6th sts over first st and off needle – **called MB**, K3, P2, K12, P2, K4, (K2 tog, yfwd) twice, K5, MB, K5, (yfwd, sl 1, K1, psso) twice, K4, P2, K12, P2, K3, MB, K3, (yfwd, sl 1, K1, psso) twice, K3, P2, K5[7:9].

17th row K5[7:9], P2, K2, (K2 tog, yfwd) twice, K8, P2, C6F, P2, K3, (K2 tog, yfwd) twice, K13, (yfwd, sl 1, K1, psso) twice, K3, P2, C6F, P2, K8, (yfwd, sl 1, K1, psso) twice, K2, P2, K5[7:9].

19th row K5[7:9], P2, K1, (K2 tog, yfwd) twice, K9, P2, K12, P2, K2, (K2 tog, yfwd) twice, K15, (yfwd, sl 1, K1, psso) twice, K2, P2, K12, P2,

K9, (yfwd, sl 1, K1, psso) twice, K1, P2, K5[7:9].

21st row K5[7:9], P2, (K2 tog, yfwd) twice, K2, MB, K7, P2, K12, P2, K1, (K2 tog, yfwd) twice, K4, MB, K7, MB, K4, (yfwd, sl 1, K1, psso) twice, K1, P2, K12, P2, K7, MB, K2, (yfwd, sl 1, K1, psso) twice, P2, K5 [7:9].

23rd row K5 [7:9], P2, K14, P2, K12, P2, (K2 tog, yfwd) twice, K9, inc one in next st, K9, (yfwd, sl 1, K1, psso) twice, P2, K12, P2, K14, P2, K5[7:9]. 102[106:110] sts.

24th row As 2nd.

These 24 rows form the patt. Cont in patt until work measure 33 [34:35]cm/13 [13½:13¾]in from beg, ending with a Ws row.

Shape armholes

Keeping patt correct, cast off 2 sts at beg of next 2 rows. Dec one st at beg of next 20 rows.

Cast off rem sts, working K2 tog 6 times across each cable panel when casting sts off, counting each K2 tog as one st.

Front

Work as given for back until 10 rows less in armhole shaping have been completed, ending with a Ws row.

Shape neck

Next row Dec one st, patt 33 sts, cast off 18[22:26] sts for centre neck, noting that centre panel sts have been counted as 28 and this may vary depending on patt row being worked, patt to end.

Complete right side first. Cont dec at armhole edge to match back, *at*

the same time cast off at neck edge on every alt row 6 sts twice, 5 sts once, 4 sts once and 3 sts once, working K2 tog 6 times across cable panel when casting sts off, as given for back.

With Ws of work facing rejoin yarn to rem sts and complete to match first side, reversing shaping.

Sleeves

With 3¾mm/No 9 needles cast on 41 [45:49] sts. Work 7cm/2¾in K1, P1 rib, ending with a Rs row.

Next row (inc row) Rib 4 [6:8] sts, *inc in next st, K1, rep from * 15 times more, inc in next st, rib 4 [6:8] sts. 58 [62:66] sts. Change to 5mm/No 6 needles.

1st row (Rs) K13[15:17] sts, P2, (patt 28 sts as 1st row of centre panel on back), P2, K13[15:17] sts.

Cont in patt as now set, inc one st at each end of 7th and every foll 8th row 9 times in all. 76[80:84] sts. Cont without shaping until sleeve measures 42 [43:44]cm/16½ [17:17¼] in from beg, ending with a Ws row.

Shape top

Cast off 2 sts at beg of next 2 rows. Dec one st at beg of next 20 rows. Cast off rem sts.

Yoke cable

With 5mm/No 6 needles and separate length of contrast yarn cast on 16 sts. With main yarn commence patt.

1st row K1, P1, K12, P1, K1.

2nd row P1, K1, P12, K1, P1.

Rep last 2 rows once more.

5th row K1, P1, C6F, P1, K1.

Cont in patt as now set working C6F on every foll 12th row until 18[19:20] cable twists in all have been completed, then work 7 more rows. Leave sts on holder.

Unpick contrast yarn at cast on edge and join yoke cable into a circle by grafting sts tog. Mark this point as centre back.

Yoke

With 4½mm/No 7 circular needle and with Rs of yoke cable facing, beg at centre back and pick up and K170 [176:182] sts along one side of cable, working into the P sts. Work in rounds of st st until yoke measures 3cm/1¼in from beg of st st.

Next round (dec round) K9 [3:9] sts,

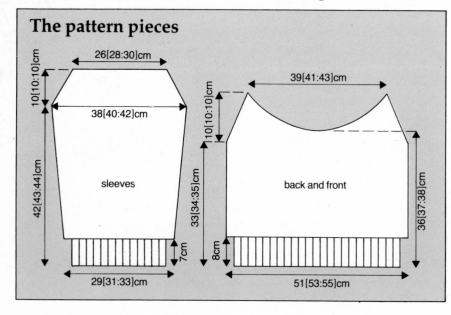

The pattern pieces

sleeves — 26[28:30]cm (top), 38[40:42]cm, 10[10:10]cm, 42[43:44]cm, 7cm, 29[31:33]cm

back and front — 39[41:43]cm, 10[10:10]cm, 33[34:35]cm, 36[37:38]cm, 8cm, 51[53:55]cm

K2 tog, *K8[6:4] sts, K2 tog, rep from * 14[20:26] times more, K9[3:9] sts. 154 sts all sizes. Cont in rounds of st st, until yoke measures 5cm/2in from beg.
Next round (dec round) *K5, K2 tog, rep from * to end. 132 sts. Cont in rounds of st st until yoke measures 7cm/3¼in from beg.

Next round (dec round) *K4, K2 tog, rep from * to end. 110 sts. Cont in st st until yoke measures 17cm/6¾in from beg. Cast off very loosely.

To make up

Do not press. Join raglan seams. Sew yoke in place to front, back and top of sleeves. Join side and sleeve seams. Roll neck edge over to Rs of work so that P side of fabric is showing.

Above: This sweater has smaller bobbles for a more delicate look. Though it looks complicated, it is very easy to knit.

Striped coat

Although large, this coat is fairly quick to make. It is knitted in a thick yarn and worked in garter stitch throughout with the minimum of shaping and so is suitable for an inexperienced knitter.

Sizes

To fit 81–86cm/32–34in bust
Length to shoulder, 108cm/42½in
Sleeve seam, 50cm/19¾in incl cuff

You will need

10×40g balls Sunbeam Sceptre Double Double (60% acrylic, 20% wool, 20% nylon) in main colour A
4×40g balls of same in contrast colours B, D and E
3×40g balls of same in contrast colours C, F, G and H
2×40g balls of same in contrast colour J
One pair of 5½mm/No 5 needles
One 5½mm/No 5 circular needle, 100cm/39½in long

Tension

16 sts and 32 rows to 10cm/4in over g st worked on 5½mm/No 5 needles

Note

The garment is worked throughout in g st stripes. The side on which broken rows of colour show is the right side

Back

With 5½mm/No 5 circular needle and B cast on 172 sts. Working from side edge to side edge and in g st throughout, beg striped patt.
Work *6 rows B, 4 rows C, 6 rows D, 6 rows E, 4 rows F, 8 rows A, 2 rows J, 6 rows G, 6 rows H, 6 rows B, 4 rows C, 6 rows D, 6 rows E, 4 rows F, 8 rows A, 2 rows J **, 6 rows G, now beg with 2 rows J work back in reverse from ** to *.
Work one more row in B.
Cast off loosely.

Right front

Cast on and work first 65 rows as given for back, ending with 1 row in E.

Left: Select plain or broken lines of colour for the right side before picking up the stitches for the front border.

Shape neck

Keeping stripe patt correct throughout, beg shaping.
1st row K to last 2 sts, turn.
2nd row K to end.
3rd row K to last 4 sts, turn.
4th row K to end.
5th row K to last 6 sts, turn.
6th row K to end.
7th row K to last 8 sts, turn.
8th row K to end.
9th row K to last 10 sts.
74 rows in all have been worked, ending with 4 rows in F.
Break off yarn and leave sts on a holder or length of spare yarn.

Left front

Work to match right front, working only 64 rows in patt before beg neck shaping, to reverse shaping. Complete as given for right front, working 1 row extra after 9 rows of neck shaping.

Sleeves

With 5½mm/No 5 needles and B cast on 96 sts. Working from top of sleeve down, K 2 rows. Cont in g st throughout and beg stripe patt. Work *6 rows H, 6 rows G, 2 rows J, 8 rows A, 4 rows F, 6 rows E, 6 rows D, 4 rows C, 6 rows B, rep from * once more then the first 32 rows again *at the same time* dec one st at each end of every 6th row until 56 sts rem.
After 128 rows of striped patt have been completed, work 10cm/4in g st in A, ending with a Ws row. Cast off.

Front border

Join shoulder seams.
With Rs of work facing, 5½mm/No 5 needles and A pick up and K23 sts across row ends of back neck. K one row.

Above: The stripe sequence continues over from the back on to the sleeves.

Next row K23 sts, then K2 sts from left front neck holder, turn.
Next row K25 sts, then K2 sts from right front holder, turn.
Next row K27 sts, then K2 sts from left front neck holder, turn.
Cont to work 2 more front neck sts in this way on every row for 7 more rows. 43 sts.
Change to 5½mm/No 5 circular needle.
Next row K43, then K across the rem 162 sts on holder for front edge.
Next row K205, then K across the rem 162 sts on holder for 2nd front edge. 367 sts.
Work 10cm/4in in g st, ending with a Ws row. Cast off loosely.

To make up

Do not press. Sew in sleeves. Join side and sleeve seams.

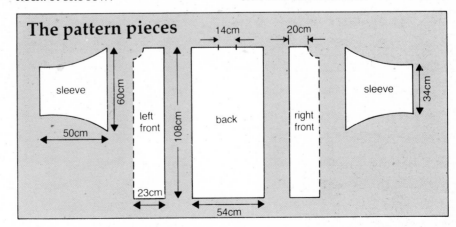

The pattern pieces

sleeve
60cm
50cm
left front
108cm
23cm
14cm
back
54cm
20cm
right front
sleeve
34cm

Cable pattern coat

This three-quarter length coat in reversed stocking stitch with twisted stitch panels combines warmth with casual elegance. Full sleeves are caught in at the cuffs with a neat rib to echo the stand-up collar.

Sizes

To fit 84 [94]cm/33 [37]in bust
Length to shoulder, 78 [80]cm/
 31 [31½]in
Sleeve seam, 45cm/17¾in
 adjustable
The figures in [] refer to the 94cm/37in size only

You will need

21 [23]×50g balls of Phildar
 Kadischa (75% acrylic, 25% wool)
One pair 6mm/No 4 needles
One pair 7mm/No 2 needles
One 7mm/No 2 crochet hook
One button

Tension

13 sts and 18 rows to 10cm/4in over patt worked on 7mm/No 2 needles

Back

With 7mm/No 2 needles cast on 78 [85] sts.
1st row (Rs) P3, *K second st on left-hand needle then K first st and sl them off needle tog – **called cr2**, P5, rep from * to last 5 sts, cr2, P3.
2nd row K3, *P2, K5, rep from * to last 5 sts, P2, K3.
These 2 rows form patt. Cont in patt until work measures 30cm/11¾in from beg, ending with a Ws row.

Shape panels

Next row P3 *cr2, P2, P2 tog, P1, rep from * to last 5 sts, cr2, P3. 68[74] sts.
Next row K3, *P2, K4, rep from * to last 5 sts, P2, K3.
Cont in patt as now set until work measures 56cm/22in from beg, ending with a Ws row.

Shape armholes

Keeping patt correct, cast off at beg of next and every row 3[4] sts twice, 2 sts twice and one st 4 times. 54[58] sts.
Cont without shaping until armholes measure 22 [24]cm/8¾ [9½]in from beg, ending with Ws row.

Shape shoulders

Cast off 7[8] sts at beg of next 4 rows. Cast off rem 26 sts.

Left front

With 7mm/No 2 needles cast on 38 [42] sts.
1st row (Rs) P3, *cr2, P5, rep from * to last 7 [4] sts, cr2, P5 [2] sts.
2nd row K5 [2] sts, *P2, K5, rep from * to last 5 sts, P2, K3.
Cont in patt as now set until work measures 30cm/11¾in from beg ending with a Ws row.

Shape panels

Next row P3, *cr2, P2, P2 tog, P1, rep from * to last 7[4] sts, cr2, P5[2] sts. 34[37] sts.

Next row K5[2] sts, *P2, K4, rep from * to last 5 sts, P2, K3.
Cont in patt as now set until work measures same as back to underarm, ending with a Ws row.

Shape armhole

Cast off at beg of next and every alt row 3[4] sts once, 2 sts once and one st twice. 27[29] sts.
Cont without shaping until armhole measures 18 [20]cm/7 [8¼]in from beg, ending with a Rs row.

Shape neck

Cast off at beg of next and every alt row 6 sts once, 3 sts once, 2 sts once and one st twice, ending with a Ws row.

Shape shoulder

Cast off at beg of next and foll alt row 7[8] sts twice.

Right front

With 7mm/No 3 needles cast on 38 [42] sts.
1st row (Rs) P5[2] sts, *cr2, P5, rep from * to last 5 sts, cr2, P3.
2nd row K3, *P2, K5, rep from * to last 7[4] sts, P2, K5[2] sts.
Cont in patt as now set until work measures 30cm/11¾in from beg, ending with a Ws row.

Shape panels

Next row P5[2] sts, *cr2, P2, P2 tog, P1, rep from * to last 5 sts, cr2, P3. 34[37] sts.
Cont in patt as now set and complete to match left front, reversing all shaping.

Sleeves

With 6mm/No 4 needles cast on 27 [29] sts.
1st row (Rs) P1, *K1, P1, rep from * to end.
2nd row K1, *P1, K1, rep from * to end.
Rep these 2 rows for 6cm/2¼in ending with a 1st row.

Small size only

Next row (inc row) K2, *inc 1 by picking up loop and K tbl, K2, inc 1, K1, rep from * 7 times more, inc 1, K1. 44 sts.

Medium size only

Next row (inc row) K1, *inc 1 by picking up loop and K tb1, K2, (inc 1, K1) twice, rep from * 6 times

---

The pattern pieces

sleeve

15[17]cm
39cm
6cm
38[43]cm
34[38]cm
21[22]cm

20cm
11[12]cm
22[24]cm
42[44]cm
52[57]cm
56cm
74[76]cm

left front   back

62[67]cm

more. 50 sts.

Both sizes

Change to 7mm/No 2 needles.
1st row (Rs) P3, *cr2, P4, rep from * to last 5 sts, cr2, P3.
2nd row K3, *P2, K4, rep from * to last 5 sts, P2, K3.
Cont in patt as now set, inc one st at each end of 21st and every foll 20th row until there are 50[56] sts.
Cont without shaping until sleeve measures 45cm/17¾in from beg, or required length to underarm, ending with a Ws row.

Shape top

Cast off at beg of next and every row 3[4] sts twice and 2 sts twice. Dec one st at each end of next and foll 7[9] alt rows, ending with a Ws row. Cast off at beg of next and every row 2 sts 4 times, 3 sts twice and 10 sts once.

Neckband

Join shoulder seams. With Rs of work facing and 6mm/No 4 needles, pick up and K55 [57] sts evenly round neck. Beg with a 2nd row, work in K1, P1 rib as given for cuff for 7cm/2¾in. Cast off in rib.

To make up

Do not press as this will flatten patt. Sew in sleeves. Join side and sleeve seams.

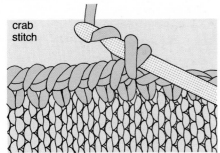

crab stitch

Front edges With Rs of left front edge facing and 7mm/No 2 hook, work one row of dc down front edge. Do not turn but work another row of dc back along same edge – **called crab st.** Work up right front edge in same way, making a button loop 4 sts from beg of last row by making 4ch, miss 3dc, 1dc into each dc to end. Sew on button to left front.

Right: This casual coat is light and warm and looks stunning worn with trousers for brisk country walks.

Cable jacket

Multi-twisted cables decorate the body and sleeves of this beautiful jacket. The cable pattern needs concentration but as it is repeated it gets easier as you go along.
All the borders are worked in Irish moss stitch and the top of the sleeves include dart shaping in moss stitch. Shoulder pads can be inserted if you wish.

Sizes
To fit 86 [91:97]cm/34 [36:38]in bust
Length to shoulder, 55 [57:59]cm/21¾ [22½:23¼]in
Sleeve seam, 40cm/15¾in
The figures in [] refer to the 91/36 and 97cm/38in sizes respectively

You will need
10 [11:12] × 50g balls of Lister-Lee Thermoknit for Aran (50% polypropylene, 30% acrylic, 20% wool)
One pair 4½mm/No 7 needles
One pair 5mm/No 6 needles
One cable needle
Five buttons

Left: Beautiful, intricate cables are the main feature on this jacket. Wear it belted or thread a twisted cord through the eyelet holes at the waist.

Tension
18 sts and 22 rows to 10cm/4in over st st worked on 5mm/No 6 needles

Cable pattern panel
This panel is worked over 20 sts, which inc to 30 sts as the pattern is worked.
1st row P10, pick up loop lying between needles and K tbl – **called M1K**, P10.
2nd row K10, M1K, P twice into next st, M1K, K10.
3rd row P9, (sl next st on to cable needle and hold at back of work, K next 2 sts tbl – **called K2B**, P1 from cable needle – **called cr3R**), (sl next 2 sts on to cable needle and hold at front of work, P1, K2B from cable needle – **called cr3L**), P9.
4th row K8, (sl next st on to cable needle and hold at front of work, P next 2 sts tbl – **called P2B**, K1 from cable needle – **called tw3R**), K2, (sl next 2 sts on to cable needle and hold at back of work, K1, P2B from cable needle – **called tw3L**), K8.
5th row P8, K2B, P4, K2B, P8.
6th row K8, P2B, K4, P2B, K8.
7th row P8, (sl next 2 sts on to cable needle and hold at front of work, K1, K2B from cable needle – **called cr3LK**), P2, (sl next st on to cable needle and hold at back of work, K2B, K1 from cable needle – **called cr3RK**), P8.
8th row K8, P next st tbl – **called P1B**, M1K, tw3L, tw3R, M1K, P1B, K8.
9th row P7, cr3R, P1, (sl next 2 sts on to cable needle and hold at back of work, K2B, K2B from cable needle – **called cr4K**), P1, cr3L, P7.
10th row K6, tw3R, K2, P next 4 sts tbl – **called P4B**, K2, tw3L, K6.
11th row P5, cr3R, P3, K next 4 sts tbl – **called K4B**, P3, cr3L, P5.
12th row K5, P2B, K4, P4B, K4, P2B, K5.
13th row P5, K2B, P4, K4B, P4, K2B, P5.
14th row K5, (sl next 2 sts on to cable needle and hold at back of work, P1, P2B from cable needle – **called tw3LP**), K3, (sl next 2 sts on to cable needle and hold at back of work, P2B, P2B from cable needle – **called cr4P**), K3, (sl next st on to cable needle and hold at front of work, P2B, P1 from cable needle – **called tw3RP**), K5.
15th row P5, K next st tbl – **called K1B**, M1K, cr3L, P2, K4B, P2, cr3R, M1K, K1B, P5.
16th row K4, tw3R, K1, tw3L, K1, P4B, K1, tw3R, K1, tw3L, K4.
17th row P3, cr3R, P3, cr3L, cr4K, cr3R, P3, cr3L, P3.
18th row K3, P2B, K5, tw3L, P2B, tw3R, K5, P2B, K3.
19th row P3, K2B, pick up loop lying between sts and P tbl – **called M1P**, P6, cr3L, cr3R, P6, M1P, K2B, P3. 30 sts.

Cable abbreviations used in this pattern

Note: Throughout these abbreviations, the front of work means the side which is facing you and the back of work means side away from you, regardless of Rs or Ws pattern row. Cable needle is referred to as cn.

K1B	K next 1, 2 or 4 sts
K2B	through back of loop
K4B	
P1B	P next 1, 2 or 4 sts
P2B	through back of loop
P4B	
M1K	pick up loop between sts and K tbl
M1P	pick up loop between sts and P tbl
cr3R	sl next st on to cable needle (cn) and hold at back of work, K2B, P1 from cn
tw3L	sl next 2 sts on to cn and hold at back of work, K1, P2B from cn
cr3L	sl next 2 sts on to cn and hold at front of work, P1, K2B from cn
tw3R	sl next st on to cn and hold at front of work, P2B, K1 from cn
cr3RK	sl next st on to cn and hold at back of work, K2B, K1 from cn
tw3LP	sl next 2 sts on to cn and hold at back of work, P1, P2B from cn
cr3LK	sl next 2 sts on to cn and hold at front of work, K1, K2B from cn
tw3RP	sl next st on to cn and hold at front of work, P2B, P1 from cn
cr4K	sl next 2 sts on to cn and hold at back of work, K2B, K2B from cn
cr4P	sl next 2 sts on to cn and hold at back of work, P2B, P2B from cn
tw2RP	sl next st on to cn and hold at front of work, P1B, P1B from cn
tw2LP	sl next st on to cn and hold at back of work, P1B, P1B from cn
cr2R	sl next st on to cn and hold at back of work, K1B, P1 from cn
tw2L	sl next st on to cn and hold at back of work, K1, P1B from cn
cr2L	sl next st on to cn and hold at front of work, P1, K1B from cn
tw2R	sl next st on to cn and hold at front of work, P1B, K1 from cn

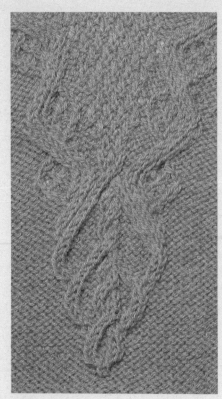

Above: An alternative colourway showing a detail of the moss stitch dart incorporated in the cable panel.

20th row K3, tw3L, K7, cr4P, K7, tw3R, K3.

21st row P3, K1B, cr3L, P6, K4B, P6, cr3R, K1B, P3.

22nd row K3, (sl next st on to cable needle and hold at back of work, P1B, P1B from cable needle – **called tw2LP**), tw3L, K5, P4B, K5, tw3R, (sl next st on cable needle and hold at front of work, P1B, P1B from cable needle – **called tw2RP**), K3.

23rd row P3, (cr3L) twice, P4, K4B, P4, (cr3R) twice, P3.

24th row K4, (tw3L) twice, K3, cr4P, K3, (tw3R) twice, K4.

25th row P5, (cr3L) twice, P2, K4B, P2, (cr3R) twice, P5.

26th row K4, tw2RP, (tw3L) twice, K1, P4B, K1, (tw3R) twice, tw2LP, K4.

27th row P3, (sl next st on to cable needle and hold at back of work, K1B, P1 from cable needle – **called cr2R**), (sl next st on to cable needle and hold at front of work, P1, K1B from cable needle – **called cr2L**), (cr3L) twice, cr4K, (cr3R) twice, cr2R, cr2L, P3.

28th row K2, tw2RP, K2, tw2LP, (tw3L) twice, P2B, (tw3R) twice, tw2RP, K2, tw2LP, K2.

29th row P1, (cr2R, cr2L) twice,

(cr3L) twice, (cr3R) twice, (cr2R, cr2L) twice, P1.

30th row K1, P1B, K2, tw2RP, K2, P1B, K1, P2B, K1, cr4P, K1, P2B, K1, P1B, K2, tw2LP, K2, P1B, K1.

31st row P1, (cr2L, cr2R) twice, cr3R, P1, K4B, P1, cr3L, (cr2L, cr2R) twice, P1.

32nd row K2, (sl next st on to cable needle and hold at back of work, K1, P1B from cable needle – **called tw2L**), K2, (sl next st on to cable needle and hold at front of work, P1B, K1 from cable needle – **called tw2R**), tw3R, K2, P4B, K2, tw3L, tw2L, K2, tw2R, K2.

33rd row P3, cr2L, cr2R, cr3R, P3, K4B, P3, cr3L, cr2L, cr2R, P3.

34th row K4, tw2R, tw3R, K4, P4B, K4, tw3L, tw2L, K4.

35th row P3, cr2R, cr3R, P5, cr4K, P5, cr3L, cr2L, P3.

36th row K2, tw2R, tw3R, tw2LP, K4, P4B, K4, tw2RP, tw3L, tw2L, K2.

37th row P1, cr2R, cr3R, cr2R, cr2L, P3, K4B, P3, cr2R, cr2L, cr3L, cr2L, P1.

38th row Tw2R, tw3R, tw2RP, K2, tw2LP, K2, P4B, K2, tw2RP, K2, tw2LP, tw3L, tw2L.

39th row P1, cr3R, (cr2R, cr2L) twice, P1, K4B, P1, (cr2R, cr2L) twice, cr3L, P1.

40th row K1, P2B, K1, P1B, K2, tw2LP, K2, P1B, K1, cr4P, K1, P1B, K2, tw2RP, K2, P1B, K1, P2B, K1.

41st row P1, cr3L, (cr2L, cr2R) twice, P1, K4B, P1, (cr2L, cr2R) twice, cr3R, P1.

42nd row K2, tw3L, tw2L, K2, tw2R, K2, P4B, K2, tw2L, K2, tw2R, tw3R, K2.

43rd row P3, cr3L, cr2L, cr2R, P3, K4B, P3, cr2L, cr2R, cr3R, P3.

44th row K4, tw3L, tw2L, K4, P4B, K4, tw2R, tw3R, K4.

45th row P5, cr3L, cr2L, P3, cr4K, P3, cr2R, cr3R, P5.

46th row K4, tw2RP, tw3L, tw2L, K2, P4B, K2, tw2R, tw3R, tw2LP, K4.

47th row P3, cr2R, cr2L, cr3L, cr2L, P1, K4B, P1, cr2R, cr3R, cr2R, cr2L, P3.

48th row K2, tw2RP, K2, tw2LP, tw3L, tw2L, P4B, tw2R, tw3R, tw2RP, K2, tw2LP, K2.

49th row P1, (cr2R, cr2L) twice, cr3L, P1, K4B, P1, cr3R, (cr2R, cr2L) twice, P1.

Rep from 30th to 49th rows inclusive throughout.

Back

With 4½mm/No 7 needles cast on 83 [87:91] sts. Commence Irish moss st.

1st row (Rs) K1, *P1, K1, rep from * to end.

2nd row P1, *K1, P1, rep from * to end.

3rd row as 2nd.

4th row as 1st.

Rep these 4 rows for 10cm/4in, ending with a Ws row and inc one st at end of last row. 84 [88:92] sts. Change to 5mm/No 6 needles.

Next row (eyelet hole row) K3, *yfwd, K2 tog, K2, rep from * to last st, K1.

Beg with a K row cont in reversed st st until work measures 23 [24:25]cm/ 9 [9½:9¾]in from beg, ending with a K row.

Commence cable patt, or cont in reversed st st, noting that sts will not be increased in this event.

Next row P10 [11:12] sts, work 1st row of cable panel, P24 [26:28] sts, work 1st row of cable panel, P10 [11:12] sts.

Next row K10 [11:12] sts, work 2nd row of cable panel, K24 [26:28] sts, work 2nd row of cable panel, K10 [11:12] sts.

Keeping each end and centre in reversed st st and beg with 3rd row on cable panel, cont in patt as now set, noting that after 19th row of panel there will be 104 [108:112] sts. Cont until work measures 35 [36:37]cm/13¾ [14¼:14½]in from beg, ending with a Ws row.

Shape armholes

Keeping patt correct throughout, cast off at beg of next and every row 3 sts twice and 2 sts twice. Dec one st at each end of next and foll 3 [4:5] alt rows. 86 [88:90] sts. Cont without shaping until armholes measure 18 [19:20]cm/ 7 [7½:7¾]in from beg, ending with a Ws row.

Shape neck

Next row Patt 35 sts, turn and leave rem sts on holder.
Complete right shoulder first.
Cast off 2 sts at beg of next row for neck. Dec one st at beg of foll alt row for neck, ending with a Ws row.

Shape shoulder

Cast off rem 32 sts for shoulder.

With Rs of work facing, rejoin yarn to rem sts on holder, cast off first 16 [18:20] sts loosely, patt to end. Work 1 row. Complete to match right shoulder, reversing shaping.

Left front

With 4½mm/No 7 needles cast on 45 [47:51] sts. Work 10cm/4in moss st as given for back, ending with a Ws row and inc 1 [2:1] sts in last row. 46 [49:52] sts.
Change to 5mm/No 6 needles.**
Next row (eyelet hole row) *K2, K2 tog, yfwd, rep from * to last 6 [9:8] sts, K0 [3:2] sts, moss st 6 sts.
Next row Moss st 6 sts, K to end.
Keeping 6 sts at front edge in moss st throughout, cont in reversed st st until work measures 23 [24:25]cm/ 9 [9½:9¾]in from beg, ending with a K row.
Commence cable patt.
Next row P10 [11:12] sts, work 1st row of cable panel, P10 [12:14] sts, moss st 6.
Next row Moss st 6 sts, K10 [12:14] sts, work 2nd row of cable panel, K10 [11:12] sts.
Keeping moss st and reversed st st correct, beg with 3rd row of cable panel and cont in patt as now set noting that after 19th row of panel there will be 56 [59:62] sts.
Cont until work measures same as back to underarm, ending with a Ws row.

Shape armhole

Keeping patt correct throughout, cast off at beg of next and foll alt row 3 sts once and 2 sts once. Dec one st at beg of foll 4 [5:6] alt rows. 47 [49:51] sts.
Cont without shaping until armhole measures 10 [11:12]cm/4 [4¼:4¾]in from beg, ending with a Ws row.

Shape neck

Next row Patt to last 6 sts, turn and leave these 6 sts on safety pin.
Cast off at beg of next and every alt row 2 sts 2 [3:4] times. Dec one st at beg of foll 5 alt rows. 32 sts.
Cont without shaping until armhole measures same as back to shoulder, ending with a Ws row.
Cast off.
Mark positions of 5 buttons on front band, first to come 15cm/6in from beg and last to come on last Rs row before neck shaping, with 3 more evenly spaced between.

Right front

Work to match left front to **
Next row (eyelet hole row) Moss st 6 sts, K0 [3:2] sts, *yfwd, K2 tog, K2, rep from * to end.
Cont as given for left front reversing position of cable panel, all shapings and making buttonholes as markers are reached on Rs rows as foll:
Next row (buttonhole row) Moss st 3 sts, cast off one st, patt to end.
Next row Patt to end, casting on one st above st cast off in previous row.

Sleeves

With 4½mm/No 7 needles cast on 43 [45:47] sts. Work 3cm/1¼in moss st as given for back, ending with a Ws row and inc one st at end of last row. 44 [46:48] sts.
Change to 5mm/No 6 needles. K one row.
Beg with a K row cont in reversed st st, inc one st at each end of every 8th row 10 times in all, *at the same time* when work measures 31cm/ 12¼in from beg, ending with a K row, work first 20 rows of cable panel in centre of sleeve sts. 74 [76:78] sts.

Shape top

Keeping patt correct throughout, cast off at beg of next and every row 3 sts 4 times, 2 sts 4 times and one st twice. 52 [54:56] sts.

Shape dart

Next row (31st cable panel row) Patt 24 [25:26] sts, (K1, P1, M1K, P1, K1, for dart), patt 24 [25:26] sts.

Next row Patt to centre 5 sts, P1, (K1, P1) twice, patt to end.
Next row P2 tog, patt to centre 5 sts, P1, (K1, P1) twice, patt to last 2 sts, P2 tog.
Next row Patt to centre 5 sts, K1, (P1, K1) twice, patt to end.
Next row Patt to centre 5 sts, M1P, K1, (P1, K1) twice, M1P, patt to end.
Next row Patt to centre 7 sts, moss st 7 as now set, patt to end.
Keeping centre dart sts in moss st as now set, inc one st on each side of these sts on 41st, 45th, 51st and 55th rows of patt, *at the same time* dec one st at each end of next and every foll 4th row 4 times in all, then at each end of foll 3 alt rows, ending with a Ws row. 47 [49:51] sts.
Cast off at beg of next and every row 2 sts twice and 43 [45:47] sts once.

Neckband

Join shoulder seams. With Rs of work facing and 4½mm/No 7 needles moss st across 6 sts of right front, pick up and K63 [65:67] sts round neck, then moss st across 6 sts of left front.
Work 3cm/1¼in moss st. Cast off in patt.

To make up

Do not press. Sew in sleeves easing in top to fit armholes. Join side and sleeve seams. Sew on buttons. Using 2 strands of yarn make a twisted cord about 100cm/40in long and thread through eyelet holes at waist.

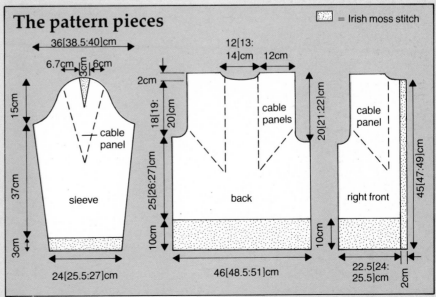

The pattern pieces

= Irish moss stitch

36[38.5:40]cm
6.7cm 3cm 6cm
15cm
cable panel
37cm
sleeve
3cm
24[25.5:27]cm

12[13:14]cm 12cm
2cm
18[19:20]cm
25[26:27]cm
10cm
cable panels
back
20[21:22]cm
46[48.5:51]cm

cable panel
right front
22.5[24:25.5]cm
45[47:49]cm
10cm
2cm

Chevron jacket

Make this warm, chunky jacket in only a few evenings, the thick yarn and large needles make it very quick to knit.

The Twilleys Minx yarn, when knitted, looks as if strips of fur have been stitched in to the knitting.

If you prefer the jacket without its furry collar then just pick up the 49 stitches round the neck and work in rib as given for the cuffs and welt.

Sizes

To fit 86–91cm/34–36in bust
Length to shoulder, 63cm/24¾in
Sleeve seam, 44cm/17¼in

You will need

11×50g balls of Twilleys Minx (62% alpaca, 30% acrylic, 8% cotton) in main colour A
4×100g balls of Twilleys Capricorn Bulky Knitting (50% nylon, 50% acrylic) in contrast colour B
One pair 6mm/No 4 needles
One pair 8mm/No 0 needles
One 60cm/24in open-ended zip fastener

Tension

9 sts and 13 rows to 10cm/4in over patt worked on 8mm/No 0 needles

Back

With 8mm/No 0 needles and B cast on 3 sts.
1st row K into front and back of first st – **called inc 1**, inc 1 in next st, K1. 5 sts.
2nd row P to end.
3rd row Inc 1, K to last 2 sts, inc 1, K1. 7 sts.
4th row P to end.
5th row With A, as 3rd row. 9 sts.
6th row With A, K to end.
7th and 8th rows As 5th and 6th. 11 sts.
9th to 12th rows With B, rep 3rd and 4th rows twice.
Rep the 5th to 12th rows twice, then the 5th and 6th rows once more. 33 sts. **
Break off yarn and leave sts on holder. Work a second piece in the same way, but do not break off yarn.

Join back pieces

31st row With A, inc 1, K to last 2 sts, sl 1, K1, psso, then working across 33 sts of first piece, K2 tog, K to last 2 sts, inc 1, K1. 66 sts.
32nd row With A, K to end.
33rd row With B, inc 1, K30, sl 1, K1, psso, K2 tog, K to last 2 sts, inc 1, K1.
34th row With B, P to end.
35th and 36th rows As 33rd and 34th.
37th to 40th rows Rep 31st and 32nd rows twice.
Rep the 33rd to 40th rows once more. 66 sts.

Shape armholes

1st row With B, cast off 3 sts, K28, sl 1, K1, psso, K2 tog, K to end. 61 sts.

Left: The diagonal stripes on the sleeves match exactly with the stripes on the front and back.

2nd row With B, cast off 3 sts, P to end. 58 sts.
3rd row With B, K27, sl 1, K1, psso, K2 tog, K to end.
4th row With B, P to end.
5th row With A, K26, sl 1, K1, psso, K2 tog, K to end.
6th row With A, K to end.
7th row With A, K25, sl 1, K1, psso, K2 tog, K to end.
8th row With A, K to end.
Working in stripes of 4 rows B, 4 rows A throughout, cont to dec in this way until 24 sts rem, ending with a Ws row. Cont to dec in centre of every Rs row, cast off 2 sts at beg of next 6 rows.
Cast off rem 6 sts.

Left front

Work as for back to **.
31st row With A, inc 1, K to last 2 sts, sl 1, K1, psso.
32nd row With A, K to end.
Cont in stripe patt as now set, rep last 2 rows until 48 rows have been worked from beg.

Shape armhole

1st row With B, cast off 3 sts, K to last 2 sts, sl 1, K1, psso.
2nd row With B, P to end.
3rd row With B, K to last 2 sts, sl 1, K1, psso.
4th row As 2nd.
Cont in patt, keep armhole edge straight and dec at front edge only on every alt row until 12 sts rem (ending with 4 rows in B). Cast off.

Right front

Work as for back to **
31st row With A, K2 tog, K to last 2 sts, inc 1, K1.
32nd row With A, K to end.
Cont in stripe patt as now set, rep last 2 rows until 48 rows have been worked from beg.

Shape armhole

1st row With B, K2 tog, K to end.
2nd row With B, cast off 3 sts, P to end.
3rd row As 1st.
4th row With B, P to end.
Complete as for left front, reversing the shaping as given.

Sleeves

Work first 22 rows as given for back. 25 sts. Break off yarn and leave sts on holder.
Work these first 22 rows again.

Join sleeve pieces

23rd row With A, inc 1, K22, sl 1, K1, psso, K2 tog from sts on holder, K to last 2 sts, inc 1, K1.
24th row With A, K to end. 50 sts.
Cont on these sts, working in stripe patt as now set until 48 rows have been worked from beg.

Shape top

1st row With A; cast off 3 sts, K20, sl 1, K1, psso, K2 tog, K to end.
2nd row With A, cast off 3 sts, K to end. 42 sts.
3rd row With A, K19, sl 1, K1, psso, K2 tog, K to end.
4th row With A, K to end. 40 sts.
Keeping patt correct, rep the last 2 rows until 8 sts rem, ending with a Ws row.
Cast off.

Cuffs

With Rs of work facing, 6mm/No 4 needles and B pick up and K31 sts along lower edge of sleeve.
1st row P1, *K1, P1, rep from * to end.
2nd row K1, *P1, K1, rep from * to end.
Rep last 2 rows for 10cm/4in. Cast off in rib.

Pockets (make 2)

With 8mm/No 0 needles and B cast on 18 sts.
Beg with a K row work 24cm/9½in st st, ending with a P row. Cast off.

Welt

With Rs facing fold pockets in half with lower cast-on edge to top cast-off edge and join side edges. Join about 4cm/1½in along cast-on and cast-off edges.
Join raglan seams. Join side seams, sewing pockets into side seams with lower edge of pocket about 4cm/1½in above lower edge of jacket.

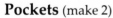

Above: A rib neckband can be knitted as an alternative to the collar.

With Rs of work facing, 6mm/No 4 needles and B pick up and K99 sts along lower edge of jacket. Work in rib as given for cuffs. Cast off in rib.

Collar

With 8mm/No 0 needles and B cast on 12 sts. P one row.
Beg with a K row, cont in st st casting on 6 sts at beg of next 6 rows. 48 sts.
Work 2 rows.
Join in A and K 8 rows. Break off A. With B, K 3 rows.
Beg with a P row work 7 rows st st. Cast off 6 sts at beg of next 6 rows.
Cast off rem 12 sts.

Ribbed neckband (alternative to collar)

With Rs of work facing, 6mm/No 4 needles and B pick up and K49 sts evenly round neck. Work as given for cuff. Cast off in rib.

To make up

Do not press. Join sleeve seams. Sew in zip, beg at centre of welt and ending at neck edge.
Fold welt and cuffs in half to inside and sl st down. Fold neckband in half if required and sl st down, or sew cast-on edge of collar to neck edge, then fold in half to inside and sl st down.

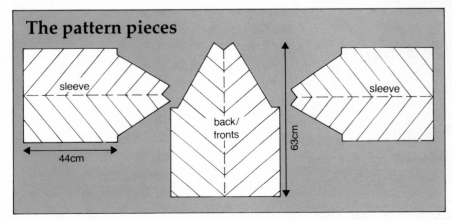

The pattern pieces

sleeve

44cm

back/fronts

63cm

sleeve

Fair Isle cardigan

The knitters of the Scottish Isles who are renowned for their skill at blending colours were probably not the originators of the art. Examples of Arabian coloured knitting indicate that it was well known by 450AD. The Moors brought the craft to Europe when they invaded Spain in the 8th century. The story goes that a ship of the Spanish Armada was wrecked on Fair Isle and the patterns on the jerseys of the dead sailors were copied by the islanders. One of the patterns is still called the Armada Cross.
Traditionally, Fair Isle patterns used natural wools that were hand dyed in muted shades of similar colours.
This cardigan has the same clever use of colour as an authentic Fair Isle pattern, but more contrasting colours are used in a smart, new design. The striking feature is the collar with multi-coloured fringing. Moss stitch has been used for the collar and cuffs to make an interesting effect. Extra instructions explain how the pattern can be adapted to a simple V neck.

Sizes

To fit 86 [91:97]cm/34 [36:38]in bust
Length to shoulder, 60 [61:62]cm/
23½ [24:24½]in
Sleeve seam, 46cm/18in
The figures in [] refer to 91/36 and 97cm/38in sizes respectively

You will need

4 [5:5] x 50g balls of 3 Suisses Suizetta 4 ply (85% Acrylic, 15% wool)
in main colour A
1 [2:2] x 50g balls of contrast colour B
1 x 50g ball each of contrast colours C, D, E, F, G and H
One 2¾mm/No 12 circular needle, 80cm/32in long
One 3¼mm/No 10 circular needle, 80cm/32in long
One pair 2¾mm/No 12 needles
One pair 3¼mm/No 10 needles
6 buttons

Tension

28 sts and 36 rows to 10cm/4in over st st and 28 sts and 28 rows to 10cm/4in over Fair Isle on 3¼mm/No 10 needles

Left: A finely knitted Fair Isle cardigan with multi-coloured fringing to add zest

Back and fronts

(worked in one piece)
With 2¾mm/No 12 circular needle and A cast on 253 [265:277] sts.
Work 4cm/1½in moss st. Change to 3¼mm/No 10 circular needle.
Beg with a K row cont in st st and patt from chart until work measures 40cm/ 15¾in from beg, ending with a P row.

Divide for armholes

Next row Keeping patt correct throughout, K56 [59:62] sts, cast off 12 sts, K117 [123:129] sts, cast off 12 sts, K56 [59:62] sts.
Cont on last 56 [59:62] sts for left front.
Next row P to end.
Next row Cast off 2 sts, K to end.
Next row P to end.
Next row K1, K2 tog, K to end.
Rep last 2 rows 6 [7:8] times more, then P one row. 47 [49:51] sts.

Shape front edge

Next row K to last 3 sts, sl 1, K1, psso, K1.
Next row P to end.
Rep last 2 rows until 27 [28:29] sts rem. Cont without shaping until armhole measures 20 [21:22]cm/7¾ [8¼: 8¾]in from beg, ending with a P row.

Shape shoulder

Cast off at beg of next and every alt row 7 sts 3 times and 6 [7:8] sts once.
With Ws of work facing, rejoin yarn

to 117 [123:129] sts for back and P to end.
Cast off 2 sts at beg of next 2 rows.
Next row K1, K2 tog, K to last 3 sts, sl 1, K1, psso, K1.
Next row P to end.
Rep last 2 rows 6 [7:8] times more.
99 [103:107] sts. Cont without shaping until armholes measure same as front to shoulder, ending with a P row.

Shape shoulders

Cast off at beg of next and every row 7 sts 6 times and 6 [7:8] sts twice. If making collar leave rem 45 [47:49] sts on holder for centre back neck. If making neckband, cast off.
With Ws of work facing, rejoin yarn to rem 56 [59:62] sts for right front and complete to match left front, reversing all shaping.

Sleeves

With 2¾mm/No 12 needles and A cast on 55 [59:63] sts. Work 4cm/1½in moss st. Change to 3¼mm/No 10 needles.
Beg with K row cont in st st patt from chart, starting on 43rd row.
Working extra sts into patt when possible, inc one st at each end of 7th

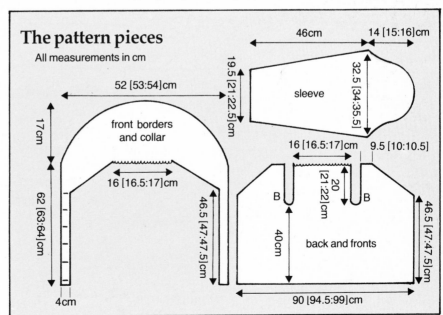

The pattern pieces
All measurements in cm

52 [53:54]cm

46cm   14 [15:16]cm

19.5 [21:22.5]cm

sleeve

32.5 [34:35.5]

17cm

front borders
and collar

16 [16.5:17]cm   9.5 [10:10.5]

16 [16.5:17]cm

20 [21:22]cm

62 [63:64]cm

16 [16.5:17]cm

46.5 [47:47.5]cm

B   B

40cm

back and fronts

46.5 [47:47.5]cm

4cm

90 [94.5:99]cm

and every foll 6th row until there are 91 [95:99] sts.

Cont without shaping until sleeve measures about 46cm/18in from beg, ending with a P row and same patt row as at underarm on body.

Shape top

Cast off 6 sts at beg of next 2 rows. Dec one st at each end of next and every alt row as given for back until 59 [61:63] sts rem, ending with a P row.

Cast off at beg of next and every row

Chart for pattern rows

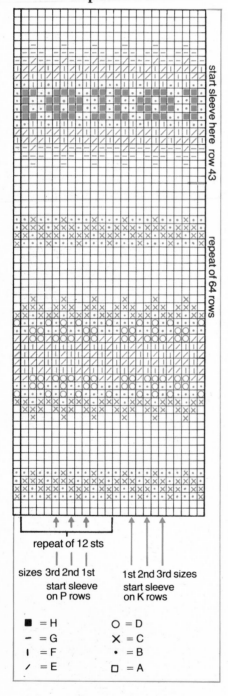

start sleeve here   row 43

repeat of 64 rows

repeat of 12 sts

sizes 3rd 2nd 1st   1st 2nd 3rd sizes
start sleeve   start sleeve
on P rows   on K rows

■ = H   O = D
— = G   X = C
I = F   • = B
∕ = E   □ = A

2 sts 10 times, 3 sts 4 times and 4 sts 4 times. Cast off rem 11 [13:15] sts.

Front borders and collar

Left front border

With 2¾mm/No 12 needles and A cast on 13 sts. Work in moss st until border is same length as front to shaping, ending with a Ws row. **. Inc one st at beg of next and every alt row until border measures same as front edge to shoulder, ending at shaped edge. Break off yarn and leave sts on holder.

Tack border in place along front edge and mark positions for buttons with pins, first pin in centre of welt and 6th pin about 2cm/¾in below beg of shaping, with 4 more evenly spaced between.

Right front border

With 2¾mm/No 12 needles and A cast on 13 sts. Work 2cm/¾in moss st ending with a Ws row.

Next row (buttonhole row) Moss st 5, cast off 3 sts, moss st to end.

Next row Moss st 5, cast on 3 sts, moss st to end.

Cont in moss st making buttonholes as markers are reached then cont until border, when slightly stretched, measures same as left front border to beg of shaping, ending with a Ws row. **

Inc one st at end of next and every alt row until border measures same as left front border, ending at straight edge.

Collar

Next row Moss st across sts of right front border, P across back neck sts

Above: The magic of Fair Isle is the way colours blend and melt together. Sketch

on holder, beg at shaped edge moss st across sts of left front border on holder.

Cont in moss st across all sts for 7cm/2¾in. Cast off at beg of next and every row 2 sts 36 times and 3 sts 12 times. Cast off rem sts.

Neckband

If collar is not required, cont in moss st on both borders from ** without shaping until borders reach to centre back neck. Cast off, join ends.

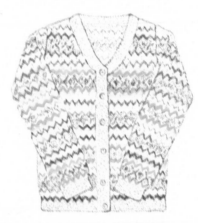

A sketch of the collarless version.

To make up

Do not press. Join shoulder seams. Set in sleeves. Join sleeve seams. Sew on front borders and collar, matching up right-front border with the left-front border which is already tacked in place. Alternatively sew on front borders and neckband only. From rem yarn cut lengths approx 15cm/6in long. Take 4 strands tog in colours as required and knot them into fringe round edge of collar. Sew on buttons.

your own colour combinations on graph paper before trying them out in knitting.

Camisole top and jacket

Sizes

To fit 81 [86:91:97]cm/32 [34:36:38]in bust

Cardigan length to shoulder, 56 [57:58:59]cm/22 [22½:22¾:23¼]in
Sleeve seam, 18cm/7in
Top length, about 42cm/16½in
The figures in [] refer to 86/34, 91/36 and 97cm/38in sizes respectively

You will need

Cardigan 12 [13:13:14]×25g balls of Wendy Shetland 4 ply, (100% wool)
Top 7 [7:8:8]×25g balls of same
One pair 2¾mm/No 12 needles
One pair 3¼mm/No 10 needles

Tension

28 sts and 36 rows to 10cm/4in over st st worked on 3¼mm/No 10 needles

Cardigan back and fronts

Worked in one piece to armholes. With 2¾mm/No 12 needles cast on 223 [235:247:259] sts. Work 6 rows in garter st.
Next row P.
Change to 3¼mm/No 10 needles.
1st row K1, *K2 tog, yfwd, K1, yfwd, sl 1, K1, psso, K1, rep from * to end.
2nd and every alt row P.
3rd row K2 tog, yfwd, *K3, yfwd, sl 1, K2 tog, psso, yfwd, rep from * to last 5 sts, K3, yfwd, sl 1, K1, psso.
5th row K2, *yfwd, sl 1, K2 tog, psso, yfwd, K3, rep from * to last 5 sts, yfwd, sl 1, K2 tog, psso, yfwd, K2.
7th, 9th and 11th rows As 1st.
13th and 15th rows as 3rd and 5th.
16th row P.
17th to 26th rows K.**
These 26 rows form the patt. Cont in patt until work measures 38cm/15in from beg ending with a Rs row.

Divide for armholes

Next row P51 [53:55:57], cast off 10 [12:14:16] sts, P101 [105:109:113], cast off 10 [12:14:16] sts, P51 [53:55:57] sts.
Complete right front first. Cont in patt dec one st at armhole edge on every row 5 times, then every alt row 3 times. 43 [45:47:49] sts.
Cont without shaping until front measures 9 [10:10:12] cm/3½ [4:4:4¾]in from beg of armhole shaping, ending at armhole edge. Mark last row at front edge.

Shape neck

Dec one st at neck edge on next 5 rows.
Cast off 6 [7:8:9] sts at beg of next row.
Dec one st at neck edge on next 5 rows. 27 [28:29:30] sts.
Cont without shaping until front measures 18 [19:20:21] cm/7 [7½:7¾:8¼]in from beg of armhole shaping, ending at armhole edge.

Shape shoulder

Cast off at beg of next and foll alt rows, 9 sts twice and 9 [10:11:12] sts once.
With Rs facing rejoin yarn to centre 101 [105:109:113] sts.
Dec one st at each end of every row 5 times, then every alt row 3 times. 85 [89:93:97] sts.
Cont without shaping until back measures same as front to shoulder, ending with a Ws row.

Shape shoulders

Cast off at beg of every row 9 [9:10:10] sts 4 times and 9 [10:9:10] sts twice. Sl rem 31 [33:35:37] sts on to a holder.

With Rs facing rejoin yarn to rem sts and work left front to match right reversing all shaping.

Sleeves

With 2¾mm/No 12 needles cast on 67 [67:73:73] sts. Work as for back and fronts to **.
Next row K.
Next row (inc row) P16 [10:13:7], (inc in next st, P1) 17 [23:23:29] times, inc in next st, P to end. 85 [91:97:103] sts.
Beg with a K row cont in st st until sleeve measures 18cm/7in from beg, ending with a P row.

Shape top

Cast off 5 [6:7:8] sts at beg of next 2 rows.
Dec one st at each end of next and every foll 4th row until 61 [63:67:67] sts rem, then every alt row until 51 [53:55:57] sts rem, then every row until 37 [39:41:43] sts rem. Cast off.

Below: The slim-line cardigan is worked in one piece to the underarm to avoid spoiling the line of the lace pattern.

Left: The lacy peplum on the camisole is well shaped to fit snugly at the waist.

Next row (dec row) P1 [4:7:10], (P2 tog, P3) 28 times, P3 tog, P to end. 115 [121:127:133] sts.
Change to 2¾mm/No 12 needles.
Beg with a 2nd row work 10 rows rib as given for border of cardigan.
Next row (eyelet hole row) K1, *yfwd, K2 tog; rep from * to end.
Beg with a 1st row, work 9 more rows in rib.
Change to 3¼mm/No 10 needles.
Beg with a K row work in st st until work measures 13cm/5in from top of rib, ending with a K row. Work 10 rows in garter st.
Next row P.
Work 26 patt rows as before.
Change to 2¾mm/No 12 needles.
Beg with 2nd row work 15 rows rib.
Cast off to form picot edge as on border of cardigan.

Back

Work as given for front.

To make up

Press each piece lightly under a damp cloth with a warm iron.
Cardigan Join sleeve seams. Sew in sleeves easing in tops of sleeves to fit armholes. Sew shoulder pads in position placing cast-on edge to armhole seam and point to shoulder seam. Join ends of borders at back neck. Press seams.
Top Join side seams. Press seams. Make one long twisted cord for waist and slot through holes in ribbing. Make 4 cords about 33cm/ 13in long, and attach to top edge of back and front and tie on shoulders.

Border

Join shoulder seams. With 2¾mm/ No 12 needles and Rs facing, pick up and K175 [179:179:183] sts up front edge to marker, 8 sts round shaped corner, 26 [29:32:35] sts to shoulder, then K across first 15 [16:17:18] sts from back neck, inc 1 in last st. 225 [233:237:245] sts.
1st row K1, *P1, K1, rep from * to end.
2nd row K2, *P1, K1, rep from * to last st, K1.
Work 7 more rows in rib.
Cast off row (picot row) Cast off 3 sts, *sl st on right-hand needle back on to left-hand needle, cast on 2 sts, cast off 6 sts, rep from * until all sts are cast off. Fasten off.
Commencing at centre back work 2nd half of border to match,

omitting inc 1 in first st, K across 16 [17:18:19] sts from back neck, pick up and K26 [29:32:35] sts from shoulder, 8 sts round shaped corner, then 175 [179:179:183] sts from marker down front edge.

Shoulder pads

With 2¾mm/No 12 needles cast on 30 sts. Work in garter st dec one st at each end of every alt row until 2 sts remain.
Next row K2 tog. Fasten off.
Make another piece the same way.

Top front

With 2¾mm/No 12 needles cast on 145 [151:157:163] sts.
Work as for back and fronts of cardigan to **.
Rep the last 26 rows once more.
Next row K.

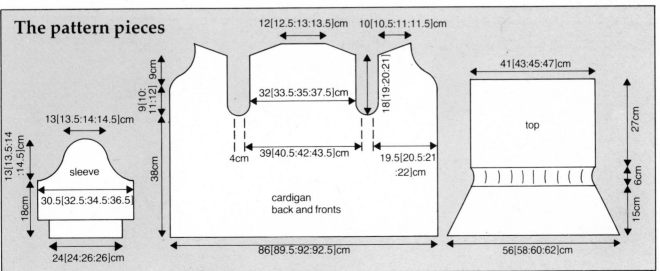

The pattern pieces

sleeve
13[13.5:14:14.5]cm
13[13.5:14 :14.5]cm
18cm
24[24:26:26]cm
30.5[32.5:34.5:36.5]

9|10: 11:12] 9cm
38cm
12[12.5:13:13.5]cm
10[10.5:11:11.5]cm
32[33.5:35:37.5]cm
4cm
39[40.5:42:43.5]cm
19.5[20.5:21 :22]cm
18[19:20:21]
cardigan
back and fronts
86[89.5:92:92.5]cm

41[43:45:47]cm
top
27cm
6cm
15cm
56[58:60:62]cm

Soft mohair cardigan

This easy fitting raglan-sleeved cardigan in soft, luxurious mohair is knitted on a circular needle, so there's blissfully little making up to do. The stitches for the front band are picked up along the row ends.

Sizes

To fit 81 [86:91:97:102]cm/ 32 [34:36:38:40]in bust
Length to back neck, 58 [60:62:64:66]cm/ 22¾ [23½:24½:25¼:26]in
Sleeve seam, 34cm/13½in, adjustable
The figures in [] refer to the 86/34, 91/36, 97/38 and 102cm/40in sizes respectively

You will need

12 [12:13:14:15]×25g balls of Sunbeam Mohair (67% mohair, 28% wool, 5% nylon)
One pair 4½mm/No 7 needles
One pair 5½mm/No 5 needles
One 4½mm/No 7 circular needle, 100cm/40in long
One 5½mm/No 5 circular needle, 100cm/40in long
7 buttons

Tension

16 sts and 21 rows to 10cm/4in over st st worked on 5½mm/No 5 needles

Cardigan back and fronts

Work in one piece to armholes.
With 4½mm/No 7 circular needle cast on 136 [144:152:160:168] sts.
1st row (Rs) P1, *K2, P2, rep from * to last 3 sts, K2, P1.
2nd row K1, *P2, K2, rep from * to last 3 sts, P2, K1.
Rep these 2 rows for 8cm/3¼in ending with a Ws row. Change to 5½mm/No 5 circular needle, beg with a K row cont in st st until work measures 40cm/15¾in from beg, end with a P row.

Divide for armholes

Next row K30 [32:34:36:38], cast off 5, K66 [70:74:78:82] including st on needle, cast off 5, K30 [32:34:36:38].
Cont on last set of sts for left front.
Next row P to end.
Next row K1, sl 1, K1, psso, K to end.
Rep last 2 rows until 16 sts rem, ending with a P row.

Shape neck

Next row K1, sl 1, K1, psso, K8, turn and leave rem 5 sts on holder.
Next row P to end.
Next row K1, sl 1, K1, psso, K to last 2 sts, K2 tog.
Rep last 2 rows twice more then P one row. 4 sts.
Next row K1, sl 1, K2 tog, psso.
Next row P2.
Cast off.
With P side of work facing, rejoin yarn to centre 66 [70:74:78:82] sts for back and P to end.
Next row K1, sl 1, K1, psso, K to last 3 sts, K2 tog, K1.
Next row P to end.
Rep last 2 rows until 28 sts rem, ending with a P row. Leave sts on holder.
With P side of work facing, rejoin yarn to rem sts for right front and P to end.
Next row K to last 3 sts, K2 tog, K1.
Complete to match left front, reversing shaping as now set.

Sleeves

With 4½mm/No 7 needles cast on 34 [34:38:38:42] sts.
1st row (Rs) K2, *P2, K2, rep from * to end.
2nd row P2, *K2, P2, rep from * to end.
Rep these 2 rows for 6cm/2¼in, ending with a Ws row and inc 4 [6:4:6:4] sts evenly in last row. 38 [40:42:44:46] sts.
Change to 5½mm/No 5 needles. Beg with a K row cont in st st, inc one st at each end of 5th and every foll 4th row until there are 54 [58:62:66:70] sts. Cont without shaping until sleeve measures 34cm/ 13½in from beg, or required length to underarm ending with a P row.

Shape top

Cast off 3 sts at beg of next 2 rows.
Next row K1, sl 1, K1, psso, K to last 3 sts, K2 tog, K1.
Next row P to end.
Rep last 2 rows until 10 sts rem, ending with a P row. Leave sts on holder.

Neckband

Join raglan seams. With Rs facing and 4½mm/No 7 needles, K5 sts on holder of right front, pick up and K6 sts up side of neck, K across sts of right sleeve, back neck and left sleeve K2 tog at each back raglan seam, pick up and K6 sts down side of neck and K5 sts on holder. 68 sts.
Next row K1, *P2, K2, rep from * to last 3 sts, P2, K1.
Work 7 more rows rib as now set. Cast off in rib.

Right front band

With Rs of work facing and 4½mm/ No 7 needles pick up and K104 [108: 112:116:120] sts along front edge and edge of neckband. Work 3 rows rib as for neckband.
Next row (buttonhole row) Rib 3 [7:5:3:7], *cast off 2, rib 14 [14:15:16:16], rep from * 5 times more, cast off 2, rib 3.
Next row Work in rib, casting on 2 sts above those cast off in previous row.
Work 3 more rows rib. Cast off in rib.

Left front band

Work as given for right front band, omitting buttonholes.

To make up

Press under a damp cloth with a cool iron. Join sleeve seams. Press seams. Sew on buttons.

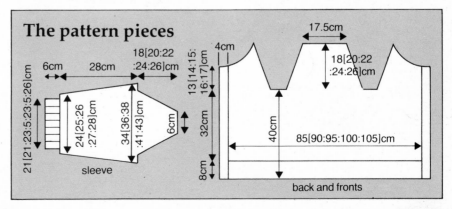

The pattern pieces

Striped cardigan and top

Sizes

To fit 81 [86:91:97]cm/32 [34:36:38]in bust

Cardigan length to shoulder, 57 [58:59:60]cm/22½ [22¾:23¼:23½]in
Sleeve seam, 43 [44:45:46]cm/ 17 [17¼:17¾:18] in
Top side length, 33.5cm/13¼in
The figures in [] refer to 86/34, 91/36 and 97cm/38in sizes respectively

You will need

Cardigan 4 [4:5:5]×50g balls of Phildar Luxe (85% acrylic, 15% wool), in main colour A
1 [1:2:2] balls of same in each of contrasts B, C, D and E
Top 2 [2:2:2] balls of same in main colour A
1 [1:1:1] ball of same in contrast B
One pair 2¾mm/No 12 needles
One pair 3mm/No 11 needles

Tension

30 sts and 40 rows to 10cm/4in over st st worked on 3mm/No 11 needles

Cardigan back

With 2¾mm/No 12 needles and A, cast on 129 [137:145:153] sts.
1st row P1, *K1, P1, rep from * to end.
2nd row K1, *P1, K1, rep from * to end.
Rep these 2 rows for 3cm/1¼in, ending with a 2nd row.
Change to 3mm/No 11 needles. Beg with a P row cont in reversed st st working in stripes of 2 rows B, 2 rows A, 2 rows C, 2 rows A, 2 rows D, 2 rows A, 2 rows E and 2 rows A.**
These 16 rows form the striped sequence throughout but, *at the same time* work bobbles on next and every foll 20th row as foll:
17th row P4, *insert right-hand needle knitwise into next st but on 4th row below, (K1, yfwd, K1, yfwd, K1, yfwd, K1) all into this st, sl the 7 loops back on to left-hand needle and K them tog with the next st tbl – **called MB**, P7, rep from * to last 5 sts, MB. P4.
Cont in striped patt working

bobbles on every foll 20th row until work measures 38cm/15in from beg, ending with a Ws row.

Shape armholes

Keeping patt correct throughout, cast off 16 [16:18:18] sts at beg of next 2 rows. 97 [105:109:117] sts.
Cont without shaping until armholes measure 19 [20:21:22]cm/7½ [7¾: 8¼:8¾]in, ending with a Ws row.

Shape shoulders

Cast off at beg of next and every row 7 [7:8:8] sts 6 times, 6 [9:7:10] sts twice and 43 [45:47:49] sts once.

Cardigan left front

With 2¾mm/No 12 needles and A, cast on 63 [67:71:75] sts and work as given for back to **.
17th row P4, *MB, P7, rep from * to last 3 [7:3:7] sts, MB, P2 [6:2:6].
Cont in patt as now set until work measures same as back to underarm, ending with a Ws row.

Shape armhole

Cast off 16 [16:18:18] sts at beg of next row. 47 [51:53:57] sts.
Cont without shaping until armhole measures 14 [15:15:16] cm/ 5½ [6:6:6¼]in ending with a Ws row.

Shape neck

Cast off at beg of next and every alt

row 7 [7:8:8] sts once, 3 sts twice, 2 sts twice and one st 3 [4:4:5] times. 27 [30:31:34] sts.
Cont without shaping until armhole measures same as back to shoulder, ending with a Ws row.

Shape shoulder

Cast off at beg of next and every alt row 7 [7:8:8] sts 3 times and 6 [9:7:10] sts once.

Cardigan right front

Work as given for left front, reversing all shaping and bobble patt row, as foll:
17th row P2 [6:2:6] sts, *MB, P7, rep from * to last 5 sts, MB, P4.

Cardigan sleeves

With 2¾mm/No 12 needles and A, cast on 59 [61:65:67] sts. Work in rib as given for back for 8cm/3¼in, ending with a 1st row.
Next row (inc row) Rib 2 [0:4:2] sts,*K twice into next st, P1, rep from * to last st, K1. 87 [91:95:99] sts.
Change to 3mm/No 11 needles. Work 16 rows striped patt as given for back, inc one st at each end of 7th and 15th rows. 91 [95:99:103] sts.
17th row P1 [3:5:7] sts, *MB, P7, rep from * to last 2 [4:6:8] sts, MB, P to end.
Cont in patt as now set, inc one st at

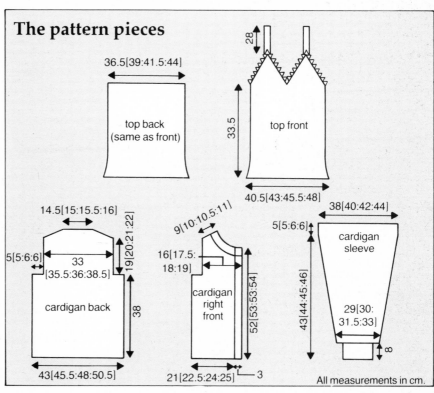

The pattern pieces

top back (same as front)
36.5[39:41.5:44]

top front
33.5
28
40.5[43:45.5:48]

cardigan back
14.5[15:15.5:16]
5[5:6:6]
33 [35.5:36:38.5]
19[20:21:22]
38
43[45.5:48:50.5]

cardigan right front
9[10:10.5:11]
16[17.5: 18:19]
52[53:53:54]
21[22.5:24:25]
3

cardigan sleeve
38[40:42:44]
5[5:6:6]
43[44:45:46]
29[30: 31.5:33]
8

All measurements in cm.

safety pin.
With Rs of work facing sl first st on to a safety pin and leave for centre neck, rejoin A to rem sts and P to end.
Complete to match left side.

Front edging

With 2¾mm/No 12 needles, B and Rs facing, *pick up and K26 [28:30:32] sts up side of point, K2 tog the sts on safety pin, pick up and K26 [28:30:32] sts down other side of point, *, K centre st from safety pin, then rep from * to * along other point.
Next row P26 [28:30:32] sts, inc one by picking up loop between sts and P tbl – **called inc 1P**, P1, inc 1P, P to next point, inc 1P, P1, inc 1P, P to end.
Next row K27 [29:31:33] sts, inc one by picking up loop between sts and K tbl – **called inc 1K**, K1, inc 1K, K to one st before centre st, sl 1, K2 tog, psso, K to next point, inc 1K, K1, inc 1K, K to end.
Keeping the number of sts correct between shapings, rep last 2 rows once more, then first of them again.
Next row (eyelet hole row) K1, *yfwd, K2 tog, rep from * to end.
Next row P to one st before point, P3 tog, P to one st before next point, P3 tog, P to end.
Next row K to one st before point, K3 tog, K to centre, inc 1K, K1, inc 1K, K to next point, K3 tog, K to end.
Keeping the number of sts correct between shapings, rep last 2 rows twice more. Cast off.

Straps (make 2)

With 2¾mm/No 12 needles and B, cast on 9 sts. Work in rib as given for cardigan back for 28cm/11in, or length required. Cast off.

To make up

Press all pieces lightly under a dry cloth with a cool iron.
Cardigan Set in sleeves, sewing last part of sleeves from markers to cast off sts of armholes. Join side and sleeve seams. Fold neckband in half to Ws and sl st down. Press seams.
Top Join side and edging seams. Fold edges in half to Ws and sl st down. Sew on straps. Press seams.

---

each end of every 8th row until there are 115 [121:127:133] sts. Cont without shaping until sleeve measures 43 [44:45:46]cm/17 [17¼: 17¾:18]in from beg. Place a marker at each end of last row, then cont in patt for a further 5 [5:6:6]cm/2 [2:2¼:2¼] in ending with a Ws row. Cast off.

Cardigan neckband

Join shoulder seams. With 2¾mm/ No 12 needles, A and Rs facing, pick up and K111 [115:119:123] sts evenly round neck. Beg with a 2nd row work 10cm/4in rib as given for back. Cast off in rib.

Cardigan front bands

With 2¾mm/No 12 needles, A and Rs of work facing, pick up and K171 [175:175:179] sts evenly along right front edge from cast-on edge to halfway up side of neckband. Beg with a 2nd row work 3cm/1¼in rib as given for back. Cast off in rib.
Work along left front edge in same way, beg halfway down side of neckband to cast-on edge.

Top back

With 2¾mm/No 12 needles and B, cast on 121 [129:137:145] sts.
**Beg with a K row work 6 rows st st.
7th row (eyelet hole row) K1, *yfwd, K2 tog, rep from * to end.
Beg with a P row work 6 rows st st. **
Break off B. Change to 3mm/No 11 needles. Join in A and P one row.
Beg with a P row cont in reversed st st, dec one st at each end of 7th and every foll 8th row until 109 [117:125: 133] sts rem. Cont without shaping until work measures 32cm/12½in from eyelet hole row, ending with a K row.*** Break off A. Change to 2¾mm/No 12 needles. Join in B and rep from **to**. Cast off.

Top front

Work as given for back to ***.

Shape front neck

Next row P54 [58:62:66] sts, turn and leave rem sts on holder.
Complete left side first. Dec one st at each end of every row until 2 sts rem. Break off yarn. Leave 2 sts on a

Fluffy cardigan and top

Delicately shaded stripes add extra interest to this pretty cardigan knitted in Trinity stitch. The soft mohair yarn provides warmth without being heavy or bulky and the basic cardigan shape is very simple, relying on the stitch texture and colour to give it that different look.

The angora and wool top is trimmed with beads and sequins, which could be chosen to tone with the cardigan if they are to be worn together.

Sizes

Cardigan to fit 86 [91:97]cm/ 34 [36:38]in bust
Length to shoulder, 60 [61:63]cm/ 23½ [24:24¾]in
Sleeve seam, 44cm/17½in
Top to fit 81 [86:91]cm/32 [34:36]in bust
Length to shoulder, 54 [55:55]cm/ 21¼ [21½:21½]in
Cardigan the figures in [] refer to the 91/36 and the 97cm/38in sizes respectively
Top the figures in [] refer to the 86/34 and the 91cm/36in sizes respectively

You will need

Cardigan 5 [6:6]×50g balls of Anny Blatt Kid Anny (80% mohair, 20% chlorofibre) in main colour A
3 [4:4]×50g balls each in contrast colours B and C
One pair 4mm/No 8 needles
One pair 5mm/No 6 needles
Five buttons
Top 6 [7:8]×20g balls Anny Blatt Angor'anny (70% angora, 30% wool)
One pair 3¼mm/No 10 needles
One pair 4mm/No 8 needles
14 cockleshell shapes, 14 round transparent pearls, and 28 drop beads, optional

Tension

Cardigan 25 sts and 22 rows to 10cm/4in over patt worked on 5mm/ No 6 needles
Top 24 sts and 32 rows to 10cm/4in over patt worked on 4mm/No 8 needles

Cardigan back

With 4mm/No 8 needles and A cast on 113 [121:129] sts.
1st row K2, *P1, K1, rep from * to last st, K1.
2nd row K1, *P1, K1, rep from * to end. Rep 1st and 2nd rows 6 times more inc one st at end of last row. 114 [122:130] sts.
Change to 5mm/No 6 needles. Working in striped sequence of 2 rows A, 2 rows B, 2 rows C, commence patt.
1st row (Rs) K1, P to last st, K1.
2nd row K1, *(K1, P1, K1) all into next st, P3 tog, rep from * to last st, K1.
3rd row K1, P to last st, K1.
4th row K1, *P3 tog, (K1, P1, K1) all into next st, rep from * to last st, K1. These 4 rows form patt. Keeping patt and striped sequence correct throughout, cont until work measures 41cm/16in from beg, ending with a Ws row.**

Shape armholes

Cast off 4 sts at beg of next 2 rows. Dec one st at each end of next 12 rows. 82 [90:98] sts.
Cont without shaping until armholes measure 19 [20:22]cm/ 7½ [7¾:8½]in from beg, ending with a Ws row.

Shape shoulders and back neck

Next row Cast off 7 [8:10] sts, patt 20 [23:25] sts, cast off 28 sts, patt 27 [31:35] sts.
Complete left shoulder first.
Next row Cast off 7 [8:10] sts, patt to end.
Next row Cast off 3 sts, patt to end.
Next row Cast off 7 [9:10] sts, patt to end.
Next row Cast off 2 sts, patt to end. Cast off rem 8 [9:10] sts.
With Ws facing, rejoin yarn to rem 20 [23:25] sts and complete to match first side reversing all shaping.

Left front

With 4mm/No 8 needles and A cast on 53 [57:61] sts. Work 14 rows K1, P1 rib as given for back inc one st at end of last row. 54 [58:62] sts. Change to 5mm/No 6 needles and work as given for back to **.

Shape armhole

Next row Cast off 4 sts, patt to end.
Next row K1, patt to end.
Dec one st at armhole edge on next

An alternative colourway for the cardigan.

12 rows. 38 [42:46] sts.
Cont without shaping until armhole measures 13 [14:15]cm/5 [5½:6]in from beg, ending with a Rs row.

Shape neck

Cast off at beg of next and every alt row 10 sts once and 2 sts 3 times. 22 [26:30] sts.
Cont without shaping until armhole measures same as back to shoulder, ending with a Ws row.

Shape shoulder

Cast off at beg of next and every alt row 7 [8:10] sts once, 7 [9:10] sts once and 8 [9:10] sts once.

Right front

Work to match left front, reversing all shapings.

Sleeves

With 4mm/No 8 needles and A cast on 45 [49:51] sts. Work 13 rows K1, P1 rib as given for back.
Next row (inc row) Rib 6 [8:5], (inc in next st, rib 3) 9 [9:11] times, rib 3 [5:2]. 54 [58:62] sts.
Change to 5mm/No 6 needles. Work in patt and striped sequence as given for back, inc one st at each end of 5th and every foll 6th row until there are 78 [82:86] sts.
Cont without shaping until work measures 44cm/17½in from beg, ending with a Ws row.

Shape top of sleeves

Cast off at the beg of every row one st 16 [20:20] times and 2 sts 18 [18:20] times.
Cast off rem 26 sts.

Right front border

With Rs facing, 4mm/No 8 needles and A, pick up and K119 [121:123] sts evenly along right front edge.
1st row K1, *P1, K1, rep from * to end.
2nd row K2, *P1, K1, rep from * to last st, K1.
3rd row As 1st.
4th row (buttonhole row) K2, (P1,

K1) 3 [4:5] times, *P1, cast off 2 sts, K1, (P1, K1) 12 times *, rep from * to * twice, P1, cast off 2 sts, K1, (P1, K1) 11 times, K1.
5th row K1, (P1, K1) 11 times, P1, *cast on 2 sts, (K1, P1) 13 times *, rep from * to * twice, cast on 2 sts, (K1, P1) 4 [5:6] times, K1.
Rep 2nd and 3rd rows once. Cast off in rib.

Left front border
Work as given for right front border omitting buttonholes.

Neckband
Join shoulder seams.
With Rs facing, 4mm/No 8 needles and A, commence at cast off edge of right front border, pick up and K32 sts up right side of neck, 37 sts from back of neck, and 32 sts down left side of neck, ending at cast off edge of left front border. 101 sts.
1st row K1, *P1, K1, rep from * to end.
2nd row K2, P1, K1, cast off 2 sts, *P1, K1, rep from * to last st, K1.
3rd row K1, *P1, K1, rep from * to last 4 sts, cast on 2 sts, (P1, K1) twice.
4th row K2, *P1, K1, rep from * to

last st, K1.
5th row As 1st.
Rep 4th and 5th rows once. Cast off in rib.

Top back
With 3¼mm/No 10 needles cast on 95 [101:107] sts. Work 10cm/4in rib as given for cardigan back, ending with a Ws row.
Change to 4mm/No 8 needles.
Commence patt.
1st row K to end.
2nd row P to end.
3rd row K to end.
4th row K2, *P1, K1, rep from * to last st, K1.
These 4 rows form patt. Keeping patt correct throughout, cont until work measures 34cm/13½in from beg, ending with a Ws row.

Shape armholes
Cast off at the beg of every row 3 sts twice and 2 sts 6 [6:8] times. 77 [83:85] sts.
Dec one st each end of next and every alt row until 59 [61:57] sts rem. Work 3 rows **.
Dec one st each end of every foll 4th row until 45 [47:47] sts rem. Work 3 rows ending with a Ws row.

Shape neck
Next row Patt 17, cast off 11 [13:13] sts, patt to end.
Complete right neck first. Work one row.
Cast off at beg of next and every foll alt row 6 sts once, 4 sts once, 2 sts once, and 5 sts once.
With Ws facing rejoin yarn to rem 17 sts and complete to match first side, reversing all shapings.

Front
Work as given for back to **.
Dec one st each end of every foll 4th row until 49 [51:51] sts rem. Work 3 rows ending with a Ws row.

Shape neck
Next row K2 tog, patt 17, cast off 11 [13:13] sts, patt to last 2 sts, K2 tog.
Complete right front neck.
Next row Patt to end.
Still dec at armhole edge cast off at beg of next and every foll alt row 5 sts once, 3 sts once and 2 sts twice.
Work 6 rows without shaping. Cast off rem 5 sts.
With Ws facing rejoin yarn to rem 18 sts and complete to match first side reversing all shapings.

Neckband
Join right shoulder seam.
With Rs facing and 3¼mm/No 10 needles, beg at top of left shoulder, pick up and K119 [123:123] sts evenly all round neck edge.
1st row K1, *P1, K1 rep from * to end.
2nd row K2, *P1, K1, rep from * to last st, K1.
Rep 1st and 2nd rows once then 1st row once more. Cast off in rib.

Armhole borders
Join left shoulder and neckband seam.
With Rs facing and 3¼mm/No 10 needles, pick up and K139 [145:145] sts evenly all round armhole edge.
Work 5 rows K1, P1 rib as given for neckband. Cast off in rib.

To make up
Do not press.
Cardigan Join side and sleeve seams. Sew in sleeves. Sew on buttons.
Top Join side and armhole border seams. Sew on bead trimmings as shown if required.

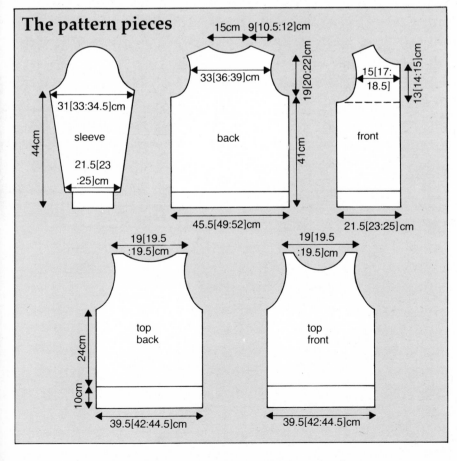

The pattern pieces

sleeve — 31[33:34.5]cm — 44cm — 21.5[23:25]cm

back — 15cm — 9[10.5:12]cm — 33[36:39]cm — 19[20:22]cm — 41cm — 45.5[49:52]cm

front — 15[17:18.5] — 13[14:15]cm — 21.5[23:25]cm

top back — 19[19.5:19.5]cm — 24cm — 10cm — 39.5[42:44.5]cm

top front — 19[19.5:19.5]cm — 39.5[42:44.5]cm

Cardigan with detachable sleeves

This boldly striped cardigan will give you two garments for the cost of one. The cleverly designed sleeves are made to be fastened in afterwards and not stitched, so if you want to ring the changes, undo the fasteners and you then have a short-sleeved cardigan.

Sizes

To fit 86 [91:97]cm/34 [36:38]in bust
Length to shoulder, 59 [60:61]cm/ 23¼ [23½:24]in
Sleeve seam, 45cm/17¾in
The figures in [] refer to the 91/36 and 97cm/38in sizes respectively

You will need

6 [7:8] × 50g balls of Robin Reward DK (60% acrylic, 40% Bri-nylon) in main colour A
1 [1:1] ball the same in each of contrast colours B, C, D, E, F, G and H
One pair 3¼mm/No 10 needles
One pair 4mm/No 8 needles
One 3¼mm/No 10 circular needle, 100cm/40in long
25 button snaps or 25 press fasteners and 25 small buttons

Tension

22 sts and 28 rows to 10cm/4in over st st worked on 4mm/No 8 needles

Back

With 3¼mm/No 10 needles and A cast on 86 [94:102] sts.
1st row P2, *K2, P2, rep from * to end.
2nd row K2, *P2, K2, rep from * to end.
Rep these 2 rows for 8cm/3¼in, ending with a 1st row.
Next row (inc row) Rib 4 [8:2], (inc in next st, rib 3 [3:4]) 19 times, inc in next st, rib 5 [9:4]. 106 [114:122] sts.
**Change to 4mm/No 8 needles and beg with a K row cont in st st until work measures 17cm/6¾in from beg, ending with a P row.
Commence patt, joining in and breaking off colours as required.

Left: Bands of boldly coloured wide rib alternate with narrow stripes of the main colour to highlight the body and sleeves of this useful cardigan-cum-waistcoat design.

1st row With B, K to end. **
2nd row With B, P3, *K4, P4, rep from * to last 7 sts, K4, P3.
3rd row With B, K3, *P4, K4, rep from * to last 7 sts, P4, K3.
4th and 5th rows As 2nd and 3rd.
6th row As 2nd.
7th row With A, K to end.
8th row With A, P to end.
9th row With C, K to end.
10th row With C, as 3rd.
11th row With C, as 2nd.
12th and 13th rows As 10th and 11th.
14th row As 10th.
15th and 16th rows As 7th and 8th.
Rep these 16 rows twice more, using D and E, then F and G instead of B and C, then work the first 6 rows again using H instead of B. Cont in A only, beg with a K row work in st st until back measures 57 [58:59]cm/22½ [22¾:23¼]in from beg, ending with a P row.

Shape neck

Next row K41 [44:47], turn and leave rem sts on holder. Complete right shoulder first. Cast off 3 sts at beg of next row and 2 sts at beg of foll alt row. 36 [39:42] sts.
Work 2 rows without shaping. Cast off.
Slip the first 24 [26:28] sts of the rem sts on to a holder for back neck, with Rs of work facing, rejoin yarn to sts for left shoulder and K to end.
Complete to match right shoulder reversing all shaping.

Above: Use ready-made button snaps which fasten to the jersey with a special tool or buy press studs and buttons.

Right front

With 3¼mm/No 10 needles and A cast on 42 [46:50] sts.
1st row P2, *K2, P2, rep from * to end.
2nd row K2, *P2, K2, rep from * to end. Rep the last 2 rows for 8cm/ 3¼in, ending with a 1st row.
Next row (inc row) Rib 3 [5:3], (inc in next st, rib 4 [4:5]) 7 times, inc in next st, rib 3 [5:4]. 50 [54:58] sts. ***
Work as given from ** to ** on back.
2nd row With B, P3, *K4, P4, rep from * to last 7 [3:7] sts, K4 [3:4], P3 [0:3].

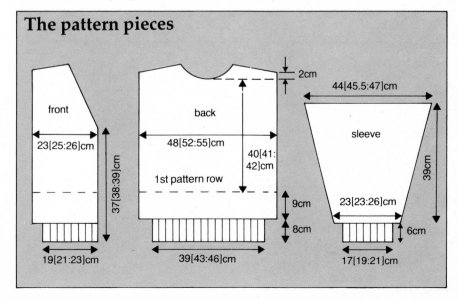

The pattern pieces

front
23[25:26]cm
37[38:39]cm
19[21:23]cm

back
48[52:55]cm
40[41:42]cm
1st pattern row
39[43:46]cm
2cm
9cm
8cm

44[45.5:47]cm
sleeve
23[23:26]cm
39cm
17[19:21]cm
6cm

beg with a K row cont in st st inc one st at each end of the 5th and every foll 4th row until there are 74 [74:82] sts, ending with a P row. Beg with a 1st row, work in patt as given for back, *at the same time* cont inc as before, working the extra sts in patt, until there are 96 [100:104] sts.

Cont without shaping until patt is complete, then cont in A only in st st until work measures 45cm/17¾in from beg, ending with a P row. Cast off loosely.

Armhole borders

Join shoulder seams. Place a marker each side of body 22 [23:24]cm/ 8¾ [9:9½]in down from shoulders. With Rs facing, 3¼mm/No 10 needles and A, pick up and K98 [102:106] sts evenly around armhole between markers. Beg with a 2nd row, work 4cm/1½in in rib as given for back. Cast off loosely in rib.

Front band

With Rs facing, 3¼mm/No 10 circular needle and A, pick up and K85 [86:87] sts up right front edge to beg of shaping, 48 sts to shoulder, 8 sts down right back neck, K across 24 [26:28] sts of back neck, pick up and K8 sts up left back neck, 48 sts down left front edge to beg of shaping and 85 [86:87] sts to lower edge. 306 [310:314] sts. K one row. Beg with a 1st row, work in rib as given for back for 3cm/1¼in. Cast off loosely in rib.

To make up

Do not press. Join side and armband seams. Join sleeve seams. Attach 7 button snaps to front bands, the first 2cm/¾in from lower edge, second level with top stripe of patt, then 5 more equally spaced in between. Attach the rem button snaps to sleeve tops and armhole borders. Fasten sleeves in position. If button snaps are not available, sew on press fasteners and stitch buttons over top of them.

3rd row With B, K3 [0:3], P4 [3:4], *K4, P4, rep from * to last 3 sts, K3. Cont in patt as now set to match back until work measures 37 [38:39]cm/14½ [15:15¼]in from beg, ending with a P row.

Shape front edge

Next row K1, sl 1, K1, psso, K to end. Work 3 rows. Rep these 4 rows until 36 [39:42] sts rem, then cont without shaping until work measures the same as back to shoulder, ending with a P row. Cast off.

Left front

Work as given for right front to ***.

Work as given from ** to ** on back. **2nd row** With B, P3 [0:3], K4 [3:4], *P4, K4, rep from * to last 3 sts, P3. **3rd row** K3, *P4, K4, rep from * to last 7 sts, P4 [3:4], K3 [0:3]. Complete as for right front, reversing shaping.

Sleeves

With 3¼mm/No 10 needles and A cast on 38 [42:46] sts and work in rib as given for back for 6cm/2¼in, ending with a 1st row. **Next row** (inc row) Rib 2 [3:6], (inc in next st, rib 2 [4:2]) 11 [7:11] times, inc in next st, rib 2 [3:6]. 50 [50:58] sts. Change to 4mm/No 8 needles and

Norwegian-type cardigan

This attractive Norwegian-style cardigan is knitted in a slightly fluffy yarn. It has a simple Fair Isle pattern worked over the body with a border The round neckline fits neatly and the tops of the sleeves are full and gathered in at the shoulders.

Sizes

To fit 86cm/34in bust loosely
Length to shoulder, 54cm/21¼in
Sleeve seam, 41cm/16¼in

You will need

5 × 50g balls of Scheepjeswol Voluma (85% acrylic, 15% kid mohair) in main colour A
1 ball of same in contrast colour B
1 ball of same in contrast colour C
One pair 3¼mm/No 10 needles
One pair 4mm/No 8 needles
One 3¼mm/No 10 circular needle, 80cm/30in long
One 4mm/No 8 circular needle, 80cm/30in long
Eight buttons

Tension

22 sts and 26 rows to 10cm/4in over patt worked on 4mm/No 8 needles

Note

Strand yarn not in use across back of work. When more than 5 sts are worked in any colour, weave in yarn not in use across back of work.

Jacket body

With 3¼mm/No 10 circular needle and A cast of 215 sts and work in one piece to underarm.
1st row K1, *P1, K1, rep from * to end.
2nd row P1, *K1, P1, rep from * to end.
Rep these 2 rows once more.
5th row (buttonhole row) Rib 2 sts, cast off 2 sts, rib to end.
6th row Rib to end, casting on 2 sts above those cast off in previous row.
Work 3 more rows in rib.
Next row (inc row) Rib 7 sts and sl these on to a saftey pin and leave for front band, change to 4mm/No 8 circular needle, P6, (inc in next st, P8) 21 times, inc in next st, P5, turn

and leave rem 7 sts on safety pin for other front band. 223 sts.
Beg with a K row cont in st st and work the first 7 rows of patt from chart 1, then P one row with A.
**Next row K3 A, *1 B, 3 A, rep from * to end.
Beg with a P row, work 3 rows st st in A.
Next row K1 A, *1 B, 3 A, rep from * to last 2 sts, 1 B, 1 A.
Beg with a P row work 3 rows st st in A.**
Rep last 8 rows until work measures about 29cm/11½in from beg, ending with 3 rows st st in A.
Beg with a K row work 8 rows of patt from chart 2.

Divide for armholes

Next row Using B, K52 sts, cast off 8 sts for armhole, K103 sts for back cast off 8 sts for other armhole, K52 sts.
Cont on last set of 52 sts for left front and P one row in A.

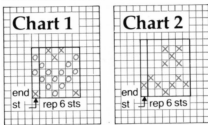

Beg with a K row work 2 rows in patt from chart 3.

Shape armhole

Keeping patt correct throughout as shown on chart 3, cast off at beg of next and every alt row 2 sts twice and one st twice. 46 sts.
Cont in patt from chart 3 until 41 rows have been worked, ending with a K row.

Shape neck

Keeping patt correct throughout as shown on chart 3, cast off at beg of next and every alt row 10 sts once, 4 sts once, 2 sts once and one st once, ending with a P row.

Shape shoulder

Cast off at beg of next and foll alt row 14 sts once and 15 sts once.
With Ws of work facing rejoin A to 103 sts for back and P one row.
Beg with a K row work 2 rows in patt from chart 3.

Shape armholes

Keeping patt correct throughout as shown on chart 3, cast off at beg of next and every row 2 sts 4 times and one st 4 times. 91 sts.
Cont in patt from chart 3 until 43 rows have been worked, ending with a K row.

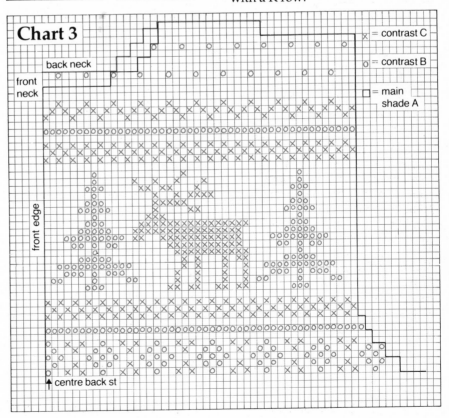

61

Shape neck
Next row Keeping patt correct throughout P35 sts, cast off 21 sts for centre back neck, P35 sts. Complete right shoulder first. K one row. Cast off 2 sts at beg of next and foll alt row, ending with a P row.

Shape shoulder
Cast off at beg of next and every row 14 sts for shoulder, 2 sts for neck and 15 sts for shoulder.
With Rs of work facing rejoin yarn to rem 35 sts and complete to match right shoulder, reversing shapings. With Ws of work facing rejoin A to rem 52 sts for right front. Complete to match left front, reversing all shapings.

Sleeves
With 3¼mm/No 10 needles and A cast on 43 sts. Work 4cm/1½in rib as given for body, ending with a 1st row.
Next row (inc row) P2, *inc in next st, P1, rep from * to last st, P1. 63 sts.
Change to 4mm/No 8 needles. Beg with a K row cont in st st and work first 7 rows of patt from chart 1, then P one row with A.
Cont in patt as given for body from ** to **, inc one st at each end of next and every foll 6th row until there are 83 sts, then cont without shaping until sleeve measures 37cm/14½in from beg, ending with 3 rows in A.

Shape top
Beg with a K row, cont in patt as given on chart 4, shaping top as shown on chart.

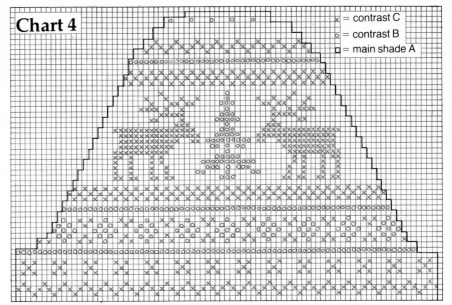

Chart 4

x = contrast C
o = contrast B
□ = main shade A

Button band
With Rs of work facing and 3¼mm/No 10 needles rejoin A to 7 sts on safety pin on left front edge, inc in first st, rib to end. 8 sts.
Cont in rib until band, when slightly stretched, fits along front edge to neck edge, ending with a Ws row. Leave sts on holder. Tack band in place.
Mark positions for 8 buttons, first to come on 5th row of welt and last to come in neckband, 5 rows above sts on holder, with 6 more evenly spaced between.

Buttonhole band
With Ws of work facing and 3¼mm/No 10 needles rejoin A to 7 sts on safety pin on right front edge, inc in first st, rib to end.
Work as given for button band,

making buttonholes as markers are reached as before. Do not cut yarn.

Neckband
Join shoulder seams.
With Rs of work facing, 3¼mm/No 10 needles and A rib across 8 sts of right front band, pick up and K24 sts up right front neck and 8 sts down right back neck, K across back neck sts on holder, pick up and K8 sts up left back neck and 24 sts down left front neck, then rib across rem 8 sts of left front band. 101 sts.
Cont in rib for 4cm/1½in, making buttonhole as before on 4th row. Cast off in rib.

To make up
Do not press. Join sleeve seams. Set in sleeves. Sew on button and buttonhole bands. Sew on buttons.

The pattern pieces

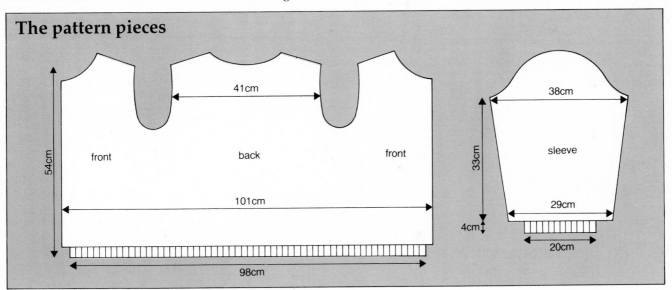

Overblouse with drawstring welt

This simple blouson shape is worked in an unusual textured bouclé yarn with panels of lace and bobbles against a reversed stocking stitch background.
The blouson effect is achieved by a cord threaded through the hem and tied to fit your hips.
The overblouse is sleeveless and has an edge-to-edge neck opening.

Sizes

To fit 81 [86:91:97]cm/32 [34:36:38]in bust
Length to shoulder, 60 [61:61:62]cm/23½ [24:24:24½]in
The figures in [] refer to the 86/34, 91/36 and the 97cm/38in sizes respectively

Below: Pick out any of the colours in this random cotton/courtelle yarn to tone with your clothes. Neck has no fastenings and forms an attractive V shape.

You will need

7 [7:7:8] × 50g balls of Wendy Capri (51% cotton, 49% Courtelle/acrylic)
One pair 3¾mm/No 9 needles
One pair 4½mm/No 7 needles

Tension

20 sts and 29 rows to 10cm/4in over st st worked on 4½mm/No 7 needles

Front

With 3¾mm/No 9 needles cast on 93 [98:103:108] sts.
Beg with a K row, work 15 rows st st.
Next row (making holes for cord) P42 [44:47:49], yrn, P2 tog, P5 [6:5:6], P2 tog, yrn, P to end.
Beg with a K row, work 4 more rows st st.
Next row (turning up hem) With the K side to the outside, fold work in half and K to end of row knitting each st on needle tog with corresponding loop from cast-on edge.
Next row P.
Change to 4½mm/No 7 needles. Commence patt.
1st row P5, *K1, yfwd, K2 tog tb1, K3, K2 tog, yfwd, K1, P15 [17:19:21], K1, yfwd, K2 tog tb1, K3, K2 tog, yfwd, K1*, P17 [18:19:20], rep from * to * once, P5.
2nd and every alt row K5, *P9, K15 [17:19:21], P9*, K17 [18:19:20], rep from * to * once, K5.
3rd row As 1st.
5th row P5, *K1, yfwd, K2 tog tb1, K1, K into front, back, front and back of next st, turn and K4, turn and P4, use left-hand needle to lift 2nd, 3rd and 4th sts over 1st st and off needle – **called MB**, K1, K2 tog, yfwd, K1, P15 [17:19:21], K1, yfwd, K2 tog tb1, K1, MB, K1, K2 tog, yfwd, K1*, P17 [18:19:20], rep from * to * once, P5.
7th row P5, *K2, yfwd, K2 tog tb1, K1, K2 tog, yfwd, K2, P15 [17:19:21], K2, yfwd, K2 tog tb1, K1, K2 tog, yfwd, K2*, P17 [18:19:20], rep from * to * once, P5.
9th row P5, *K3, yfwd, sl 1, K2 tog, psso, yfwd, K3, P15 [17:19:21], K3, yfwd, sl 1, K2 tog, psso, yfwd, K3*, P17 [18:19:20], rep from * to * once, P5.

11th row P5, *K4, yfwd, sl 1, K1, psso, K3, P15 [17:19:21], K4, yfwd, sl 1, K1, psso, K3*, P17 [18:19:20], rep from * to * once, P5.
12th row As 2nd.
These 12 rows form patt. Cont in patt until work measures 34cm/13¾in from beg, ending with a Ws row.

Armhole borders

Working the 5 sts at each end of the rows in garter st to form armhole borders, cont in patt on rem sts. Work 2 rows.**

Divide for neck opening

Next row Patt across 44 [46:49:51] sts, cast off 5 [6:5:6] sts, patt to end.
Complete right shoulder on these 44 [46:49:51] sts.
Keeping patt correct dec one st at neck edge on foll 16th row, then every 8th row until 40 [42:45:47] sts rem.
Cont without shaping until front opening measures 18 [19:19:20]cm/7 [7½:7½:8]in, ending at neck edge.

Shape neck

Cast off 3 [3:4:4] sts at beg of next row.
Dec one st at neck edge on next 5 rows. 32 [34:36:38] sts.
Cont without shaping until armhole measures 26 [27:27:28]cm/10¼ [10¾:10¾:11]in, ending at side edge.

Shape shoulders

Cast off at the beg of next and every foll alt row 8 [8:9:9] sts 3 times and 8 [10:9:11] sts once.
With Ws facing, rejoin yarn to rem 44 [46:49:51] sts and complete left shoulder to match right shoulder, reversing all shaping.

Back

Work as given for front to ** omitting holes made for cord.
Cont as given for last 2 rows until back measures same as front to shoulders.

Shape shoulders

Cast off at the beg of next and every row 8 [8:9:9] sts 6 times and

8 [10:9:11] sts twice.
Slip the rem 29 [30:31:32] sts on to a
holder for centre back neck.

Neckband

Join shoulder seams.
With Rs of work facing and 3¾mm/
No 9 needles, pick up and knit
16 [19:20:21] sts from right front
neck, 29 [29:31:31] sts from holder at
back neck dec one st on 2nd and 4th
sizes, and 16 [19:20:21] sts from left
front neck. 61 [67:71:73] sts.
1st row K1, *P1, K1, rep from * to
end.
2nd row K2, *P1, K1, rep from * to
last st, K1.
Rep these 2 rows twice more.
Cast off.

Front neck borders

With 3¾mm/No 9 needles cast on
7 sts.
Work in rib as given for neckband
until border is long enough to fit up
right front neck edge. Cast off
firmly in rib.
Work left front edge in same way.

To make up

Do not press.
Join side seams up to garter st
border. Sew side and lower edges of
front neck borders in position.
Make a twisted cord and slot
through hem to tie at centre front.

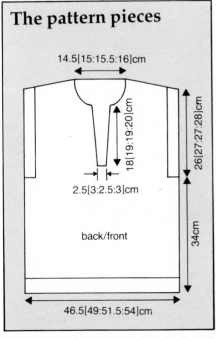

The pattern pieces

14.5[15:15.5:16]cm

18[19:19:20]cm

26[27:27:28]cm

2.5[3:2.5:3]cm

back/front

34cm

46.5[49:51.5:54]cm

*Right: The shoulders are cleverly shaped
so that the armhole edges form neatly
fitting cap sleeves.*

Feather-weight waistcoat

This attractive waistcoat with its pretty lacy peplum is flattering to all figure types. Knitted in alpaca yarn, it lends warmth without weight so it is ideal to wear over a blouse or dress. You can make it either with lacy armbands as shown in the illustration or with plain ribbed ones.

Sizes

To fit 86 [91:97]cm/34 [36:38] in bust
Length to shoulder, 49 [50:51]cm/ 19¼ [19¾:20]in, adjustable
The figures in [] refer to 91/36 and 97cm/38in sizes respectively

You will need

4 [4:5]×50g balls of Jaeger Alpaca, (100% alpaca)
One pair 3¾mm/No 9 needles
One pair 3mm/No 11 needles
Five buttons

Tension

28 sts and 36 rows to 10cm/4in over st st worked on 3mm/No 11 needles

Back

With 3¾mm/No 9 needles cast on 128 [135:142] sts. Commence lace patt for peplum.
1st row (Rs) K1, K2 tog, K1, yfwd, *K1, yfwd, K1, sl 1, K1, psso, K2 tog, K1, yfwd, rep from * to last 5 sts, K1, yfwd, K1, sl 1, K1, psso, K1.
2nd row K1, P to last st, K1.
Rep these 2 rows 13 times more, then 1st row once more.
Next row (dec row) K1, P44 [44:51] sts, (P2 tog, P3 [4:3] sts) 7 times, P2 tog, P45 [45:52] sts, K1. 120 [127:134] sts.
Change to 3mm/No 11 needles.
Next row K22 [22:29] sts, *(K2 tog, K1, yfwd, K1, yfwd, K1, sl 1, K1, psso) twice, *, K48 [55:48] sts, rep from * to * once more, K22 [22:29] sts.
Next row P to end
Cont in patt as now set until work measures 20cm/7¾in from end of lace patt or required length to underarm less 2cm/¾in, ending with a Ws row.

Shape armholes

Keeping patt correct, cast off at beg of next and every row 7 sts twice, 4 sts twice and 2 sts twice. Dec one st at each end of next and every alt row 2 [3:4] times in all.
90 [95:100] sts.
Cont in patt without shaping until armholes measure 19 [20:21]cm/7½ [7¾:8¼]in, ending with Ws row.

Shape shoulders

Keeping patt correct cast off at beg of next and every row 9 [9:10] sts 4 times and 8 [9:9] sts twice. Cast off rem 38 [41:42] sts.

Left front

With 3¾mm/No 9 needles cast on 72 [79:86] sts. Work 29 rows as given for back.**
Next row (dec row) K1, P9, (P2 tog, P3 [4:3] sts) 5 [6:7] times, P36 [32:40] sts, K1. 67 [73:79] sts.
Change to 3mm/No 11 needles.
Next row K22 [22:29] sts, (K2 tog, K1, yfwd, K1, yfwd, K1, sl 1, K1, psso) twice, K23 [29:28] sts, turn and leave rem 8 sts on holder for front band. 59 [65:71] sts.
Next row P to end.
Cont in patt as now set until work measures 15cm/6in from end of lace patt or 5cm/2in less than back to underarm, ending at front edge.

Shape front

Dec one st at beg of next row and at same edge on every foll 3rd row 18 [22:25] times in all, *at the same time* shape armhole when work measures same as back to underarm, ending at armhole edge.

Shape armhole

Keeping patt correct cast off at beg of next and every alt row 7 sts once, 4 sts once and 2 sts once, ending at armhole edge. Dec one st at beg of next and every alt row 2 [3:4] times in all. 26 [27:29] sts rem when front shaping has been completed.
Cont without shaping until armhole measures same as back to shoulder ending at armhole edge.

Shape shoulder

Keeping patt correct cast off at beg of next and every alt row 9 [9:10] sts twice and 8 [9:9] sts once.

Right front

Work as given for left front to **.
Next row (dec row) K1, P36 [32:40] sts, (P3 [4:3] sts, P2 tog) 5 [6:7] times, P2, sl rem 8 sts on to holder for front band. 59 [65:71] sts.
Change to 3mm/No 11 needles.
Next row K23 [29:28] sts, (K2 tog, K1, yfwd, K1, yfwd, K1, sl 1, K1, psso) twice, K22 [22:29] sts.
Next row P to end.
Complete as given for left front, reversing all shaping.

Left front band

Join shoulder seams. With Rs of work facing and 3mm/No 11 needles, rejoin yarn at inner edge of 8 sts on holder.
1st row Inc in first st, (K1, P1) 3 times, K1. 9 sts.

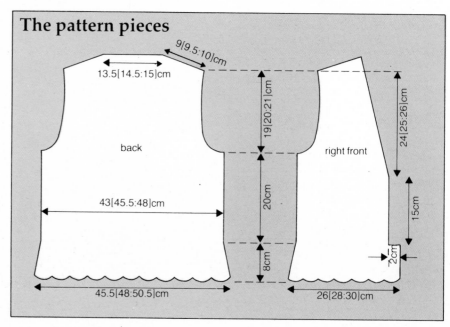

The pattern pieces

9[9.5:10]cm

13.5[14.5:15]cm

back

43[45.5:48]cm

45.5[48:50.5]cm

19[20:21]cm

right front

20cm

8cm

24[25:26]cm

15cm

2cm

26[28:30]cm

2nd row K1, *K1, P1, rep from * to last 2 sts, K2.

3rd row K1, *P1, K1, rep from * to end.

Rep 2nd and 3rd rows until band, when slightly stretched, fits along front edge and round to centre back neck. Cast off.

Tack band along front edge. Mark positions for 5 buttons, first to come level with beg of front shaping and last to come 1cm/½in above end of lace patt with 3 more evenly spaced between.

Right front band

With Ws facing and 3mm/No 11 needles rejoin yarn at inner edge of 8 sts on holder, inc in first st and beg with a 2nd row. Work as given for left front band, making buttonholes as markers are reached on Rs rows.

Next row (buttonhole row) Rib 4, cast off 2, rib 3.

Next row Rib to end, casting on 2 sts above those cast off in previous row.

Ribbed armbands

With Rs of work facing and 3mm/ No 11 needles pick up and K119 [125:131] sts round armhole. Work 7 rows K1, P1 as given for front band, beg with a 2nd row and dec one st at each end of next and every alt row. Cast off in rib.

Frilled armbands (alternative to rib)

With 3¾mm/No 9 needles cast on 128 [135:142] sts. Work 11 rows lace patt as given for back. Change to 3mm/No 11 needles.

Next row (dec row) K1, P34 (P2 tog, P5) 8 [9:10] times, P2 tog, P34, K1. 119 [125:131] sts.

Cast off.

To make up

Press each piece lightly under a damp cloth with a warm iron. Sew on front bands and sew tog at centre back neck. Sew on frilled armbands if required. Join side seams. Press seams. Sew on buttons. Make a crochet ch or twisted cord about 125cm/50in long and thread through last row of holes in lace patt, to tie at centre front. Add two small pompoms.

Right: For extra interest pompoms or tassels can be added to each end of the cord at the waist.

Striped camisole top

This boldly striped camisole top in mohair is knitted diagonally, starting from the bottom left-hand corner and working across to the top right-hand corner. Ideal to wear with shorts for the beach, it looks just as good with trousers or, for evenings, with a full-length skirt.

Size

To fit 81-86cm/32-34in bust
Length to shoulder, 59cm/23¼in

You will need

1×50g of Chat Botte Kid Mohair, (80% mohair, 20% Chlorofibre) in colours A, B, C, D, E and F
One pair 3¼mm/No 10 needles
One pair 4mm/No 8 needles
One 3¼mm/No 10 circular needle, 60cm/24in long

Tension

19 sts and 27 rows to 10cm/4in over st st worked on 4mm/No 8 needles

Back

With 4mm/No 8 needles and A cast on 3 sts.
1st row K to end.
2nd row Inc in first st, P to last st, inc in last st.
3rd row Inc in first st, K to last st, inc in last st.
4th row P to end.
5th row As 3rd.
6th row As 2nd. 11 sts.
Rep these 6 rows 9 times more, working 6 rows each in B, C, D, E, F, A, B, C, and D. 83 sts.
61st row With E, K to end.
62nd row Inc in first st, P to last 2 sts, P2 tog.
63rd row K2 tog, K to last st, inc in last st.
64th row P to end.
65th row As 63rd.
66th row As 62nd.
Rep these 6 rows once more, using F.
73rd row With A, K to end.
74th row P2 tog, P to last 2 sts, P2 tog.

Left: Soft enough to be worn immediately next to the skin, this sun-bright top is worked in a sequence of six-row stripes cleverly matched at the side seams.

75th row K2 tog, K to last 2 sts, K2 tog.
76th row P to end.
77th row As 75th.
78th row As 74th. 75 sts.
Rep these 6 rows 9 times more, using B, C, D, E, F, A, B, C and D. Cast off rem 3 sts.

Front

Work as for back.

Welt

Join side seams, matching the stripes. With 3¼mm/No 10 circular needle and A, pick up and K130 sts round lower edge.
Work 5cm/2in in rounds of K1, P1 rib. Cast off loosely in rib.

Top edge

With 3¼mm/No 10 circular needle and B, pick up and K130 sts round top edge. Work 2cm/¾in in rounds of K1, P1 rib. Cast off in rib.

Above: Think about colours and include shades that tone with other clothes.

Straps (make 2)

With 3¼mm/No 10 needles and B, cast on 5 sts.
1st row K1, *P1, K1, rep from * once.
2nd row P1, *K1, P1, rep from * once.
Rep these 2 rows until strap measures 40cm/15¾in. Cast off.

To make up

Do not press. Sew on straps, crossing at back.

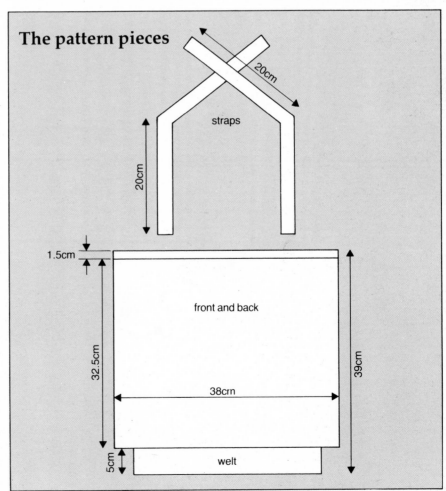

The pattern pieces

20cm

straps

20cm

20cm

1.5cm

front and back

32.5cm

38cm

39cm

5cm

welt

Lacy slipover

Sizes

To fit 84 [91:99]cm/33 [36:39]in bust
Length to shoulder, 55 [56:57]cm/
21¾ [22:22½]in
The figures in [] refer to the 91/36
and 99cm/39in sizes respectively

You will need

5 [6:6]×50g balls of Sirdar Country
 Style Double Knitting (45% acrylic,
 40% nylon, 15% wool)
One pair 3mm/No 11 needles
One pair 3¾mm/No 9 needles
Set of four 3mm/No 11 needles
One cable needle

Tension

24 sts and 33 rows to 10cm/4in over
st st worked on 3¾mm/No 9 needles

Back

With 3mm/No 11 needles cast on
103 [113:123] sts.
1st row K1, *P1, K1, rep from * to end.
2nd row P1, *K1, P1, rep from * to
end. Rep these 2 rows 15 times more.
Next row (inc row) (K1, P1) twice,
*K3 [4:5] sts, (M1, K3) 3 times, M1,
K3 [4:5] sts, P1, (K1, P1) twice, rep
from * 4 times more omitting last P1
at end of row. 123 [133:143] sts.
Change to 3¾mm/No 9 needles.
1st row (Rs) P1, sl 1 in a purlwise
direction keeping yarn at back of
work – **called sl 1**, P1, *sl 1,
P19 [21:23] sts, (sl 1, P1) twice, rep
from * to end.
2nd row K1, P1, K1, *P1, K19 [21:23]
sts, (P1, K1) twice, rep from * to end.
Rep these 2 rows 3 times more.
9th row P1, sl 1, P1, *sl 1, P5 [6:7] sts,
P2 tog tbl, yon and hold across
needle, sl next st on to cable needle
and hold at back of work, sl 1 from
left-hand needle, yfwd between
needles ready to P1 from cable
needle – **called cr2R**, P1, sl next st
on to cable needle and hold at front
of work, P1, sl 1 from cable needle
(on to right hand needle) – **called
cr2L**, yrn, P2 tog, P5 [6:7] sts, (sl 1,
P1) twice, rep from * to end.
Note: When working cr2R take care
not to lose the st formed by the yon.
10th row K1, P1, K1, *P1, K7 [8:9] sts,
P1, K3, P1, K7 [8:9] sts, (P1, K1)
twice, rep from * to end.
11th row P1, sl 1, P1, *sl 1, P4 [5:6] sts
P2 tog tbl, yon, cr2R, P3, cr2L, yrn,
P2 tog, P4 [5:6] sts, (sl 1, P1) twice,

rep from * to end.
12th row K1, P1, K1, *P1, K6 [7:8] sts,
P1, K5, P1, K6 [7:8] sts, (P1, K1)
twice, rep from * to end.
13th row P1, sl 1, P1, *sl 1, P3 [4:5] sts,
P2 tog tbl, yon, cr2R, P5, cr2L, yrn,
P2 tog, P3 [4:5] sts, (sl 1, P1) twice,
rep from * to end.
14th row K1, P1, K1, *P1, K5 [6:7] sts,
P1, K7, P1, K5 [6:7] sts, (P1, K1)
twice, rep from * to end.
15th row P1, sl 1, P1, *sl 1, P2 [3:4]
sts, P2 tog tbl, yon, cr2R, P1, cr2R, P1,
cr2L, P1, cr2L, yrn, P2 tog, P2 [3:4]
sts, (sl 1, P1) twice. rep from * to end.
16th row K1, P1, K1, *P1, K4 [5:6] sts,
P1, K2, P1, K3, P1, K2, P1, K4 [5:6]
sts, (P1, K1) twice, rep from * to end.
17th row P1, sl 1, P1, *sl 1, P1 [2:3] sts,
P2 tog tbl, yon, cr2R, P1, cr2R, P3,
cr2L, P1, cr2L, yrn, P2 tog, P1 [2:3]
sts, (sl 1, P1) twice, rep from * to end.
18th row K1, P1, K1, *P1, K3 [4:5] sts,
P1, K2, P1, K5, P1, K2, P1, K3 [4:5]
sts, (P1, K1) twice, rep from * to end.
19th row P1, sl 1, P1, *sl 1, P5 [6:7] sts,
cr2R, P5, cr2L, P5 [6:7] sts, (sl 1, P1)
twice, rep from * to end.
20th row K1, P1, K1, *P1, K5 [6:7] sts,
P1, K7, P1, K5 [6:7] sts, (P1, K1)
twice, rep from * to end.
21st row P1, sl 1, Pl, *sl 1, P4 [5:6] sts,
cr2R, P7, cr2L, P4 [5:6] sts, (sl 1, P1)
twice, rep from * to end.
22nd row K1, P1, K1, *P1, K4 [5:6]
sts, P1, K9, P1, K4 [5:6] sts, (P1, K1)
twice, rep from * to end.
23rd row P1, sl 1, P1, *sl 1, P3 [4:5]
sts, cr2R, P9, cr2L, P3 [4:5] sts, (sl 1,
P1) twice, rep from * to end.
24th row K1, P1, K1, *P1, K3 [4:5] sts,
P1, K11, Pl, K3 [4:5] sts, (P1, K1)
twice, rep from * to end.
These 24 rows form patt and are rep
throughout. Cont in patt until work
measures 33cm/13in from beg,
ending with a Ws row.

Shape armholes

Cast off at beg of next and every row
4 [5:6] sts twice, 3 sts 4 times, 2 sts 8
times and one st 4 [6:8] times. 83
[89:95] sts. Work 6 [8:10] rows
without shaping.
Inc one st at each end of next and
every foll 6th row until there are 99
[105:111] sts. Cont without shaping
until armholes measure 22 [23:24]cm/
8¾ [9:9½]in from beg, ending with
a Ws row.

Shape shoulders and neck

Cast off 5 sts at beg of next 4 rows.

Next row Cast off 5 sts, patt 18 [20:22]
sts, turn and leave rem sts on holder.
Complete right side first.
Cast off at beg of next and every row
4 sts once, 5 [6:7] sts once, 4 sts once
and 5 [6:7] sts once.
With Rs of work facing sl next 33
[35:37] sts on to holder for centre
neck, rejoin yarn to rem sts and patt
to end. Complete to match first side
reversing shaping.

Front

Work as given for back until point
where you have inc to 93 [99:105] sts
in armhole shaping, ending with a
Ws row.

Shape neck

Next row Patt 39 [41:43] sts, turn and
leave rem sts on holder.
Cont inc at armhole edge on every
6th row 3 times more, *at the same time*
cast off at neck edge on next and
every alt row 3 sts once, 2 sts 3 times
and one st 8 times. Cont without
shaping until armhole measures
same as back to shoulder, ending
with a Ws row.

Shape shoulder

Cast off at beg of next and every alt
row 5 sts 3 times and 5 [6:7] sts twice.
With Rs of work facing sl next 15
[17:19] sts on to holder for centre
neck, rejoin yarn to rem sts and patt
to end. Complete to match first side
reversing shaping.

Neckband

Join shoulder seams. With four 3mm/
No 11 needles and Rs facing, pick up
and K9 sts down right back neck, K
across back neck sts, pick up and K9
sts up left back neck and 26 sts down
left front neck, K across front neck
sts, pick up and K26 sts up right front
neck. 118 [122:126] sts.
Work 8 rounds K1, P1 rib. Cast off
loosely in rib.

Armbands

With 3mm/No 11 needles and Rs
facing, pick up and K103 [109:115]
sts round armhole. Beg with 2nd rib
row, work 6 rows rib as for back,
dec one st at each end of 2nd and
every alt row. Cast off in rib.

To make up

Press each piece under a dry cloth
with a warm iron, omitting ribbing.
Join side seams. Press seams.

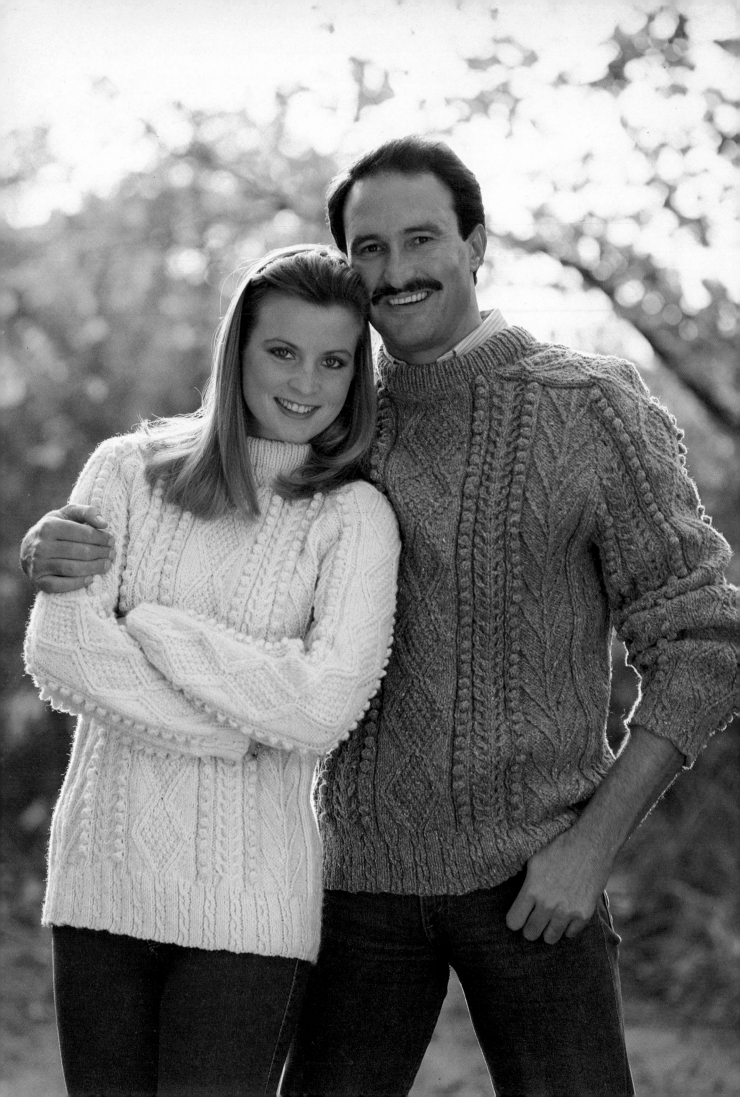

Aran sweaters

Aran sweaters traditionally come from the islands off the western coast of Ireland. These authentic jerseys are knitted in Aran wool with moss stitch diamonds on the centre panel of the body and sleeves, with panels of bobbles, lobster claw cables and the tree of life design on either side. The centre panel on the sleeves continues to form a saddle-top shoulder line. The sweaters are finished with a neat ribbed crew neck for comfort.

Sizes

To fit 86/91 [97/102]cm/
34/36 [38/40]in bust/chest
Length to shoulder 66 [70]cm/
26 [27½]in
Sleeve seam, 46 [48]cm/18 [19]in
The figures in [] refer to 97-102cm/
38-40in size only

You will need

21 [25] x 50g balls of Sunbeam Aran
  Knit or Aran Tweed
One pair 3¾mm/No 9 needles
One pair 4½mm/No 7 needles
Set of four 3¾mm/No 9 needles
1 cable needle

Tension

20 sts and 28 rows to 10cm/4in over st
st worked on 4½mm/No 7 needles

Back

With 3¾mm/No 9 needles cast on 123 [139] sts. Commence rib.
1st row K3, *P1, (K1 tbl, P1) twice, K3, rep from * to end.
2nd row P3, *K1, (P1 tbl, K1) twice, P3, rep from * to end.
3rd and 4th rows As 1st and 2nd
5th row K3, *P1, sl next st on to cable needle and hold at front of work, K second st on left-hand needle then P first st and sl both sts off needle tog, K1 tbl from cable needle – **called cr3**, P1, K3, rep from * to end.
6th row As 2nd.
Rep these 6 rows twice more, then first 2 rows once more. Change to 4½mm/No 7 needles.
1st row (Rs) K3, (P1, (K1 tbl, P1) twice, K3) once [twice], *P8, K next 3

Left: Traditional patterns and authentic yarn have been used for these practical Aran sweaters for a man or a woman.

sts tbl, P8, **, K3, P2, K9, P2, K3, ***, P2, K7, (K1 tbl, P1) 3 times, K1 tbl, K7, P2, rep from ** to *** once, then from * to ** once, K3, (P1, (K1 tbl, P1) twice, K3) once [twice].
2nd row P3, (K1, (P1 tbl, K1) twice, P3) once [twice], *K8, P next 3 sts tbl, K8, **, P3, K2, P9, K2, P3, ***, K2, P7, (P1 tbl, K1) 3 times, P1 tbl, P7, K2, rep from ** to *** once, then from * to ** once, P3, (K1, (P1 tbl, K1) twice, P3) once [twice].
3rd row K3, (P1, cr3, P1, K3) once [twice], *P7, sl next st on to cable needle and hold at back of work, K1 tbl from left-hand needle then P1 from cable needle – **called tw2R**, K1 tbl, sl next st on to cable needle and hold at front of work, P1 from left-hand needle then K1 tbl from cable needle – **called tw2L**, P7, **, K3, P2, K9, P2, K3, ***, P2, K6, (tw2R) twice, K1, (tw2L) twice, K6, P2, rep from ** to *** once, then from * to ** once, K3, (P1, cr3, P1, K3) once [twice].
4th row Patt 11 [19] sts as 2nd row, *K7, (P1 tbl, K1) twice, P1 tbl, K7,** P3, K2, P9, K2, P3, ***, K2, P6, (P1 tbl, K1) twice, P1, (K1, P1 tbl) twice, P6, K2, rep from ** to *** once, then from * to ** once, patt 11[19]sts as 2nd row.
5th row Patt 11 [19] sts as 1st row, *P6, tw2R, P1, K1 tbl, P1, tw2L, P6, **, K1, K into front, back, front and back of next st making 4 sts, turn, sl 1, P3, turn, pass the 2nd, 3rd and 4th sts on left-hand needle over the first then K this st tbl – **called MB**, K1, P2, sl next 3 sts on to cable needle and hold at back of work, K1 from left-hand needle, K3 from cable

needle, K1 from left-hand needle, sl next st on to cable needle and hold at front of work, K3 from left-hand needle then K1 from cable needle – **called cable 9**, P2, K1, MB, K1, ***, P2, K5, (tw2R) twice, K1, P1, K1, (tw2L) twice, K5, P2, rep from ** to *** once, then from * to ** once, patt 11[19]sts as 1st row.
6th row Patt 11 [19] sts as 2nd row, *K6, (P1 tbl, K2) twice, P1 tbl, K6, **, patt 19 sts as 2nd row, ***, K2, P5, (P1 tbl, K1) twice, P1, K1, P1, (K1, P1 tbl) twice, P5, K2, rep from ** to *** once, then from * to ** once, patt 11 [19] sts as 2nd row.
7th row Patt 11 [19] sts as 1st row, *P5, tw2R, P2, K1 tbl, P2, tw2L, P5, **, patt 19 sts as 1st row, ***, P2, K4, (tw2R) twice, K1, (P1, K1) twice, (tw2L) twice, K4, P2, rep from ** to *** once, then from * to ** once, patt 11 [19] sts as 1st row.
8th row Patt 11 [19] sts as 2nd row, *K5, (P1 tbl, K3) twice, P1 tbl, K5, **, patt 19 sts as 2nd row, ***, K2, P4, (P1 tbl, K1) twice, (P1, K1) twice, P1, (K1, P1 tbl) twice, P4, K2, rep from ** to *** once, then from * to ** once, patt 11 [19] sts as 2nd row.
9th row Patt 11 [19] sts as 3rd row, *P4, tw2R, P3, K1 tbl, P3, tw2L, P4, **, patt 19 sts as 5th row, ***, P2, K3, (tw2R) twice, K1, (P1, K1) 3 times, (tw2L) twice, K3, P2, rep from ** to *** once, then from * to ** once, patt 11 [19] sts as 3rd row.
10th row Patt 11 [19] sts as 2nd row, *K4, (P1 tbl, K4) 3 times, **, patt 19 sts as 2nd row, ***, K2, P3, (P1 tbl, K1) twice, (P1, K1) 3 times, P1, (K1, P1 tbl) twice, P3, K2, rep from ** to *** once, then from * to ** once, patt 11

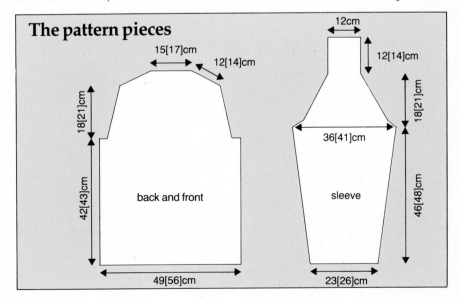

The pattern pieces

15[17]cm
12[14]cm
18[21]cm
42[43]cm
back and front
49[56]cm

12cm
12[14]cm
18[21]cm
36[41]cm
sleeve
46[48]cm
23[26]cm

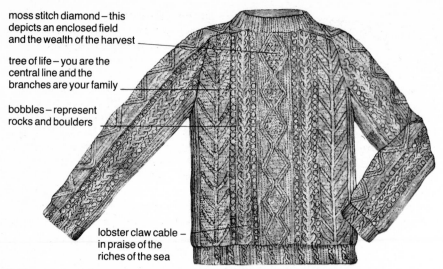

moss stitch diamond – this depicts an enclosed field and the wealth of the harvest

tree of life – you are the central line and the branches are your family

bobbles – represent rocks and boulders

lobster claw cable – in praise of the riches of the sea

[19] sts as 2nd row.

11th row Patt 11 [19] sts as 1st row, *P3, tw2R, P4, K1 tbl, P4, tw2L, P3, **, patt 19 sts as 1st row, ***, P2, K2, (tw2R) twice, K1, (P1, K1) 4 times, (tw2L) twice, K2, P2, rep from ** to *** once, then from * to ** once, patt 11 [19] sts as 1st row.

12th row Patt 11 [19] sts as 2nd row, *K3, P1 tbl, (K5, P1 tbl) twice, K3, **, patt 19 sts as 2nd row, ***, K2, P2, (P1 tbl, K1) twice, (P1, K1) 4 times, P1, (K1, P1 tbl) twice, P2, K2, rep from ** to *** once, then from * to ** once, patt 11 [19] sts as 2nd row.

13th row Patt 11 [19] sts as 1st row, *P2, tw2R, P4, K next 3 sts tbl, P4, tw2L, P2, **, patt 19 sts as 5th row, ***, P2, K1, (tw2R) twice, K1, (P1, K1) 5 times, (tw2L) twice, K1, P2, rep from ** to *** once, then from * to ** once, patt 11 [19] sts as 1st row.

14th row Patt 11[19] sts as 2nd row, *K2, P1 tbl, K5, P next 3 sts tbl, K5, P1 tbl, K2, **, patt 19 sts as 2nd row, ***, K2, P1, (P1 tbl, K1) twice, (P1, K1) 5 times, P1, (K1, P1 tbl) twice, P1, K2, rep from ** to *** once, then from * to ** once, patt 11[19] sts as 2nd row.

15th row Patt as 3rd row to centre panel of 25 sts, P2, K1, sl next st on to cable needle and hold at front of work, K1 from left-hand needle then K1 tbl from cable needle – **called tw2LK**, tw2L, (P1, K1) 5 times, P1, tw2R, sl next st on to cable needle and hold at back of work, K1 tbl from left-hand needle then K1 from cable needle – **called tw2RK**, K1, P2, patt as 3rd row to end.

16th row Patt as 4th row to centre panel, patt centre 25 sts as 12th row, patt as 4th row to end.

17th row Patt as 5th row to centre panel, P2, K2, tw2LK, tw2L, (P1, K1) 4 times, P1, tw2R, tw2RK, K2, P2, patt as 5th row to end.

18th row Patt as 6th row to centre panel, patt centre 25 sts as 10th row, patt as 6th row to end.

19th row Patt as 7th row to centre panel, P2, K3, tw2LK, tw2L, (P1, K1) 3 times, P1, tw2R, tw2RK, K3, P2, patt as 7th row to end.

20th row As 8th row.

21st row Patt as 9th row to centre panel, P2, K4, tw2LK, tw2L, (P1, K1) twice, P1, tw2R, tw2RK, K4, P2, patt as 9th row to end.

22nd row Patt as 10th row to centre panel, patt centre 25 sts as 6th row, patt as 10th row to end.

23rd row Patt as 11th row to centre panel, P2, K5, tw2LK, tw2L, P1, K1, P1, tw2R, tw2RK, K5, P2, patt as 11th row to end.

24th row Patt as 12th row to centre panel, patt centre 25 sts as 4th row, patt as 12th row to end.

25th row Patt as 13th row to centre panel, P2, K6, tw2LK, tw2L, P1, tw2R, tw2RK, K6, P2, patt as 13th row to end.

26th row Patt as 14th row to centre panel, patt centre 25 sts as 2nd row, patt as 14th row to end.

The 3rd to 26th rows form patt and are rep throughout. Cont in patt until back measures 42 [43]cm/16½ [17]in from beg, ending with a Ws row. Adjust length if required.

Shape armholes

Keeping patt correct, cast off at beg of next and every row 8 sts twice and 2[3] sts twice.

Dec one st at each end of next and every foll 4th row until 81[91] sts rem, then work one row ending with a Ws row.

Shape shoulders

Cast off at beg of next and every row 8[9] sts 4 times and 9[10] sts twice. Leave rem 31[35] sts on holder for neck.

Front

Work as given for back.

Sleeves

With 3¾mm/No 9 needles cast on 51 [59] sts. Work 13 rows rib patt as given for back.

14th row Patt 4[7] sts, *M1, P3, M1, P2[3] sts, rep from * 8[7] times more, patt 2 [4] sts. 69 [75] sts. Change to 4½mm/No 7 needles. Cont in Aran patt as foll:

1st row P0[1] st, K1[3] sts, P2, *K3, P2, K9, P2, K3, *, P2, K7, (K1 tbl, P1) 3 times, K1 tbl, K7, P2, rep from * to *, P2, K1[3] sts, P0[1] st.

2nd row K0[1] st, P1[3] sts, K2, *P3, K2, P9, K2, P3, *, K2, P7, (P1 tbl, K1) 3 times, P1 tbl, P7, K2, rep from * to *, K2, P1[3] sts, K0[1] st.

Cont in patt as now set, working centre panel with cable and bobble panels at each side as for back, inc one st at each end of 9th and every foll 8th row, working extra sts into welt patt, until there are 89[99] sts. Cont without shaping until sleeve measures 46 [48]cm/18 [19]in from beg, ending with a Ws row.

Shape top

Cast off at beg of next and every row 8 sts twice and 2[3] sts twice. Dec one st at each end of next and every alt row until 25 sts rem.

Cont in patt on these 25 sts for length of shoulder, ending with a Ws row. Leave sts on holder.

Neckband

Sew saddle top of sleeves to shoulders.

With set of four 3¾mm/No 9 needles and Rs of work facing, K across all sts on holders, K2 tog at each seam. 108 [116] sts. Cont in rounds of K1, P1 rib for 6cm/2¼in. Cast off loosely in rib.

To make up

Do not press as this will flatten the patt. Sew in sleeves. Join side and sleeve seams.

Fold neckband in half to inside and sl st down.

Press seams only under a damp cloth with a warm iron.

Look-alike slipovers in authentic Fair Isle

Well worth a second look, these attractive slipovers in traditional patterns and colours can be knitted to match – or in the same colours but different patterns.

The patterns have already been handed down over several centuries and such is their timeless appeal they will never date. So, your slipovers need not be discarded with the next fashion trend but can be among the treasured mainstays of your wardrobe for many years to come.

If you have a favourite Fair Isle pattern, you can use it to knit these slipovers. Count how many stitches and rows your pattern is worked over and, provided it corresponds to one of the charts given overleaf, substitute your own chart, working the colours in the sequence given.

Sizes

To fit 81 [86:91:97:102:107]cm/ 32 [34:36:38:40:42]in bust/chest
Length to shoulder 58 [60:63:65:67:69] cm/22¾ [23½:24¾:25½:26½:27¼]in
The figures in [] refer to 86/34, 91/36, 97/38, 102/40 and 107cm/42in sizes respectively

Below: These slipovers are machine washable and will keep their shape well.

Chart A

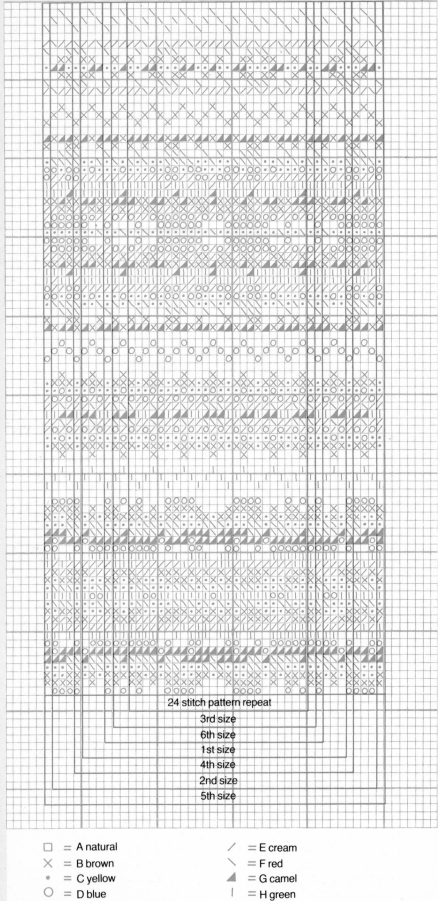

24 stitch pattern repeat
3rd size
6th size
1st size
4th size
2nd size
5th size

Chart B

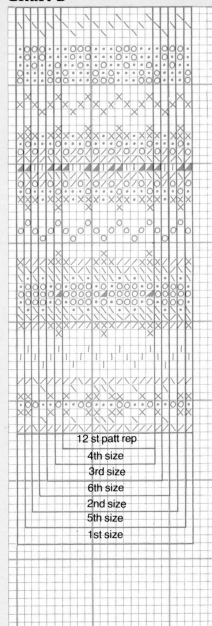

12 st patt rep
4th size
3rd size
6th size
2nd size
5th size
1st size

□ = A natural	/	= E cream
✕ = B brown	\	= F red
• = C yellow	◣	= G camel
○ = D blue	|	= H green

The pattern piece

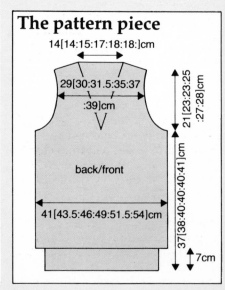

14[14:15:17:18:18:]cm

29[30:31.5:35:37
:39]cm

21[23:23:25
:27:28]cm

back/front

41[43.5:46:49:51.5:54]cm

37[38:40:40:40:41]cm

7cm

You will need

Version A 2 [3:3:3:4:4]×50g balls of Patons Clansman 4 ply (100% wool) in main colour A
1 [1:1:1:1:2] balls of same in contrast colour B
1 [1:1:1:1:1] ball of same in each of contrast colours C, D, E, F, G and H
Version B 2 [3:3:3:4:4]×50g balls of same in main colour A
1 [1:1:1:1:1] ball of same in each of contrast colours B, C, E, F, G and H
1 [1:1:1:1:2] balls of same in contrast colour D
One pair 2¾mm/No 12 needles
One pair 3¼mm/No 10 needles

Tension

28 sts and 36 rows to 10cm/4in over st st and 32 sts and 32 rows to 10cm/4in over Fair Isle patt worked on 3¼mm/No 10 needles

Note

When working patt from charts carry yarn not in use loosely across back of work. Read all K rows from right to left and all P rows from left to right.

Back version A

With 2¾mm/No 12 needles and A cast on 114 [122:128:136:144:150] sts.
Work 7cm/2¾in K1, P1 rib, ending with a Rs row.
1st, 2nd, 3rd and 5th sizes only
Next row (inc row) Rib 1 [5:1:2] sts, *pick up loop lying between needles and K tbl – **called M1**, rib 7 sts, rep from * to last 1 [5:1:2] sts, M1, rib to end. 131 [139:147:165] sts.
4th and 6th sizes only
Next row (inc row) Rib 3 [4] sts, *pick up loop lying between needles and K tbl – **called M1**, rib 6 sts, M1, rib 7 sts, rep from * to last 3 [3] sts, M1, rib to end. 157 [173] sts.

All sizes

Change to 3¼mm/No 10 needles. Join in and break colours as required. Work in patt from chart A, rep the 24 patt sts 5 [5:6:6:6:7] times, and K the first 5 [9:1:6:10:2] and last 6 [10:2:7:11:3] sts and P the first 6 [10:2:7:11:3] and last 5 [9:1:6:10:2] sts as indicated. Cont in patt until back measures 37 [38:40:40:40:41]cm/14½ [15:15¾:15¾:15¾:16¼]in from beg, or length to underarm, ending on a Ws row.**

Shape armholes

Keeping patt correct throughout, cast off 5 sts at beg of next 2 rows. Dec one st at each end of next 7 [9:11:7:9:11] rows, then at each end of every foll alt row until 93 [97:101:113:119:125] sts rem. Cont without shaping until armholes measure 21 [22:23:25:27:28]cm/8¼ [8¾:9:9¾:10¾:11]in from beg, ending with a Ws row.

Shape shoulders

Cast off at beg of next and every row 8 [9:9:10:10:11] sts 4 times and 8 [8:8:9:11:12] sts twice.
Leave rem 45 [45:49:55:57:57] sts on holder for back neck.

Front version A

Work as given for back to **.
Keeping patt correct throughout shape armholes and divide for neck as foll:
Next row Cast off 5 sts, patt 58 [62:66:71:75:79] sts, K2 tog, turn and leave rem sts on holder.
Complete left shoulder on these 59 [63:67:72:76:80] sts. Work one row.
Dec one st at armhole edge on next 7 [9:11:7:9:11] rows then on every foll alt row 7 [7:7:10:9:8] times more, *at the same time* dec one st at neck edge on next and every alt row until 34 [35:36:41:44:47] sts rem.
Cont dec one st at neck edge only on every foll 4th row from previous dec until 24 [26:26:29:31:34] sts rem. Cont without shaping until front measures same as back to shoulder, ending with a Ws row.

Shape shoulder

Cast off at beg of next and every alt row 8 [9:9:10:10:11] sts twice and 8 [8:8:9:11:12] sts once.
With Rs of work facing sl centre st on to safety pin for centre front neck, rejoin appropriate colour to rem sts, sl 1, K1, psso, patt to end. Complete to match first side reversing all shapings.

Back and front version B

Work as given for version A but working in patt from chart B instead of chart A, rep the 12 patt sts 10 [11:12:13:13:14] times, and K the first 5 [3:1:0:4:2] and last 6 [4:2:1:5:3] sts and P the first 6 [4:2:1:5:3] and last 5 [3:1:0:4:2] sts as indicated.

Above: The pattern is worked on the back and front of traditional slipovers. If preferred the back could be knitted plain.

Neckband (both versions)

Join right shoulder seam. With Rs facing, 2¾mm/No 12 needles and A, pick up and K66 [70:74:82:90:94] sts down left side of neck, K centre st from safety pin and mark this with coloured thread, pick up and K66 [70:74:82:90:94] sts up right side of neck then K across 45 [45:49:55:57:57] sts from back neck holder dec 5 sts evenly. 173 [181:193:215:233:241] sts.
1st row (Ws) *P1, K1, rep from * to within 2 sts of marked centre st, P2 tog, P centre st, P2 tog tbl, **K1, P1, rep from ** to end.
2nd row *K1, P1, rep from * to within 2 sts of marked centre st, P2 tog tbl, K centre st, P2 tog, **K1, P1, rep from ** to last st, K1.
Rep these 2 rows 3 times more then 1st row again.
Cast off in rib, dec at either side of centre st as before.

Armbands (both versions)

Join left shoulder and neckband seam. With Rs facing, 2¾mm/No 12 needles and A, pick up and K128 [136:144:160:176:184] sts evenly round armhole. Work 9 rows K1, P1 rib. Cast off in rib.

To make up (both versions)

Press each piece under a damp cloth with a warm iron, omitting ribbing. Join side and armband seams. Press seams.

Man's striped jersey

Sizes

To fit 97 [102:107]cm/38 [40:42]in chest

Length to back neck, 76 [77:78]cm/ 30 [30¼:30¾]in

Sleeve seam, 50cm/19¾in adjustable

The figures in [] refer to the 102/40 and 107cm/42in sizes respectively

You will need

13 [13:14]×50g balls of Patons Shetland Chunky in main colour M, (50% acrylic, 25% nylon, 25% wool)

About 25×13.7m/14¾yd skeins of Coats/Anchor Tapisserie wool in assorted colours C, (100% wool)

Or oddments of Patons Shetland Chunky in assorted colours to give a total of 150g, C

One pair 4½mm/No 7 needles

One pair 6mm/No 4 needles

Set of four 4½mm/No 7 needles

Tension

15 sts and 20 rows to 10cm/4in over st st worked with M on 6mm/No 4 needles

Note

Only the Tapisserie wool is used double throughout. Colours are used at random in any order but take care to match back and front body and raglan stripes

Back

With 4½mm/No 7 needles and M, cast on 83 [87:91] sts.

1st row (Rs) K1, *P1, K1, rep from * to end.

2nd row P1, *K1, P1, rep from * to end.

Rep these 2 rows for 4cm/1½in, ending with a 2nd row.

Change to 6mm/No 4 needles. Beg with a K row work 2 rows st st.

1st row K3 M, *1 C, 3 M, rep from * to end.

Beg with a P row work 3 rows st st with M.

5th Row K1 M, *1 C, 3 M, rep from * to last 2 sts, 1 C, 1 M.

Beg with a P row work 3 rows st st with M.

These 8 rows form striped patt,

using colours as required. Cont until work measures 53cm/20¾in from beg, ending with a P row.

Shape armholes

Cast off 5 sts at beg of next 2 rows.

Next row K2, sl 1, K1, psso, K to last 4 sts, K2 tog, K2.

Next row P to end.

Rep last 2 rows until 27 [29:31] sts rem, ending with a P row. Leave sts on holder for back neck.

Front

Beg with a 5th patt row work as given for back until 43 [45:47] sts rem in armhole shaping, ending with a P row.

Shape neck

Next row K2, sl 1, K1, psso, K11, turn and leave rem sts on holder. Complete left side first.

Next row P to end.

Next row K2, sl 1, K1, psso, K to last 2 sts, K2 tog.

Rep last 2 rows 4 times more, then P one row.

Next row K2, sl 1, K1, psso.

Next row P3.

Next row K1, sl 1, K1, psso.

Next row P2.

Cast off.

With Rs of work facing, leave first 13 [15:17] sts on holder for front neck, rejoin yarn to rem sts, K to last 4 sts, K2 tog, K2.

Next row P to end.

Next row Sl 1, K1, psso, K to last 4 sts, K2 tog, K2.

Complete to match left side, reversing shaping.

Sleeves

With 4½mm/No 7 needles and M,

cast on 31 [33:35] sts. Work 4cm/1½in rib as for back, ending with a 2nd row and inc 4 sts evenly in last row. 35 [37:39] sts.

Change to 6mm/No 4 needles. Beg with a K row work 2 rows st st.

1st row (Rs)K3 [2:3] M, *1 C, 3 M, rep from * to last 4 [3:4] sts, 1 C, 3 [2:3] M.

Cont in patt as now set, inc one st at each end of 5th patt row and every foll 6th row until there are 63 [65:67] sts. Cont without shaping until sleeve measures 50cm/19¾in from beg, or required length to underarm ending with same patt row as at back and front armholes.

Shape top

Keeping striped patt as back and front correct, cast off 5 sts at beg of next 2 rows. Dec one st at each end of next and every alt row as given for back until 7 sts rem, ending with a P row.

Leave sts on holder.

Neckband

Join raglan seams. With Rs facing, set of four 4½mm/No 7 needles and M, K across sts of back neck and left sleeve top K2 tog at seam, pick up and K8 sts down left front neck, K across front neck sts, pick up and K8 sts up right front neck, K across sts of right sleeve top K last st of sleeve tog with first st of back neck. 68 [72:76] sts.

Work 3cm/1¼in in rounds of K1, P1 rib. Cast off in rib.

To make up

Do not press. Join side and sleeve seams.

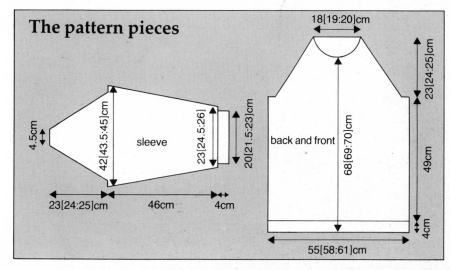

The pattern pieces

18[19:20]cm

23[24:25]cm

4.5cm

42[43.5:45]cm

sleeve

23[24.5:26]cm

23[24:25]cm

46cm

4cm

20[21.5:23]cm

back and front

68[69:70]cm

49cm

4cm

55[58:61]cm

V-necked jerseys for father and son

Knit this jersey in the colours shown or even in the colours of a favourite football team.

The main part of the jersey is knitted in garter stitch with the welts and cuffs in rib.

The pattern is given in a range of sizes so that you can knit one for each member of your family, including your daughter.

Sizes

To fit 66 [81:97]cm/26 [32:38]in chest
Length to shoulder, 45 [55:65]cm/17¾ [21¾:25½]in
Sleeve seam, 35 [43:51]cm/13¾ [17:20]in
The figures in [] refer to the 81/32 and 97cm/38in sizes respectively

You will need

6 [7:8]×50g balls Neveda Bistro (52% wool, 48% acrylic) in main colour A
2 [3:3] balls of same in contrast colour B
2 [2:3] balls of same in contrast colour C
One pair 4½mm/No 7 needles
One pair 5½mm/No 5 needles
One set of four 4½mm/No 7 needles

Tension

15 sts and 30 rows to 10cm/4in over garter stitch worked on 5½mm/No 5 needles

Back

With 4½mm/No 7 needles and A cast on 55 [65:75] sts.
1st row K1, *P1, K1, rep from * to end.
2nd row P1, *K1, P1, rep from * to end.
Rep these 2 rows for 5 [6:7]cm/2 [2¼:2¾]in, ending with a 2nd row and inc 0 [2:4] sts evenly on last row. 55 [67:79] sts. Break off A. Join in C.
Change to 5½mm/No 5 needles and work in g st for 16 [26:36] rows.
Using a separate ball of yarn for each section of colour, and twisting the yarns on the Ws of work on

Left: The simple shape of these garter stitch jerseys makes it easy to work the geometric design. The pattern is worked on both front and back.

every row commence chevron patt.
1st and 2nd rows K1 B, *K17 [21:25] C, K1 B, rep from * twice more.
3rd and 4th rows K2 B, *K15 [19:23] C, K3 B, rep from * once more, K15 [19:23] C, K2 B.
5th and 6th rows K3 B, *K13 [17:21] C, K5 B, rep from * once more, K13 [17:21] C, K3 B.
Cont inc the number of sts worked in B in this way until all sts are worked in B.
Work in B for 20 [24:28] rows.
Commence 2nd chevron.
1st and 2nd rows K9 [11:13] B, *K1 A, K17 [21:25] B, rep from * once more, K1 A, K9 [11:13] B.
3rd and 4th rows K8 [10:12] B, *K3 A, K15 [19:23] B, rep from * once more, K3 A, K8 [10:12] B.
Cont inc as before until all sts are worked in A.
Cont in A only until work measures 45 [55:65]cm/17¾ [21¾:25½]in from beg, ending with a Ws row.

Shape shoulders

Cast off at beg of next and every foll row 8 [7:8] sts 2 [4:4] times, and 8 [6:8] sts twice.
Leave rem 23 [27:31] sts on holder.

Front

Work as given for back until 10 [12:14] rows of the 2nd chevron have been worked.

Divide for neck

Next row Still working in patt K27 [33:39], turn and leave rem sts on holder for right shoulder.

Working on sts for left shoulder, cont in g st without shaping for 3 rows.
Dec one st at neck edge on next and every foll 4th row until 16 [20:24] sts rem.
Cont without shaping until work measures same as back to shoulder, ending at armhole edge.

Shape shoulder

Cast off at beg of next and every foll alt row 8 [7:8] sts 1 [2:2] times and 8 [6:8] sts once.
With Rs of work facing, slip first st from holder on to safety pin for neckband, rejoin A and complete right shoulder to match left reversing all shaping.

Sleeves

With 4½mm/No 7 needles and A cast on 29 [33:37] sts. Work 5 [6:7]cm/2 [2¼:2¾]in rib as given for back, ending with a first row.
Next row (inc row) Rib 5 [4:4], (inc in next st, rib 5 [4:3]) 3 [5:7] times, inc in next st, rib 5 [3:4], 33 [39:45] sts.
Change to 5½mm/No 5 needles.
Work in g st inc one st at each end of 13th [9th:5th] and every foll 12th row until there are 47 [57:67] sts.
Cont in g st without shaping until sleeve measures 35 [43:51]cm/ 13¾ [17:20] in from beg, or length required, ending with a Ws row.
Cast off loosely.

Neckband

Join shoulder seams.
With set of four 4½mm/No 7 needles and A K across 23 [27:31] sts from back neck, pick up and K30 [36:42] sts down left front neck, K centre front st from safety pin, then pick up and K30 [36:42] sts up right front neck. 84 [100:116] sts.
Next round Work in K1, P1 rib to 2 sts before centre front st, P2 tog, K1 (centre front st), P2 tog tbl, work in rib to end.
Rep this round until neckband measures 2 [2.5:3]cm/¾ [1:1¼]in. Cast off in rib working dec as before.

To make up

Do not press.
Sew in sleeves. Join side and sleeve seams.

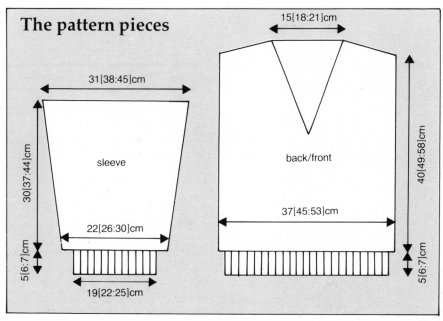

The pattern pieces

15[18:21]cm

31[38:45]cm

sleeve

30[37:44]cm

5[6:7]cm

22[26:30]cm

19[22:25]cm

back/front

40[49:58]cm

37[45:53]cm

5[6:7]cm

A new look for the traditional Argyle

This stylish waistcoat in Argyle pattern sounds two new fashion notes: it is knitted in pastel shades and a cotton yarn, cool and crisp worn with light-weight trousers and an open-necked shirt.

If you prefer to have only one contrast colour, you can use the main colour within the pattern, too.

Sizes

To fit 91 [97:102]cm/36 [38:40]in chest
Length to shoulder, 59 [62:65]cm/23¼ [24½:25½]in
The figures in [] refer to 97/38 and 102cm/40in sizes respectively

You will need

3 [4:4]×50g balls of Pingouin Corrida No 3, (60% cotton, 40% acrylic) in colour A
1×50g ball each of contrasts B and C
One pair 2¾mm/No 12 needles
One pair 3mm/No 11 needles
Five buttons

Tension

28 sts and 37 rows to 10cm/4in over st st worked on 3mm/No 11 needles

Note

For the Argyle pattern on the fronts work from the chart using a separate small ball for each block of colour.

Twist the yarns round each other when changing colour during a row.

Back

With 2¾mm/No 12 needles and A cast on 126 [132:138] sts. Work in K1, P1 rib for 6cm/2¼in ending with Rs row.
Next row (inc row) Rib 6 [12:18], (inc in next st, rib 14) 8 times. 134 [140:146] sts.
Change to 3mm/No 11 needles. Beg with a K row work in st st until back measures 37 [39:41]cm/14½ [15¼: 16¼]in from beg, ending on a P row.

Shape armholes

Cast off at the beg of next and every following row 5 sts twice, 2 sts 8 times, and one st 4 [6:8] times. 104 [108:112] sts. Cont without shaping until armholes measure 22 [23:24]cm/8¾ [9:9½]in from beg, ending with a P row.

Shape shoulders and neck

Cast off 8 sts at beg of next 4 rows.
Next row Cast off 8 sts, K10 [11:12] sts and leave these for right shoulder, cast off next 36 [38:40] sts for centre back neck, K18 [19:20] sts. Complete left shoulder first.
Cast off at beg of next and every row 8 sts once, 4 sts once and 6 [7:8] sts once.

With Ws of work facing rejoin yarn to neck edge of right shoulder. Cast off at beg of next 2 rows 4 sts once and 6 [7:8] sts once.

Right front

With 2¾mm/No 12 needles and A cast on 64 [66:68] sts. Work in K1, P1 rib for 6cm/2¼in ending with Rs row.
Next row (inc row) Rib 20 [16:10], (inc in next st, rib 10) 3 [4:5] times, rib 11 [6:3]. 67 [70:73] sts.
Change to 3mm/No 11 needles. Beg with a K row cont in st st, working the Argyle patt from the chart and joining in colours as required.
1st row K1 B, (23 C, 1 B) 2 [2:3] times, then 18 [21:0] C.
Cont in patt as now set until work measures 37 [39:41] cm/14½ [15¼: 16¼]in from beg, ending with a P row.

Shape front and armhole

Dec one st at beg of next (front edge) and every alt row 6 [7:8] times, then every 4th row 16 times, *at the same time* cast off at beg of every Ws row (armhole edge) 5 sts once, 2 sts 4 times and one st 2 [3:4] times. 30 [31:32] sts.
Cont in patt without shaping until work measures same as for back to shoulder ending at armhole edge.

Shape shoulder

Cast off at beg of next and every alt row 8 sts 3 times and 6 [7:8] sts once.

Left front

Work as given for right front, reversing the patt from the chart and all shapings.

Left front border

With 2¾mm/No 12 needles and A cast on 172 [182:192] sts. Work in K1, P1 rib for 4 rows.
Next row (buttonhole row) Rib to last 95 [102:109] sts, cast off 2 sts, *rib 20 [22:24], cast off 2 sts, rep from * 3 more times, rib to end.
Next row Rib to end casting on 2 sts above those cast off in previous row.
Work 4 more rows in rib. Cast off loosely in rib.

Right front and back neck border

With 2¾mm/No 12 needles and A cast on 218 [230:242] sts. Work in K1, P1 rib for 10 rows. Cast off in rib.

Chart for Argyle pattern

☐ = colour B   ☐ = colour C

52 row pattern repeat

commence 1st row here

Note: for left front reverse pattern from chart

3rd 2nd 1st size

side edge

centre front edge

Above: A modern interpretation of a traditional pattern in pastel colours. The true Argyle patterns are knitted in grey or beige, with red and yellow diamonds and a dark green criss-cross.

Armhole borders

With 2¾mm/No 12 needles and A cast on 150 [156:162] sts. Work in K1, P1 rib for 10 rows. Cast off in rib.

Making up

Do not press the pieces as this will spoil the yarn. Join right shoulder seam. Sew on borders with the ends meeting at left shoulder. Join left shoulder seam and ends of borders. Sew on armhole borders easing them slightly around the curves. Join side seams and ends of borders. Sew on buttons.

The pattern pieces

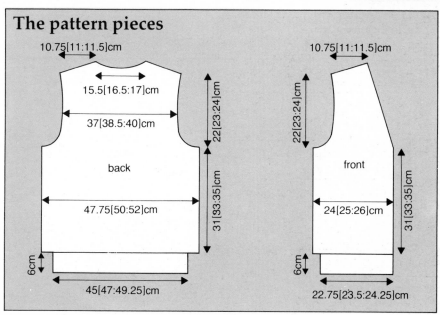

10.75[11:11.5]cm

15.5[16.5:17]cm

37[38.5:40]cm

back

22[23:24]cm

31[33:35]cm

47.75[50:52]cm

6cm

45[47:49.25]cm

10.75[11:11.5]cm

22[23:24]cm

front

24[25:26]cm

31[33:35]cm

6cm

22.75[23.5:24.25]cm

Traditional baby layette

This layette for a new baby comprises a dress, crossover and raglan cardigans, dungarees, bonnet, mitts, bootees and socks with an heirloom shawl. The co-ordinating stitch patterns are designed to mix and match.

Knit this beautiful wardrobe for a new arrival or pick out just one or two garments. The patterns for the dress, crossover cardigan and bootees are given here – the rest follow in the next two chapters.

A dainty eyelet hole pattern worked on the reversed side of stocking stitch and an old Scottish lace cable pattern are the two main patterns. Picot hems and edges are used on some of the garments with garter stitch sometimes used as a basic fabric.

The set is designed to fit a 40cm/16in chest and will suit a baby from birth to six months.

Bootees

You will need

1×20g ball of Wendy Peter Pan Darling 3 ply (55% Bri-nylon, 45% Courtelle acrylic)
One pair 3mm/No 11 needles
One cable needle
70cm/¾yd ribbon

Tension As for dress (overleaf)

Left foot

With 3mm/No 11 needles cast on 40 sts and beg at sole.
1st and every alt row (Ws) K to end.
2nd row K19, M1, K2, M1, K19.
4th row K19, M1, K4, M1, K19.
6th row K19, M1, K6, M1, K19.
8th row K19, M1, K8, M1, K19.
10th row K1, M1, K18, M1, K10, M1, K18, M1, K1. 52 sts.
12th row P25, (K1, P1) in next st, (P1, K1) in next st, P25. 54 sts.
13th and every alt row K25, P1, yrn, P2 tog, P1, K25.
14th row P25, K1, yrn, P2 tog, K1, P25.
16th row P3, (yrn, P2 tog, P6) twice, yrn, P2 tog, P4, sl next 2 sts on to cable needle and hold at back of work, K2 from left-hand needle, then K2 from cable needle – **called C4B**, P5, (yrn, P2 tog, P6) twice, yrn, P2 tog, P2.
18th row As 14th.
19th row As 13th.

Shape top of foot

20th row P25, K1, yrn, P2 tog, K1, P3, sl 1 purlwise, turn.
21st row K2 tog tbl, K2, P1, yrn, P2 tog, P1, K2, K2 tog, turn.
22nd row P3, K1, yrn, P2 tog, K1, P3, sl 1 purlwise, turn.
Rep 21st and 22nd rows twice more, then 21st row again.
28th row P3, C4B, P3, sl 1 purlwise, turn.
Rep 21st and 22nd rows 4 times more, then 21st row again.
38th row P3, K1, yrn, P2 tog, K1, P to end of row.
39th row K12, K2 tog tbl, K2, P1, yrn, P2 tog, P1, K2, K2 tog, K12. 34 sts.
40th row (ribbon slotting row) P1, *(yrn) twice, P2 tog*, rep from * to * 6 times more, C4B, **P2 tog, (yrn) twice**, rep from ** to ** 6 times more, P1.
41st row K15 dropping 1 extra loop made on previous row, P1, yrn, P2 tog, P1, K15 dropping extra loops. 34 sts.
42nd row P15, K1, yrn, P2 tog, K1, P15.
43rd row K15, P1, yrn, P2 tog, P1, K15.
Rep 42nd and 43rd rows once more.
46th row P7, yrn, P2 tog, P6, K1, yrn, P2 tog, K1, P7, yrn, P2 tog, P6.
47th row As 43rd.
Rep 42nd and 43rd rows twice more.
52nd row P3, yrn, P2 tog, P6, yrn, P2 tog, P2, C4B, P3, yrn, P2 tog, P6, yrn, P2 tog, P2.
Rep 43rd row once, then 42nd row once.
55th and 56th rows K to end.
Cast off loosely.
Knit right foot as left foot.

To make up

Press pieces lightly under a dry cloth with a cool iron.
Join seam at back and undersole.
Cut ribbon in half and thread one piece through each bootee.

Dress

You will need

5×20g balls of Wendy Peter Pan
  Darling 3 ply (55% Bri-nylon, 45%
  Courtelle acrylic)
One pair 2¾mm/No 12 needles
Set of four 2¾mm/No 12 needles
  pointed at both ends
One pair 3mm/No 11 needles
One cable needle
Four buttons
1.20m/1½yd narrow ribbon

Tension

34 sts and 44 rows to 10cm/4in over
lace cable patt worked on 3mm/
No 11 needles
30 sts and 44 rows to 10cm/4in over
eyelet hole patt worked on 3mm/
No 11 needles

Front

With 2¾mm/No 12 needles cast on
127 sts. Beg with a P row work 6
rows reversed st st.
Next row (picot hem) P1, *yrn, P2
tog, rep from * to end.
Work 2 rows reversed st st. Change
to 3mm/No 11 needles.
Next row (inc row) K2, P2, *K3, P1,
yrn, P2, K3, P2, rep from * to last
2 sts, K2. 138 sts.
Commence lace cable patt.
1st row (Rs) P2, yon, K2 tog, *P3, sl
next 2 sts on to cable needle and
hold at back of work, K2 from
left-hand needle, then K2 from
cable needle – **called C4B**, P3, yon,
K2 tog, rep from * to last 2 sts, P2.
2nd and every alt row K2, P2, *K3,
P1, yrn, P2 tog, P1, K3, P2, rep from
* to last 2 sts, K2.
3rd row P2, K2 tog, yrn, *P3, K1,
yrn, P2 tog, K1, P3, K2 tog, yrn, rep
from * to last 2 sts, P2.
5th row P2, yon, K2 tog, *P3, K1,
yrn, P2 tog, K1, P3, yon, K2 tog, rep
from * to last 2 sts, P2.
7th row As 3rd.
9th row As 5th.
11th row As 3rd.
12th row As 2nd.
These 12 rows form the patt.
Cont in patt until work measures
28cm/11in from hemline, ending
with an 11th row.
Next row (dec for bodice) K2 tog,
(P2, K1, K2 tog, P4 tog, K2 tog, K1)
11 times, P2, K2 tog. 81 sts.
Next row P to end.
Next row (ribbon slotting row) P1,
*yrn twice, P2 tog, rep from * to end.
Next row P to end, dropping 1 extra

loop made on previous row.
Work 3 rows reversed st st.
Commence eyelet hole patt.
1st row P4, yrn, P2 tog, *P6, yrn, P2
tog, rep from * to last 3 sts, P3
2nd row K to end.
Cont eyelet hole patt and
commence armhole shaping, as foll:

Shape armholes

3rd row Cast off 4 sts, P to end.
4th row Cast off 4 sts, K to end.
5th row P2 tog, P to last 2 sts, P2 tog.
6th row K2 tog, K to last 2 sts, K2
tog.
7th row P2 tog, P8, *yrn, P2 tog, P6,
rep from * to last 3 sts, P1, P2 tog.
8th row As 6th.
9th row As 5th.
10th row K to end.
11th row As 5th. 61 sts.
12th row K to end.
13th row P2, *yrn, P2 tog, P6, rep
from * to last 3 sts, yrn, P2 tog, P1.
Work 5 rows reversed st st.
19th row *P6, yrn, P2 tog, rep from *
to last 5 sts, P5.
Work 5 rows reversed st st, then rep
13th to 20th rows.

Shape neck

Next row (Rs) P23 sts, P2 tog, turn
and leave rem sts on holder.
Complete left shoulder first.
Keeping patt correct throughout,
dec one st at neck edge on next 8
rows. 16 sts.
Work 3 rows without shaping.

Shape shoulder

Cast off at beg of next and every alt
row 5 sts twice and 6 sts once.
With Rs of work facing, sl first 11 sts
on to length of yarn, rejoin yarn to
rem sts, P2 tog, P to end. 24 sts.
Complete to match first side,
reversing shapings.

Back

Work as given for front until back
measures 23cm/9in from hemline,
ending with a Ws row.

Divide for back opening

Next row Patt 67 sts, P2, turn and
leave rem 69 sts on holder.
Next row K2, patt to end.
Cont in patt on these 69 sts for right
back, working 2 sts at opening in
reversed st st, until work measures
28cm/11in from hemline, ending
with an 11th row.
Next row (dec for bodice) (K2 tog)
twice, (K1, P2, K1, K2 tog, P4 tog,

K2 tog) 5 times, K1, P2, K2 tog.
41 sts.
Next row P to end.
Next row (ribbon slotting row) P1,
*yrn twice, P2 tog, rep from * to end.
Next row P to end, dropping 1 extra
loop made on previous row.
Work 3 rows reversed st st.
Commence eyelet hole patt.
1st row P4, yrn, P2 tog, *P6, yrn, P2
tog, rep from * to last 3 sts, P3.
2nd row K to end.

Shape armhole

3rd row Cast off 4 sts, P to end.
4th row K to end.
5th row P2 tog, P to end.
6th row K to last 2 sts, K2 tog.
7th row P2 tog, P8, *yrn, P2 tog, P6,
rep from * to last 7 sts, P7.
8th row As 6th.
9th row As 5th.
10th row K to end.
11th row As 5th. 31 sts.
12th row K to end.
13th row P2, *yrn, P2 tog, P6, rep
from * to last 5 sts, yrn, P2 tog, P3.
Work 5 rows reversed st st.
19th row *P6, yrn, P2 tog, rep from *
to last 7 sts, P7.
Work 5 rows reversed st st, then rep
last 12 rows until back measures
same as front to shoulder, ending
with a Ws row.

Shape shoulder

Cast off at beg of next and every alt
row 5 sts twice and 6 sts once.
Leave rem 15 sts on holder for back
neck.
With Rs of work facing, rejoin yarn
to rem 69 sts and complete to match
right back, reversing all shapings
and noting that 1st and 7th eyelet
hole patt rows will read as foll:
1st row P3 , *P2 tog, yrn, P6, rep
from * to last 6 sts, P2 tog, yrn, P4.
7th row P7, *P6, P2 tog, yrn, rep
from * to last 10 sts, P8, P2 tog.

Sleeves

With 2¾mm/No 12 needles cast on
33 sts. Beg with a P row work 7
rows reversed st st.
Next row (ribbon slotting row) K16,
yfwd, yrn, K2 tog, K15.
Next row P to end, dropping extra
loop at centre.
Work 2 rows reversed st st. Change
to 3mm/No 11 needles.
Next row (inc row) K1, *M1, K1, rep
from * to end. 65 sts.
Commence eyelet hole patt.
1st row P to end.

2nd row K to end.
3rd row P4, *yrn, P2 tog, P6, rep from * to last 5 sts, yrn, P2 tog, P3.
Work 5 rows reversed st st.
9th row P8, *yrn, P2 tog, P6, rep from * to last st, P1.
Work 3 rows reversed st st.
These 12 rows form the patt.

Shape top
Keeping patt correct throughout, cast off 4 sts at beg of next 2 rows. Dec one st at each end of every row until 27 sts rem. Cast off at beg of next and every row 3 sts twice, 4 sts twice and 13 sts once.

Neck border
Join shoulder seams. With Rs of work facing and 2¾mm/No 12 needles, P15 sts from left back neck, pick up and K12 sts down left front neck, P11 sts from front neck, pick up and K12 sts up right front neck and P15 sts from right back neck. 65 sts.
Beg with a K row work 4 rows reversed st st.
Next row (picot row) K1, *yfwd, K2 tog, rep from * to end.
Work 5 rows reversed st st. Cast off loosely. Fold in half to Ws and sl st in place.

Back borders
With Rs of work facing and set of four 2¾mm/No 12 needles, beg at top of neck border, pick up and K38 sts down right back to top of skirt, 19 sts to base of opening, 19 sts up left side of skirt and 38 sts up left back to top of neck border. 114 sts.
1st row (buttonhole row) K56 sts, K2 tog, K17, (yfwd, K2 tog, K10) 3 times, yfwd, K2 tog, K1.
2nd row P56 sts, P2 tog, P55 sts.
Cast off, dec one st at base of opening as before.

To make up
See pattern pieces diagram on next page.
Press all pieces lightly under a dry cloth with a cool iron.
Fold hem at lower edge to Ws and sl st in place. Join side and sleeve seams. Set in sleeves. Fold first 5 rows of sleeve to Ws and sl st in place. Thread ribbon through holes.

Right: This pretty dress has a dainty picot trim worked on the purl side round the hem, sleeve and neck edges.

Crossover cardigan

You will need

2×20g balls of Wendy Peter Pan
 Darling 3 ply (55% Bri-nylon, 45%
 Courtelle acrylic)
One pair 2¾mm/No 12 needles
One pair 3mm/No 11 needles
One cable needle
Two buttons

Tension

34 sts and 44 rows to 10cm/4in over
lace cable patt worked on 3mm/
No 11 needles
30 sts and 44 rows to 10cm/4in over
eyelet hole patt worked on 3mm/
No 11 needles

Left front

With 2¾mm/No 12 needles cast on
66 sts. Work 5 rows g st noting that
1st row is Ws. Change to 3mm/
No 11 needles.
Next row (inc row) P13 sts, (M1,
P13) 3 times, K2 tog, yrn, P1, M1,
P1, K1, yrn, P2 tog, K1, P1, M1, P1,
K2 tog, yfwd, K2. 71 sts.
Next row Sl 1, K1, P2, K3, P1, yrn,
P2 tog, P1, K3, P2, K to end.
Commence eyelet hole and cable
panel patts, *at the same time* dec for
front edge at inside of cable panel.
1st row P7, *yrn, P2 tog, P6, rep
from * to last 24 sts, yrn, P2 tog, P3,
P2 tog, P1, yon, K2 tog, P3, C4B as
1st row of dress front, P3, yon, K2
tog, K2.
2nd and every alt row Sl 1, K1, P2,
K3, P1, yrn, P2 tog, P1, K3, P2, K to
end.
3rd row P to last 19 sts, P2 tog, P1,
K2 tog, yrn, P3, K1, yrn, P2 tog, K1,
P3, K2 tog, yfwd, K2.
5th row P to last 19 sts, P2 tog, P1,
yon, K2 tog, P3, K1, yrn, P2 tog, K1,
P3, yon, K2 tog, K2.
7th row P3, *yrn, P2 tog, P6, rep

from * to last 25 sts, yrn, P2 tog, P4,
P2 tog, P1, K2 tog, yrn, P3, K1, yrn,
P2 tog, K1, P3, K2 tog, yfwd, K2.
9th row As 5th.
11th row As 3rd.
12th row As 2nd.
These 12 rows form eyelet and cable
panel patts.
Keeping patts correct, cont dec at
inside edge of cable panel as before
until 52 sts rem. Work one row.

Shape armhole

Next row (Rs) Cast off 5 sts, P27 sts,
P2 tog, patt to end.
Work one row.
Cont dec at front edge as before on
every alt row, *at the same time* dec
one st at armhole edge on next
5 rows, then one st on foll alt row.
36 sts.
Cont dec at front edge only until
19 sts rem. Work one row.

Shape shoulder

Cast off at beg of next and every alt
row 6 sts twice and 7 sts once.

Right front

With 2¾mm/No 12 needles cast on
66 sts. Work 2 rows g st, noting that
1st row is Ws.
Next row (buttonhole row) K12 sts,
cast off 2 sts, K to last 5 sts, cast off
2 sts, K to end.
Next row K to end, casting on 2 sts
above those cast off in previous row.
Next row K to end.
Change to 3mm/No 11 needles.
Next row (inc row) Sl 1, K1, K2 tog,
yrn, P1, M1, P1, K1, yrn, P2 tog,
K1, P1, M1, P1, K2 tog, yrn, (P13,
M1) 3 times, P13. 71 sts.
Next row K to last 16 sts, P2, K3, P1,
yrn, P2 tog, P1, K3, P2, K2.
Commence eyelet and cable panel
patts, *at the same time* dec for front
edge at inside of cable panel.

1st row Sl 1, K1, yfwd, K2 tog, P3,
C4B, P3, yon, K2 tog, P1, P2 tog tbl
for front edge, P4, *yrn, P2 tog, P6,
rep from * to end.
2nd and every alt row K to last
16 sts, P2, K3, P1, yrn, P2 tog, P1,
K3, P2, K2.
Cont in patt as now set and
complete to match left front,
reversing all shapings.

Back

With 2¾mm/No 12 needles cast on
78 sts. Work 5 rows g st. Change to
3mm/No 11 needles.
Next row (inc row) P6, M1, (P11,
M1) 6 times, P6. 85 sts.
Next row K to end.
Commence eyelet hole patt.
1st row P2, *yrn, P2 tog, P6, rep
from * to last 3 sts, yrn, P2 tog, P1.
Work 5 rows reversed st st.
7th row *P6, yrn, P2 tog, rep from *
to last 5 sts, P5.
Work 5 rows reversed st st.
These 12 rows form the patt. Cont
in patt until work measures same as
left front to underarm, ending with
a Ws row.

Shape armholes

Cast off 5 sts at beg of next 2 rows.
Dec one st at each end of next
5 rows. Work one row. Dec one st
at each end of next row. 63 sts.
Cont without shaping until work
measures same as fronts to
shoulder, ending with a Ws row.

Shape shoulders

Cast off 6 sts at beg of next 4 rows.
Cont shaping shoulders and work
back neck border.
Next row Cast off 5 sts, K6, (K2 tog,
K6) twice, K2 tog, K5, P5.
Next row Cast off 5 sts, K26 sts.
Next row K26 sts. Cast off.

Armhole borders

Join shoulder seams. With Rs of
work facing and 2¾mm/No 12
needles, pick up and K72 sts round
armhole. Work 2 rows g st. Cast off
loosely.

To make up

Press all pieces lightly under a dry
cloth with a cool iron.
Join side and armhole border
seams. Sew on buttons.

*Right: The border of this cardigan is
knitted in one with the main fabric.*

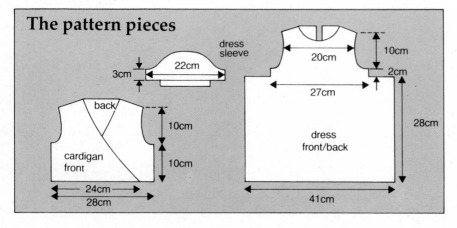

The pattern pieces

dress sleeve

3cm 22cm

back

10cm

cardigan front

10cm

24cm
28cm

dress front/back

20cm 10cm

27cm 2cm

28cm

41cm

Dungarees

These dungarees are suitable for a boy or girl and are shaped to allow plenty of room for a nappy. The leg ends are open so as not to restrict the baby's feet.

You will need

5×20g balls of Wendy Peter Pan Darling 3 ply (55% Bri-nylon, 45% Courtelle acrylic)
One pair 2¾mm/No 12 needles
One pair 3mm/No 11 needles
One cable needle
Four buttons
1m/1yd narrow ribbon

Tension

34 sts and 44 rows to 10cm/4in over lace cable patt worked on 3mm/No 11 needles
30 sts and 44 rows to 10cm/4in over eyelet hole patt worked on 3mm/No 11 needles

Back and front (both alike)

Pattern for panel worked over 14 sts.
1st row (Rs) K2 tog, yrn, P3, K1, yrn, P2 tog, K1, P3, K2 tog, yrn.
2nd and every alt row P2, K3, P1, yrn, P2 tog, P1, K3, P2.
3rd row Yon, K2 tog, P3, sl next 2 sts on to cable needles and hold at back of work, K2 from left-hand needle, then K2 from cable needle – **called C4B**, P3, yon, K2 tog.
5th row As 1st.
7th row Yon, K2 tog, P3, K1, yrn, P2 tog, K1, P3, yon, K2 tog.
9th row As 1st.
11th row As 7th.
12th row As 2nd.
These 12 rows form the panel patt.
With 3mm/No 11 needles cast on 15 sts for gusset and leave on a holder.

First leg

**With 2¾mm/No 12 needles cast on 26 sts. Work 7 rows g st, noting that 1st row is Ws.
Next row (inc row) (K1, M1, K2, M1) 8 times, K2. 42 sts.
Change to 3mm/No 11 needles.**
Next row K14, P2, K3, P1, yrn, P2, K3, P2, K15. 43 sts.
Commence patt.
1st row (Rs) P15 sts, patt 14 sts as 1st row of panel, P14 sts.
2nd and every alt row K14 sts, patt 14 sts as 2nd row of panel, K15 sts.
3rd row P3, yrn, P2 tog, P6, yrn, P2 tog, P2, patt 14 sts as 3rd row of panel, P3, yrn, P2 tog, P6, yrn, P2 tog, P1.
5th row P15 sts, patt 14 sts as 5th row of panel, P14 sts.
7th row P15 sts, patt 14 sts as 7th row of panel, P14 sts.
9th row P7, yrn, P2 tog, P6, patt 14 sts as 9th row of panel, P7, yrn, P2 tog, P5.
11th row P15 sts, patt 14 sts as 11th row of panel, P14 sts.
12th row As 2nd.
These 12 rows form panel and eyelet hole patts.
Cont in patt until leg measures 22cm/8¾in from beg, ending with a 4th patt row. Break off yarn. Leave sts on holder.

Second leg

Work as first leg from ** to **.
Next row K15, P2, K3, P1, yrn, P2, K3, P2, K14. 43 sts.
Commence patt.
1st row (Rs) P14 sts, patt 14 sts as 1st row of panel, P15 sts.
2nd and every alt row K15 sts, patt 14 sts as 2nd row of panel, K14 sts.
Cont in patt as now set noting that 9th row will read as foll:
9th row P6, yrn, P2 tog, P6, patt 14 sts as 9th row of panel, P7, yrn, P2 tog, P6.
Complete to match first leg. Do not break off yarn.

Join legs and work gusset

Next row (Rs) Patt 43 sts from second leg, P15 gusset sts, patt 43 sts from first leg. 101 sts.
Next row Patt 43 sts, K15 sts, patt 43 sts.

Shape gusset

Next row Patt 42 sts, P2 tog tbl, P13, P2 tog, patt 42 sts.
Next row Patt to end.
Next row Patt 42 sts, P2 tog tbl, P11, P2 tog, patt 42 sts.
Next row Patt to end.
Cont dec 2 sts in this way on next and every alt row until 89 sts rem.
Next row Patt 42 sts, P2 tog tbl, P1, P2 tog, patt 42 sts. 87 sts.
Cont in patt without shaping until work measures 20cm/7¾in from beg

of gusset, ending with a 6th patt row. Change to 2¾mm/No 12 needles.
Next row (Rs) (K3, K2 tog) twice, K27 sts, K2 tog, K9, K2 tog, K27 sts, (K2 tog, K3) twice. 81 sts.
Work 5 rows g st.
Next row (ribbon slotting row) K1, *yfwd, yrn, K2 tog, rep from * to end.
Next row K to end, dropping 1 extra loop.
Work 4 rows g st. Change to 3mm/No 11 needles. Commence patt.
1st row (Rs) P12 sts, patt 14 sts as 1st row of panel, P29 sts, patt 14 sts as 1st row of panel, P12 sts.
2nd and every alt row K12 sts, patt 14 sts as 2nd row of panel, K29 sts, patt 14 sts as 2nd row of panel, K12 sts.
Cont in patt as now set, noting that 9th row will read as foll:
9th row P5, yrn, P2 tog, P5, patt 14 sts as 9th row of panel, P2, (yrn, P2 tog, P6) 3 times, yrn, P2 tog, P1, patt 14 sts as 9th row of panel, P6, yrn, P2 tog, P4.
Cont until work measures 9cm/3½in from ribbon slotting at waist, ending with a Ws row.

Shape armholes

Keeping patt correct throughout cast off 5 sts at beg of next 2 rows. Dec one st at each end of next 7 rows. Work one row. Dec one st at each end of next row. 55 sts.
Cont without shaping until armholes measure 4cm/1½in from beg, ending with a Ws row.

Shape neck

Next row Patt 22 sts, P2 tog, turn and leave rem sts on holder.
Complete this side first. Dec one st at neck edge on next 5 rows, then on every foll alt row 6 times more. 12 sts.
Cont without shaping until armhole measures 10cm/4in from beg, ending with a Rs row.

Shape shoulder

Next row Patt 6 sts, turn.
Next row Patt to end.
Next row Patt across all sts.
Break yarn. Leave sts on a safety pin.
With Rs of work facing, sl first 7 sts on to a safety pin for centre neck,

rejoin yarn to rem sts, P2 tog, patt to end.
Complete to match first side, reversing all shapings.

Armhole borders

Join side seams. With Rs of work facing and 2¾mm/No 12 needles, pick up and K68 sts round armhole. Work 2 rows g st. Cast off.

Neck borders

With Rs of front facing and 2¾mm/No 12 needles, pick up and K19 sts down left side of neck, K7 sts from safety pin and pick up and K19 sts up right side of neck. 45 sts. Work 2 rows g st. Cast off. Work back neck in same way.

Back shoulder borders

With Rs of work facing and 2¾mm/No 12 needles, pick up and K1 st from border, K12 sts from safety pin and pick up and K1 st from border. 14 sts. Work 4 rows g st. Cast off.

Front shoulder borders

Work as given for back shoulder borders making buttonholes on 2nd row as foll:
Next row (buttonhole row) K2, yfwd, K2 tog, K7, yfwd, K2 tog, K1.

To make up

Press pieces lightly under a dry cloth with a cool iron.
Join inside leg and gusset seams.
Sew on buttons to shoulders.
Thread ribbon through eyelet holes.

Right: Easy to get in and out of, the dungarees button on the shoulders.

The pattern pieces

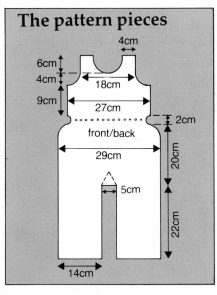

Raglan cardigan

The skirt of the cardigan is worked in lace cable pattern and the bodice and sleeves in eyelet pattern.

You will need

4×20g balls of Wendy Peter Pan Darling 3 ply
One pair 2¾mm/No 12 needles
One pair 3mm/No 11 needles
One cable needle
Four buttons

Tension

34 sts and 44 rows to 10cm/4in over lace cable patt worked on 3mm/No 11 needles
30 sts and 44 rows to 10cm/4in over eyelet hole patt worked on 3mm/No 11 needles

Back

With 2¾mm/No 12 needles cast on 94 sts. **Beg with a P row work 6 rows reversed st st.
Next row (picot hem) P2, *yrn, P2 tog, rep from * to end.
Work 2 rows reversed st st.**
Change to 3mm/No 11 needles.
Next row (inc row) K2, P2, *K3,.P1, yrn, P2, K3, P2, rep from * to last 2 sts, K2. 102 sts.
Cont in lace cable patt as given for dress front (see Knitwear Collection 43), rep these 12 rows until work measures 14cm/5½in from hemline, ending with an 11th row.
Next row (dec row) K2, (P2, K3, (P2 tog) twice, K3) 4 times, P2 tog, (K3, (P2 tog) twice, K3, P2) 4 times, K2. 85 sts.

Shape raglans

Cont in reversed st st.
Cast off 3 sts at beg of next 2 rows.
Commence eyelet hole patt.
1st row P2 tog, P5, *yrn, P2 tog, P6, rep from * to last 8 sts, yrn, P2 tog, P4, P2 tog.
2nd and every alt row K to end.
3rd and 5th rows P2 tog, P to last 2 sts, P2 tog.
7th row P2 tog, *P6, yrn, P2 tog, rep from * to last 7 sts, P5, P2 tog.
9th and 11th rows As 3rd and 5th.
12th row K to end.
These 12 rows form the patt.
Keeping patt correct cont dec one st at each end of next and every alt row until 35 sts rem. Dec one st at each end of next 3 rows. Leave rem 29 sts on holder.

Left front

With 2¾mm/No 12 needles cast on 45 sts.
Work as given for back from ** to ** noting that picot row will beg with P1.
Change to 3mm needles.***
Next row (inc row) (K2, P1, yrn, P2, K3, P2, K1) 4 times, K1. 49 sts.
Commence patt.
1st row (Rs) P2, yon, K2 tog, *P3, C4B, P3, yon, K2 tog, rep from * to last 9 sts, P3, C4B, P2.
2nd row *K2, P1, yrn, P2 tog, P1, K3, P2, K1, rep from * to last st, K1.
Cont in patt as now set until front measures same as back to dec row before raglan shaping, ending with an 11th row.
Next row (dec row) (K2, (P2 tog) twice, K3, P2, K1) 4 times, K1. 41 sts.

Shape raglan

Next row Cast off 3 sts, P to end.
Next row K to end.
Commence eyelet hole patt.
1st row P2 tog, P5, yrn, P2 tog, *P6, yrn, P2 tog, rep from * to last 5 sts, P5.
2nd and every alt row K to end.
3rd and 5th rows P2 tog, P to end.
7th row P2 tog, P6, *yrn, P2 tog, P6, rep from * to last 3 sts, yrn, P2 tog, P1.
9th and 11th rows As 3rd and 5th.
12th row K to end.
These 12 rows form the patt.
Keeping patt correct cont dec one st at beg of next and every alt row until 23 sts rem.
Next row (Ws) K to end.

Shape neck

Next row P2 tog, patt 16 sts, P2 tog, turn and leave rem 3 sts on safety pin.
Cont in patt, dec one st at neck edge on next 4 rows, *at the same time* dec one st at raglan on alt rows as before. 12 sts. Work one row.
Cont dec at raglan as before, dec one st at neck edge on next and foll 2 alt rows. 6 sts. Work one row.
Dec one st at raglan only on next 4 rows. P2 tog and fasten off.

Right front

Work as given for left front to ***.
Next row (inc row) (K2, P2, K3, P1, yrn, P2, K1) 4 times, K1. 49 sts.
Commence patt.
1st row (Rs) *P2, C4B, P3, yon, K2 tog, P1, rep from * 3 times, P1.
2nd row *K2, P2, K3, P1, yrn, P2 tog, P1, K1, rep from * 3 times, K1.
Cont in patt as now set until front measures same as back to dec row

---

Mitts

There are panels of eyelet and lace cable pattern on both front and back.

You will need

1×20g ball of Darling 3 ply
One pair 2¾mm/No 12 needles
One pair 3mm/No 11 needles
One cable needle
70cm/¾yd narrow ribbon

Cuff

With 2¾mm/No 12 needles cast on 30 sts.
Work 7 rows g st (1st row is Ws).
Next row (ribbon slotting row) K2, *yfwd, yrn, K2 tog, rep from * to end.
Next row K to end, dropping 1 extra

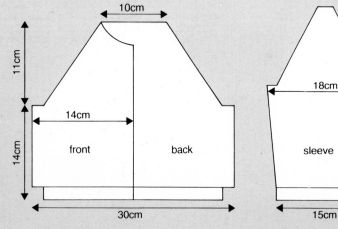

The pattern pieces

front — 14cm — back
11cm
14cm
10cm
30cm

sleeve
18cm
15cm
15cm
2cm

before raglan shaping, ending with an 11th row.
Next row (dec row) (K2, P2, K3, (P2 tog) twice, K1) 4 times, K1. 41 sts.
Next row P to end.

Shape raglan
Next row Cast off 3 sts, K to end. Commence eyelet hole patt.
1st row P6, *yrn, P2 tog, P6, rep from * to last 8 sts, yrn, P2 tog, P4, P2 tog.
2nd and every alt row K to end.
3rd and 5th rows P to last 2 sts, P2 tog.
7th row P2, *yrn, P2 tog, P6, rep from * to last 9 sts, yrn, P2 tog, P5, P2 tog.
Cont in patt as now set and complete to match left front, reversing all shapings.

Sleeves
With 2¾mm/No 12 needles cast on 44 sts. Work 2cm/1in g st (1st row is Ws and ends with a Rs row).
Next row (inc row) K8, M1, (K14, M1) twice, K8. 47 sts.
Change to 3mm/No 11 needles. Commence eyelet hole patt.
1st row (Rs) P to end.
2nd row K to end.
3rd row P3, *yrn, P2 tog, P6, rep from * to last 4 sts, yrn, P2 tog, P2. Work 5 rows reversed st st.
9th row P7, *yrn, P2 tog, P6, rep from * to end.
Work 3 rows reversed st st.
These 12 rows form the patt. Cont in patt, inc one st at each end of next and every foll 14th row until there are 55 sts. Work a few rows

without shaping until sleeve measures 17cm/6½in from beg, ending with a 4th or 10th patt row.

Shape raglan
Keeping patt correct, cast off 3 sts at beg of next 2 rows.
Next row P2 tog, patt to last 2 sts, P2 tog.
Work 3 rows.
Cont in patt, dec one st at each end of next and every alt row until 5 sts rem. Work one row. Leave on safety pin.

Neck border
Join raglan seams. With Rs of work facing and 2¾mm/No 12 needles, P3 sts from right front safety pin, pick up and K12 sts up right front neck, P5 sts from right sleeve, 29 from back neck and 5 from left sleeve, pick up and K12 sts down left front neck and P3 sts from left front safety pin. 69 sts.
Work 4 rows reversed st st.
Next row (picot row) K1, *yfwd, K2 tog, rep from * to end.
Work 5 rows reversed st st. Cast off loosely. Fold in half to Ws and sl st in place.

Above: The neckband has a picot edge.

Button border
With 2¾mm/No 12 needles cast on 5 sts. Work in g st noting that 1st row is Ws until border fits up left front edge to top of neck border, sewing in place as you go and ending with a Rs row. Cast off.

Buttonhole border
Work as given for button border making 4 buttonholes as foll, first to come level with dec row at beg of raglan and last to come level with beg of neck border and 2 more, evenly spaced between.
Next row (buttonhole row) K2, cast off 2 sts, K1.
Next row K to end casting on 2 sts above those cast off in previous row.

To make up
Press pieces lightly under a dry cloth with a cool iron.
Fold hem at lower edge to Ws and sl st in place. Join seams. Sew on buttons.

loop.
Next row K to end.
Change to 3mm/No 11 needles.
Next row (inc row) K1, M1, K1, P2, K1, M1, K1, P1, yrn, P2, K1, M1, K1, P2, K1, M1, K2, M1, K1, P2, K1, M1, K1, P1, yrn, P2, K1, M1, K1, P2, K1, M1, K1. 40 sts.
Commence lace cable patt.
1st row (Rs) P3, *K2 tog, yrn, P3, K1, yrn, P2 tog, K1, P3, K2 tog, yrn*, P6, rep from * to *, P3.
2nd and every alt row K3, *P2, K3, P1, yrn, P2 tog, P1, K3, P2*, K6, rep from * to *, K3.
3rd row P3, *yon, K2 tog, P3, C4B as 3rd row of bonnet, P3, yon, K2 tog*, P6, rep from * to *, P3.
5th row As 1st.

7th row P3, *yon, K2 tog, P3, K1, yrn, P2 tog, K1, P3, yon, K2 tog*, P6, rep from * to *, P3.
9th row As 1st.
11th row As 7th.
13th row As 1st.
14th row As 2nd.
The 3rd to 14th rows form the patt. Rep 3rd to 8th rows once more.

Shape top
Keep patt correct throughout.
9th row P1, P2 tog, patt 14 sts, P2 tog tbl, P2, P2 tog, patt 14 sts, P2 tog tbl, P1.
10th and every alt row Patt to end.
11th row P1, P2 tog, patt 12 sts, P2 tog tbl, P2, P2 tog, patt 12 sts, P2 tog tbl, P1.

13th row P1, P2 tog, patt 10 sts, P2 tog tbl, P2, P2 tog, patt 10 sts, P2 tog tbl, P1.
15th row P1, P2 tog, patt 8 sts, P2 tog tbl, P2, P2 tog, patt 8 sts, P2 tog tbl, P1.
16th row As 10th. 24 sts.
Sl 12 sts on to each of 2 needles, points both to the centre, fold work in half with Rs tog, cast off by knitting tog one st from each needle. Fasten off.

To make up
Press each piece lightly under a dry cloth with a cool iron.
Join side seams. Cut ribbon in half and thread one piece through each mitt at wrist.

Shawl

The central square in garter stitch is surrounded by a deep flounce in lace cable pattern with mitred corners and is worked entirely in one piece.

Size of shawl 137cm/54in square

You will need

11×20g balls of Wendy Peter Pan Darling 2 ply
One pair 5½mm/No 5 needles
One 5½mm/No 5 circular needle, 80cm/30in long
One cable needle
5m/5yd narrow ribbon

Tension

18 sts and 30 rows to 10cm/4in over g st worked on 5½mm/No 5 needles

Note

The border is worked on a circular needle, inc at each corner. Make 3 marker loops in one colour and one in another. The first 3 will be slipped on to the needle at appropriate point to mark the corners of the shawl and the 4th to mark end of rounds. These markers are slipped from one needle point to the other without being worked into.

Shawl centre

With 5½mm/No 5 needles cast on 3 sts.
1st row Yfwd and over needle to inc 1 – **called L1**, K to end. 4 sts.
Rep this row until there are 119 sts, thus making 58 loops along each side.
Next row K to end.

Next row L1, K3 tog, K to end.
Rep this row until 3 sts rem, thus making 58 loops along each side.
Next row K3 tog, do not break off yarn, turn and leave ready to beg border.

Shawl border

Sl rem st from centre on to 5½mm/No 5 circular needle, *pick up and K58 sts from first side of centre working into *back* of loops, pick up and K1 st at centre row, sl first marker on to needle, pick up and K58 sts along 2nd side as before, pick up and K1 st at centre of cast-on sts, sl 2nd marker on to

Below: Although traditionally made in white, the baby's shawl can be trimmed in contrasting ribbon if preferred.

needle, rep from * along 3rd and 4th sides, placing different coloured marker on end of needle to mark end of round. 236 sts.

1st round *Yrn, P1, M1, P1, K1, yrn, P2 tog, K1, P1, M1, P1, (K2 tog, yrn, P1, M1, P1, K1, yrn, P2 tog, K1, P1, M1, P1) 5 times, yon, K1 at corner, rep from * 3 times more. 292 sts.

2nd round *P4, K1, K2 tog, yfwd, K1, P3, (K2, P3, K1, K2 tog, yfwd, K1, P3) 5 times, P1, K1 at corner, rep from * 3 times more.

3rd round *Yrn, P4, sl next 2 sts on to cable needle and hold at back of work, K2 from left-hand needle, then K2 from cable needle – **called C4B**, P3, (yon, K2 tog, P3, C4B, P3) 5 times, P1, yon, K1 at corner, rep from * 3 times more. 300 sts.

4th round *P5, K1, K2 tog, yfwd, K1, P3, (K2, P3, K1, K2 tog, yfwd, K1, P3) 5 times, P2, K1 at corner, rep from * 3 times more.

5th round *Yrn, P5, K1, yrn, P2 tog, K1, P3, (K2 tog, yrn, P3, K1, yrn, P2 tog, K1, P3) 5 times, P2, yon, K1 at corner, rep from * 3 times more. 308 sts.

6th round *P1, K2, P3, K1, K2 tog, yfwd, K1, P3, (K2, P3, K1, K2 tog, yfwd, K1, P3) 5 times, K2, P1, K1 at corner, rep from * 3 times more.

7th round *Yrn, P1, yon, K2 tog, P3, K1, yrn, P2 tog, K1, P3, (yon, K2 tog, P3, K1, yrn, P2 tog, K1, P3) 5 times, yon, K2 tog, P1, yon, K1 at corner, rep from * 3 times more. 316 sts.

8th round *P2, K2, P3, K1, K2 tog, yfwd, K1, P3, (K2, P3, K1, K2 tog, yfwd, K1, P3) 5 times, K2, P2, K1 at corner, rep from * 3 times more.

9th round *Yrn, P2, (K2 tog, yrn, P3, K1, yrn, P2 tog, K1, P3) 6 times, K2 tog, yrn, P2, yon, K1 at corner, rep from * 3 times more. 324 sts.

10th round *P3, (K2, P3, K1, K2 tog, yfwd, K1, P3) 6 times, K2, P3, K1 at corner, rep from * 3 times more.

11th round *Yrn, P3, (yon, K2 tog, P3, K1, yrn, P2 tog, K1, P3) 6 times, yon, K2 tog, P3, yon, K1 at corner, rep from * 3 times more. 332 sts.

12th round *P4, (K2, P3, K1, K2 tog, yfwd, K1, P3) 6 times, K2, P4, K1 at corner, rep from * 3 times more.

13th round *Yrn, P4, (K2 tog, yrn, P3, K1, yrn, P2 tog, K1, P3) 6 times, K2 tog, yrn, P4, yon, K1 at corner, rep from * 3 times more. 340 sts.

14th round *P5, (K2, P3, K1, K2 tog, yfwd, K1, P3) 6 times, K2, P5, K1 at

corner, rep from * 3 times more.

15th round *Yrn, P5, (yon, K2 tog, P3, C4B, P3) 6 times, yon, K2 tog, P5, yon, K1 at corner, rep from * 3 times more. 348 sts.

16th round *P6, (K2, P3, K1, K2 tog, yfwd, K1, P3) 6 times, K2, P6, K1 at corner, rep from * 3 times more.

17th round *Yrn, P6, (K2 tog, yrn, P3, K1, yrn, P2 tog, K1, P3) 6 times, K2 tog, yrn, P6, yon, K1 at corner, rep from * 3 times more. 356 sts.

18th round *P1, K2 tog, yfwd, K1, P3, (K2, P3, K1, K2 tog, yfwd, K1, P3) 6 times, K2, P3, K1, K2 tog, yrn, P1, K1 at corner, rep from * 3 times more.

19th round *Yrn, P1, yrn, P2 tog, K1, P3, (yon, K2 tog, P3, K1, yrn, P2 tog, K1, P3) 6 times, yon, K2 tog, P3, K1, yrn, P2 tog, P1, yon, K1 at corner, rep from * 3 times more. 364 sts.

20th round *P1, (K1, K2 tog, yfwd, K1, P3, K2, P3) 7 times, K1, K2 tog, yfwd, K1, P1, K1 at corner, rep from * 3 times more.

21st round *Yrn, P1, (K1, yrn, P2 tog, K1, P3, K2 tog, yrn, P3) 7 times, K1, yrn, P2 tog, K1, P1, yon, K1 at corner, rep from * 3 times more. 372 sts.

22nd round *P2, (K1, K2 tog, yfwd, K1, P3, K2, P3) 7 times, K1, K2 tog, yfwd, K1, P2, K1 at corner, rep from * 3 times more.

23rd round *Yrn, P2, (K1, yrn, P2 tog, K1, P3, yon, K2 tog, P3) 7 times, K1, yrn, P2 tog, K1, P2, yon, K1 at corner, rep from * 3 times more. 380 sts.

24th round *P3, (K1, K2 tog, yfwd, K1, P3, K2, P3) 7 times, K1, K2 tog, yfwd, K1, P3, K1 at corner, rep from * 3 times more.

25th round *Yrn, P3, (K1, yrn, P2 tog, K1, P3, K2 tog, yrn, P3) 7 times, K1, yrn, P2 tog, K1, P3, yon, K1 at corner, rep from * 3 times more. 388 sts.

26th round *P4, (K1, K2 tog, yfwd, K1, P3, K2, P3) 7 times, K1, K2 tog, yfwd, K1, P4, K1 at corner, rep from * 3 times more.

The 3rd to 26th rounds inclusive form the patt.

Rep 3rd to 26th round 3 times more, noting that patt will be worked 7, 8 then 9 times along each side on first rep; 9, 10 then 11 for 2nd rep and 11, 12 then 13 times for 3rd rep.

99th round As 3rd, rep patt 13 times along each side. 684 sts.

100th round As 4th, rep patt 13 times along each side.

Lace edging

Sl last corner st on to left-hand point of circular needle, with separate 5½mm/No 5 needle cast on 12 sts loosely.

Cont in rows and dec at inside edge as foll:

Next row K11 of the cast-on sts, K tog last cast-on st and first border st. Turn.

Commence lace patt.

1st row (Ws) K3, yfwd, K2 tog, K1, (K2 tog, yfwd) twice, K2.

2nd row K2, yfwd, K2 tog, yfwd, K5, yfwd, (K2 tog) twice, turn.

3rd row K3, yfwd, K2 tog, K4, yfwd, K2 tog, yfwd, K2.

4th row K2, yfwd, K2 tog, yfwd, K7, yfwd, (K2 tog) twice, turn.

5th row K3, yfwd, (K2 tog) twice, yfwd, yrn, K2 tog, M1, (K2 tog, yfwd) twice, K2.

6th row K2, yfwd, K2 tog, yfwd, K5, P1, K3, yfwd, (K2 tog) twice, turn.

7th row K3, yfwd, K2 tog, K2, K2 tog, yfwd, yrn, K2 tog, (K2 tog, yfwd) twice, K2.

8th row K1, (K2 tog, yfwd) twice, K2 tog, K1, P1, K5, yfwd, (K2 tog) twice, turn.

9th row K3, yfwd, (K2 tog) twice, yfwd, yrn, K2 tog, (K2 tog, yfwd) twice, K2 tog, K1.

10th row K1, (K2 tog, yfwd) twice, K2 tog, K1, P1, K3, yfwd, (K2 tog) twice, turn.

11th row K3, yfwd, K2 tog, K2, (K2 tog, yfwd) twice, K2 tog, K1.

12th row K1, (K2 tog, yfwd) twice, K2 tog, K3, yfwd, (K2 tog) twice, turn.

These 12 rows form the patt.

Rep these 12 rows, thus using 6 sts from border in every patt rep, until 28 reps have been worked. On 29th patt rep dec at inside edge on 4th, 8th and 12th rows *only* and work 2nd, 6th and 10th rows as 'K2 tog, K1, turn'.

Rep from ** to ** until all sts from shawl border have been worked off and 12 sts from lace edging rem. Cast off.

To make up

Join cast-off sts to cast-on sts. Do not press. Thread ribbon through eyelet holes at inner edge of border and tie in a bow at one corner.

Socks

There is a panel of eyelet lace worked up the side of the leg of the socks

You will need

1×20g ball of Wendy Peter Pan
  Darling 3 ply (55% Bri-nylon,
  45% Courtelle acrylic)
One pair 3mm/No 11 needles

Left sock

With 3mm/No 11 needles cast on 38 sts.
Work 2cm/¾in K1, P1 rib.
Commence patt.
1st row (Rs) P6, (yon, K2 tog, P3) twice, P9, (yon, K2 tog, P3) twice, P3.
2nd and every alt row K6, (P2, K3) twice, K9, (P2, K3) twice, K3.
3rd row P6, (K2 tog, yrn, P3) twice, P9, (K2 tog, yrn, P3) twice, P3.

4th row As 2nd.
These 4 rows form the patt. Cont in patt dec one st at each end of 13th and foll 8th row. 34 sts. Work 11 rows without shaping.

Top of foot

Cont in reversed st st.
Next row (Rs) P9, P2 tog, place a coloured marker at this point, P2 tog, P8, P2 tog, turn.
Next row K10, turn.
Beg with a P row work 22 more rows on these 10 sts. Break off yarn. Leave sts on holder.
With Rs of work facing, rejoin yarn at marker, pick up and K20 sts along side of foot, P10 sts from holder, pick up and K20 sts along other side of foot, P2 tog, P9. 70 sts.
Next row (dec row) K29, K2 tog, (K3, K2 tog) twice, K29. 67 sts.
Work 6 rows reversed st st.

Above: The raglan cardigan, mitts and socks worn with a dress or romper suit, make an ideal set for an outing on cooler days.

Shape sole

1st row P2, P2 tog, P26, P2 tog tbl, P3, P2 tog, P26, P2 tog tbl, P2.
2nd and every alt row K to end.
3rd row P2, P2 tog, P24, P2 tog tbl, P3, P2 tog, P24, P2 tog tbl, P2.
5th row P2, P2 tog, P22, P2 tog tbl, P3, P2 tog, P22, P2 tog tbl, P2.
7th row P2, P2 tog, P20, P2 tog tbl, P3, P2 tog, P20, P2 tog tbl, P2.
Cast off rem 51 sts.
Right sock is knitted in exactly the same way.

To make up

Press pieces lightly under a dry cloth with a cool iron.
Join seam at back and undersole.

Bonnet

A dainty bonnet for a baby girl knitted in lace cable pattern with a neat garter stitch neck edging.

You will need

1×20g ball of Wendy Peter Pan
  Darling 3 ply
One pair 2¾mm/No 12 needles
One pair 3mm/No 11 needles
One cable needle
1m/1yd wide ribbon

Tension

As raglan cardigan

Brim

With 2¾mm/No 12 needles cast on 116 sts. Beg with a P row work 6 rows reversed st st.
Next row (picot hem) P2, *yrn, P2 tog, rep from * to end.
Work 2 rows reversed st st. Change to 3mm/No 11 needles.
Next row (inc row) K2, P2, *K3, P1, yrn, P2, K3, P2, rep from * to last 2 sts, K2. 126 sts.
Commence lace cable patt.
1st row (Rs) P2, yon, K2 tog, *P3, sl next 2 sts on to cable needle and hold at back of work, K2 from left-hand needle, then K2 from cable needle – **called C4B**, P3, yon, K2 tog, rep from * to last 2 sts, P2.
2nd and every alt row K2, P2, *K3, P1, yrn, P2 tog, P1, K3, P2, rep from * to last 2 sts, K2.
3rd row P2, K2 tog, yrn, *P3, K1, yrn, P2 tog, K1, P3, K2 tog, yrn, rep from * to last 2 sts, P2.
5th row P2, yon, K2 tog, *P3, K1, yrn, P2 tog, K1, P3, yon, K2 tog, rep from * to last 2 sts, P2.
7th row As 3rd.
9th row As 5th.
11th row As 3rd.
12th row As 2nd.

Left: If preferred, add ribbons of a different colour to the bonnet.

These 12 rows form the pattern. Cont in patt until work measures 12cm/5in from hemline, ending with a 2nd row.

Divide for crown

Next row Cast off 42 sts, patt to end.
Next row Cast off 42 sts, (one st left on right-hand needle), (P1, P2 tog, P1, K3, P2 tog, K3) 3 times, P1, P2 tog, P1, K1. 35 sts.
Commence eyelet hole patt.
1st row (Rs) P to end.
2nd row K to end.
3rd row P1, *yrn, P2 tog, P6, rep from * to last 2 sts, yrn, P2 tog.
Work 3 rows reversed st st.

Shape back of crown

7th row P2 tog, P to last 2 sts, P2 tog.
8th row K to end.
9th row P4, *yrn, P2 tog, P6, rep from * to last 5 sts, yrn, P2 tog, P3.
Work 3 rows reversed st st.
These 12 rows form patt. Cont in patt dec one st at each end of every foll 8th row from last dec until 23 sts rem.
Work a few rows without shaping until edge of back fits along cast-off sts, ending with a Ws row. Break off yarn. Leave sts on holder.

Neck edge

Join back crown seams.
With Rs of work facing and 2¾mm/No 12 needles, pick up and K20 sts along side of neck, work across sts on holder as foll: K3, (K2 tog, K3) 3 times, K2 tog, K3, pick up and K20 sts along other side of neck. 59 sts. Work 6 rows g st. Cast off.

To make up

Press lightly under a dry cloth with a cool iron.
Fold hem to Ws and sl st in place.
Cut ribbon in half. Make a rosette at each end and attach to bonnet.

Helmet

This close-fitting helmet is knitted in plain garter stitch for a boy.

You will need

1× 20g ball of Wendy Peter Pan
  Darling 3 ply
One pair 3mm/No 11 needles
One button

Right flap

**With 3mm/No 11 needles cast on 3 sts for right flap. K one row.
Next row (Rs) (K1, M1) twice, K1. 5 sts.
K 3 rows g st.
Next row (buttonhole row) K1, M1, cast off 2 sts, K1, M1, K1.
Next row K to end, casting on 2 sts above those cast off in previous row. K 2 rows g st.
Next row K to end, casting on 2 sts above those cast off in previous row. K 2 rows g st.
Rep last 4 rows 3 times more. 15 sts.
Cont in this way, inc one st at each end of next and every alt row until there are 39 sts. Work one row after last inc.
Inc one st at beg *only* of next and foll alt row. 41 sts.**
Leave sts on holder. Do not break off yarn.

Work left flap as given for right flap from ** to **, reversing shaping and omitting buttonhole and casting on 21 sts for centre at end of last row. Break off yarn.

Join flaps

Next row (Ws) Beg with right flap, cast on 3 sts, K3 then K41 from right flap, K21 sts cast on for centre, K41 from left flap, turn and cast on 3 sts. 109 sts.
Work 5cm/2in g st, ending with a Ws row.

Shape top

Next row K2, (K2 tog, K13) 7 times, K2. 102 sts.
Work 3 rows g st.
Next row K2, (K2 tog, K12) 7 times, K2. 95 sts.
Work 3 rows g st.
Next row K2, (K2 tog, K11) 7 times, K2. 88 sts.
Work one row g st.
Cont dec in this way on next and every alt row until 39 sts rem. Work one row.
Next row K2, (K3 tog, K2) 7 times, K2. 25 sts.
Work one row g st.
Next row K2, (K3 tog) 7 times, K2. 11 sts.
Break off yarn, thread through rem sts, draw up and fasten off.

To make up

Do not press.
Join back seam. Sew on button.

Bootee boutique

A new baby can never have too many pairs of bootees. These three delightful styles will keep tiny feet snug and warm and make a welcome gift. They are knitted in Patons Fairytale, which has the advantage of being machine-washable in warm water and the added bonus of needing no ironing. There is a range of soft pastel shades to choose from.

If you are a beginner, tackle the blue and white bootees first, as these are the easiest. They can form the first part of a matinée set – a whole wardrobe of babies' clothes will be featured in later chapters.

Size

For foot length of about 9cm/3½in

You will need

Button-strap bootees 1×20g ball of Patons Fairytale 4 ply with Lambswool (25% wool, 50% acrylic, 25% nylon) in main shade A
1×20g ball of contrast colour B
One pair 3¼mm/No 10 needles
2 small buttons
Lacy bootees 1×20g ball of Patons Fairytale 4 ply (50% acrylic, 50% nylon)
One pair 2¾mm/No 12 needles
One pair 3mm/No 11 needles
50cm/20in ribbon, 1cm/½in wide
Ruffled bootees 1×20g ball of Patons Fairytale 3 ply (50% acrylic, 50% nylon)
One pair 2¼mm/No 13 needles
One pair 2¾mm/No 12 needles
50cm/20in ribbon, 1cm/½in wide

Tension

Button-strap bootees 28 sts and 36 rows to 10cm/4in over st st worked on 3¼mm/No 10 needles; **lacy bootees** 30 sts and 38 rows to 10cm/4in over st st worked on 3mm/No 11 needles; **ruffled bootees** 34 sts and 42 rows to 10cm/4in over st st worked on 2¾mm/No 12 needles

Button-strap bootees

With 3¼mm/No 10 needles and A cast on 37 sts.
1st and every alt row (Ws) K to end.
2nd row (K1, M1, K17, M1) twice, K1.
4th row (K1, M1, K19, M1) twice, K1.
6th row (K1, M1, K21, M1) twice, K1.
8th row (K1, M1, K23, M1) twice, K1.
K15 rows g st.

Shape instep

Note: Instep in a knitting pattern refers to the top of the bootee.
1st row K31, sl 1, K1, psso, turn.
2nd row K10, sl 1, K1, psso, turn.
Rep 2nd row 4 times more. Break off A. Join in B. Cont using B only.
7th row As 2nd.
8th row (P1, K1) 5 times, P2 tog, turn.
9th row (K1, P1) 5 times, sl 1, K1, psso, turn.
Rep 8th and 9th rows 3 times more, then 8th row once more.
Next row (K1, P1) 5 times, K to end. 37 sts.
Next row (K1, P1) 12 times, P to end.
Next row P1, *K1, P1, rep from * to end.

Next row K1, *P1, K1, rep from * to end.
Rep last 2 rows 10 times more. Cast off in rib.

Straps
With 3¼mm/No 10 needles and A cast on 15 sts.
1st row (Ws) K to end.
2nd row (buttonhole row) K12, yfwd, K2 tog, K1.
Cast off.

Lacy bootees

With 3mm/No 11 needles cast on 41 sts.
1st row (K1, inc 1 in next st, K17, inc 1 in next st) twice, K1.
2nd and every alt row K to end.
3rd row (K1, inc 1, K19, inc 1) twice, K1.
5th row (K1, inc 1, K21, inc 1) twice, K1.
Cont inc in this way, working 2 extra sts between inc twice on every alt row until there are 61 sts.
Next row K2 tog, K to last 2 sts, K2 tog. 59 sts.
K 6 rows g st.

Shape instep
1st row K34, K2 tog tbl, turn.
2nd and every alt row Sl 1, P9, P2 tog, turn.
3rd row Sl 1, K1, yfwd, sl 1, K1, psso, K3, K2 tog, yfwd, K1, K2 tog tbl, turn.
5th row Sl 1, K2, yfwd, sl 1, K1, psso, K1, K2 tog, yfwd, K2, K2 tog tbl, turn.
7th row Sl 1, K3, yfwd, sl 1, K2 tog, psso, yfwd, K3, K2 tog tbl, turn.
8th row As 2nd.
Rep 3rd to 8th rows twice more. 39 sts.
Next row Sl 1, K9, K2 tog tbl, turn.
Next row Sl 1, P9, P2 tog, turn.
Next row Sl 1, K to end. 37 sts.
Next row P to end.
Next row (eyelet hole row) K1, *yfwd, K2 tog, rep from * to end.
Next row P to end.
Change to 2¾mm/No 12 needles.
Next row K2, *P1, K1, rep from * to last st, K1.
Next row K1, *P1, K1, rep from * to end.
Rep last 2 rows twice more. K 13 rows g st. Cast off loosely.

Ruffled bootees

With 2¾mm/No 12 needles cast on

47 sts
1st row (Rs) (K1, inc 1 in next st, K20, inc 1 in next st) twice, K1.
2nd and every alt row K to end.
3rd row (K1, inc 1, K22, inc 1) twice, K1.
5th row (K1, inc 1, K24, inc 1) twice, K1.
7th row (K1, inc 1, K26, inc 1) twice, K1.
9th row (K1, inc 1, K28, inc 1) twice, K1. 67 sts.
10th row K2 tog, K to last 2 sts, K2 tog. 65 sts.
K 10 rows g st.

Shape instep
1st row K37, K2 tog tbl, turn.
2nd row Sl 1 purlwise, P9, P2 tog, turn.
3rd row Sl 1 knitwise, K9, K2 tog tbl, turn.
Rep 2nd and 3rd rows until 45 sts rem, ending with a 2nd row.
Next row Sl 1, K to end.
Next row P to end.
Next row (eyelet hole row) K1, *yfwd, K2 tog, rep from * to end.
Next row P to end.
Next row K1, *P1, K1, rep from * to end.
Next row P1, *K1, P1, rep from * to end.
Rep last 2 rows once more. Beg with a P row work 8 rows in reversed st st. Cast off loosely.

Ruffles
With 2¼mm/No 13 needles cast on 7 sts.
1st row (Rs) K to end.
2nd row P5, turn.
3rd row K5.
4th row P5, K2.
5th row K2, P5.
6th row K5, turn.
7th row P5.
8th row K to end.

Above: Knit a pair of dainty bootees for the latest member of the family.

These 8 rows form the patt. Rep last 8 rows 19 times more. Cast off.

To make up
Do not press any of the bootees.
Button-strap bootees Join sole and back seam, reversing seam half-way up ribbing. Fold rib in half to right side. Sew one edge of strap in place on inside edge of each bootee to fasten across instep. Sew on button to correspond with buttonhole.
Lacy bootees Join foot and back seam. Cut ribbon in half, or make 2 twisted cords 25cm/9¾in long, and thread through row of eyelet holes to tie at centre of instep.
Ruffled bootees Join foot and back, reversing seam for 1cm/½in for cuff. With right side facing, begin at back seam and sew ruffles to top of each bootee. Join ruffle seam and fold over to right side. Complete as given for lacy bootees.

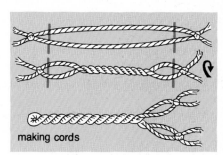

making cords

To make fine twisted cords
Ask a friend to help you. Cut 2 lengths of yarn 50cm/20in long for each bootee cord. Knot both ends. together. Put a pencil in front of each knot between the 2 strands. Each person holds a pencil and facing the other, turns the pencil in a clockwise direction.
Continue until the strands are tightly twisted. Fold cord in half by putting the pencils together and allowing cord to twist. Remove pencils and knot each end of cord.

Romper suit with crossover top

Knit this snug romper suit and you'll make a baby warm and comfortable. The trousers have knitted-in feet to keep baby toes cosy and there's an extra allowance knitted in to the back to accommodate bulky nappies.
The smart little jacket has cross-over fronts to give added warmth over the chest and one-button fastening at each side to make it easy to put on and remove.

Sizes

To fit 46-51cm/18-20in chest
Top length 29cm/11½in
Sleeve length, 19cm/7½in
Trousers inside leg, 29cm/11½in

You will need

4×50g balls of Phildar Anouchka (80% acrylic, 16% mohair, 4% wool) in main colour A
1 ball each of same in contrast colours B and C
One pair 2¼mm/No 13 needles
One pair 3mm/No 11 needles
One 2¼mm/No 13 circular needle, 80cm/32in long
One 3mm/No 11 circular needle, 80cm/32in long
Two buttons for top
Waist length of elastic for trousers

Tension

30 sts and 35 rows to 10cm/4in over patt worked on 3mm/No 11 needles

Top

With 2¼mm/No 13 circular needle and A cast on 223 sts and work in one piece to armhole.
1st row (Rs) P1, *K1, P1, rep from * to end.
2nd row K1, *P1, K1 rep from * to end.
Rep these 2 rows for 4cm/1½in, ending with a 2nd row. Change to 3mm/No 11 circular needle.
Commence patt. Beg with a K row cont in st st, working first 2 rows patt from chart.

Shape front edges

Next row Keeping patt correct, K1, K2 tog, K to last 3 sts, sl 1, K1, psso, K1.
Next row P to end.
Keeping patt correct throughout, rep the last 2 rows 20 times more. 181 sts.

Divide for armholes

Next row K1, K2 tog, K40, cast off 12 for underarm, K71 for back, cast off 12 for underarm, K40, sl 1, K1, psso, K1.
Cont on last 42 sts for left front, dec at front edge as before on every alt row until 21 sts rem. Cont without shaping until armhole measures 12cm/4¾in from beg, ending with a P row. Cast off.
With Ws facing rejoin yarn to 71 sts for back. Cont in patt until armholes measure 12cm/4¾in from beg, ending with a P row.
Next row Cast off 21 sts, K29, cast off rem 21 sts.

Leave 29 sts on holder for back neck. With Ws of work facing join yarn to rem 42 sts for right front and work to match left front, reversing all shapings.

Sleeves

With 2¼mm/No 13 needles and A cast on 51 sts.
Work 2cm/¾in K1, P1 rib as given for main part, ending on a 1st row.
Next row (inc row) Rib 4, (inc in next st, P1) 22 times, rib 3. 73 sts.
Change to 3mm/No 11 needles. Beg with a K row cont in st st, working in patt from chart until sleeve measures 19cm/7½in from beg. Place marker at each end of last row. Work a further 2cm/¾in in patt, ending with a P row. Cast off.

Front border

Join shoulder seams.
With Rs facing, 2¼mm/No 13 circular needle and A, pick up and K93 sts up right front edge, K across back neck sts inc 4 sts evenly, then pick up and K93 sts down left front edge. 219 sts.
Work 2cm/¾in K1, P1 rib as given for main part. Cast off loosely in rib.

Trousers right back leg

With 3mm/No 11 needles and A cast on 43 sts.
Beg with a K row cont in st st, working in patt from chart for 26cm/10¼in, or length required, ending with a K row. Break off yarn and leave sts on holder.

Left back leg

Work as for right back leg, reversing patt and ending with same patt row, do not break off yarn.

Join legs

With Ws facing P the 43 sts of left back leg, cast on 7 sts for crutch, then P the 43 sts of right back leg. 93 sts. Cont in patt until work measures 47cm/18½in from beg, ending with a P row.**

Shape back

Next row Keeping pattern correct, K86 sts, turn.
Next row P79 sts, turn.
Next row K72 sts, turn.
Cont shaping back by working 7 sts

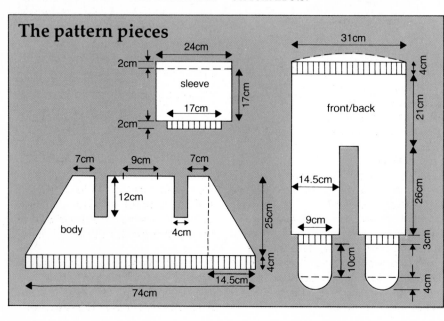

The pattern pieces

sleeve
24cm
2cm
2cm
17cm
17cm

body
7cm
9cm
7cm
12cm
4cm
74cm
14.5cm

front/back
31cm
4cm
21cm
26cm
14.5cm
9cm
25cm
4cm
3cm
10cm
4cm

100

Chart for pattern rows

rep 40 rows

end st — rep 10 sts — end sts

□ = A   ○ = B   × = C

Above: Knitted in washable yarn this baby's romper suit is pretty and practical.

less on every row for 7 more rows, ending with P23 sts, turn.
Next row K to end.
Next row P across all sts.
***Change to 2¼mm/No 13 needles. Break off B and C. Cont in A and work 4cm/1½in K1, P1 rib as given for top. Cast off in rib.

Front

Work as for back to **, noting that right back leg will be worked for left front leg and left back leg will be worked for right front leg.
Complete as given for back from *** to end.

Feet

With Rs of right back leg facing, 2¼mm/No 13 needles and A, pick up and K43 sts along cast on edge.
Next row (dec row) P1, *P2 tog, P1, rep from * to end. 29 sts.
Beg with a 2nd row work 3cm/1¼in K1, P1 rib as given for top, ending with a Ws row.
Change to 3mm/No 11 needles. Beg with a K row cont in st st working in patt from chart for 10cm/4in, *taking care to centralize patt*, ending with a Ws row.
Keeping patt correct, dec one st at each end of next and foll 2 alt rows, ending with a P row. Cast off at the beg of every row 2 sts 4 times, 3 sts twice and 9 sts once.

Work in the same way across bottom of left back leg and both front legs.

To make up

Press all pieces lightly with a cool iron.
Top Join sleeve seams. Set in sleeves. Make a button loop at the centre of each welt along the front edge. Sew one button to outside and one to inside to fasten, lapping right front over left for a girl and left front over right for a boy. Press seams.
Trousers Join side, foot and inside leg seams. Fold ribbing in half at waist and sl st down. Thread elastic through and secure. Press seams.

101

A striped baby suit

Once babies begin to be lively, they need clothes to fit their lifestyle. This brightly coloured suit is practical as well as eye-catching. Try a cheerful lollipop pink or a cool sea-green and blue combination, the two alternatives photographed above.

Remember that babies do differ in size even at an early age. Any baby hates to have his head pushed through a small opening, so if you think your baby is above average size attach poppers to the shoulder seams instead of sewing the seams together. This gives a much bigger opening for the head to pass through.

Sizes

To fit 46 [51:56]cm/18 [20:22]in chest
Jersey length to shoulder,
25 [28:31]cm/9¾ [11:12¼]in
Sleeve seam, 15 [18:21]cm/6 [7:8]in
Pants length, 37 [41:45]cm/
14½ [16¼:17¾]in Inside leg,
19 [21:23]cm/7½ [8¼:9]in
Scarf, 61 [64:67]cm/24 [25¼:26½]in
The figures in [] refer to 51/20 and 56cm/22in sizes respectively

You will need

8 [8:9] x 20g balls of Lister-Lee Nursery Time Double Knitting in main colour, A

2 [2:2] x 20g balls each of contrast colours, B and C

One pair 3¼mm/No 10 needles
One pair 4mm/No 8 needles
Waist length of 2cm/¾in wide elastic

Tension

22 sts and 28 rows to 10cm/4in over st st worked on 4mm/No 8 needles

Jersey back

With 3¼mm/No 10 needles and A cast on 54 [58:66] sts.
1st row K2, *P2, K2, rep from * to end.
2nd row P2, *K2, P2, rep from * to end.

Rep these 2 rows for 4cm/1½in ending with a 2nd row and inc one st at each end of last row on 2nd size only. 54 [60:66] sts.
Change to 4mm/No 8 needles
Beg with a K row cont in st st, working 8 rows each in C, B and A until 7 [8:9] stripes in all have been completed. Inc one st at each end of last row on 2nd size only. 54 [62:66] sts.
With A only work 4 rows rib as given for welt at bottom edge of jersey.

Shape shoulders
Keeping rib patt correct, cast off 6 [7:8] sts at beg of next 4 rows. Cast off rem 30 [34:34] sts.

Jersey front
Work as given for back.

Jersey sleeves
With 3¼mm/No 10 needles and A cast on 30 [34:38] sts. Work 5cm/2in rib as for back, ending with 1st row.
Next row Rib 4 [6:8] sts, (inc in next st, rib 2) 8 times, rib 2 [4:6] sts. 38 [42:46] sts.
Change to 4mm/No 8 needles.
Beg with a K row cont in st st and beg with B work 8 rows each in B, A, C until 3 [4:5] stripes in all have been completed, ending with same colour as body.
With A only work 4 rows rib as given for back. Cast off very loosely in rib.

Pants front
With 3¼mm/No 10 needles and using A only throughout, cast on 54 [58:66] sts.

Work in rib as given for jersey back for 10 rows, inc one st at each end of last row on 2nd size only. 54 [60:66] sts. **

***Change to 4mm/No 8 needles.
Beg with a K row cont in st st for 15 [17:19]cm/6 [6¾:7½]in ending with a P row. Mark each end of last row with coloured threads.

Divide for legs
Next row K24 [27:30] sts, cast off 6, K to end.
Complete this side first.
Dec one st at end of next and every foll alt row for inside leg until 22 [22:26] sts rem. Cont without shaping until work measures 15 [17:19]cm/6 [6¾:7½]in from marker, ending with a P row.
Change to 3¼mm/No 10 needles.
Work in rib as given for jersey back for 12 rows. Cast off in rib.
With Ws of work facing, rejoin yarn to rem sts and complete to match first side, reversing shaping.

Pants back
Work as given for front to **.
Change to 4mm/No 8 needles.

Shape back
1st row K35 [38:41] sts, turn.
2nd row P16 sts, turn.
3rd row K24 sts, turn.
4th row P32 sts, turn.
5th row K40 sts, turn.
6th row P48 sts, turn.
7th row K to end.
8th row P to end.
Complete as given for pants front from *** to end.

Scarf
With 4mm/No 8 needles and A cast on 34 sts. Work rib as given for jersey back for 61 [64:67]cm/24 [25:26]in. Cast off.

To make up all three garments
Press all st st only under a dry cloth with a warm iron.
Jersey Join shoulders. Sew in sleeves with centre of sleeve top to shoulder seam. Join side and sleeve seams.
Pants Join side, inside leg and crutch seams. Sew elastic inside waist edge with herringbone casing st.
Scarf Gather up ends of scarf with running sts. Make two pompoms (see below) about 7cm/2¾in diameter in contrast colours and sew one to each end of scarf.

To make pompoms
Cut a card circle, diameter 7cm/2¾in. Cut a circle out of the centre. The size of the hole affects the density of the pompom – the larger the hole, the denser the pompom.
Cut out another identical card and place both pieces of card together. Wind the yarn into a tight ball small enough to pass through the hole. Push the yarn through the centre hole and over the outer edge until the hole is almost filled. Thread the yarn on to a needle and continue until the hole is tightly packed.
Cut yarn along edge of outer circle. Ease the two circles slightly apart. Slip a piece of yarn between them to tie the cut lengths firmly in the middle.
Take off the circles and ruffle the cut ends of yarn into shape.

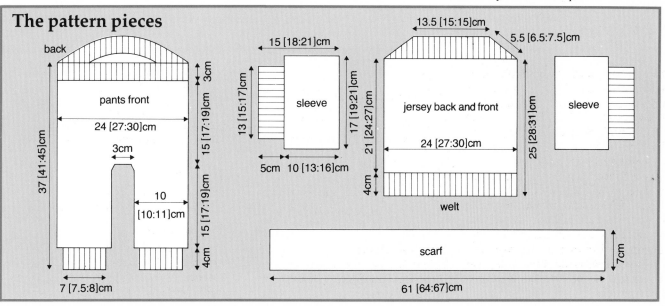

The pattern pieces

back

pants front

24 [27:30]cm

3cm

37 [41:45]cm

15 [17:19]cm

15 [17:19]cm

4cm

3cm

10 [10:11]cm

7 [7.5:8]cm

15 [18:21]cm

sleeve

13 [15:17]cm

5cm   10 [13:16]cm

17 [19:21]cm

13.5 [15:15]cm

5.5 [6.5:7.5]cm

jersey back and front

24 [27:30]cm

21 [24:27]cm

4cm

welt

25 [28:31]cm

sleeve

scarf

61 [64:67]cm

7cm

Stars and stripes jersey

This smart jersey in four sizes is scattered with stars both back and front. It is made in double knitting yarn and so is quick to knit.

If you are unsure about working the pattern into the knitting, then knit the back and front in just one colour and embroider the stars on afterwards.

It has an unusual, neat little button-up neck opening. The neckband is knitted all in one piece and then sewn on afterwards to avoid the need for picking up stitches.

Sizes

To fit 56 [61:66:71]cm/22 [24:26:28]in chest
Length to shoulder, 36 [39:44:48]cm/ 14¼ [15¼:17¼:19]in
Sleeve seam, 22 [27:32:37]cm/8¾ [10¾:12½:14½]in
The figures in [] refer to the 61/24, 66/26 and 71cm/28in sizes respectively

You will need

3 [3:4:4]×50g balls of Pingouin Confort (50% wool, 40% acrylic, 10% mohair) or Shetland DK (100% wool) in main colour A
1 ball of same in each of contrast colours B and C
One pair 3¼mm/No 10 needles
One pair 4mm/No 8 needles
Three buttons

Tension

22 sts and 28 rows to 10cm/4in over st st worked on 4mm/No 8 needles

Note

The stars can be knitted in or applied with Swiss darning. If knitting in always use a separate ball of yarn for each motif. If working in Swiss darning, work front and back all in shade A and embroider motifs from chart.

Back

With 3¼mm/No 10 needles and B cast on 65 [71:77:83] sts.
1st row (Rs) K1, *P1, K1, rep from * to end.
2nd row P1, *K1, P1, rep from * to end.
Rep these 2 rows for 5cm/2in ending with a Ws row.
Change to 4mm/No 8 needles and A. Beg with a K row work 2 rows st st. Cont in st st working in patt from chart, and complete first 37 rows.

3rd and 4th sizes only

Work 3 rows st st.
Rep first 17 rows from chart once more.

All sizes

Beg with a P and 38th row of chart cont in st st until 51st row has been completed.
Cont in st st in A until back measures 24 [27:30:33]cm/9½ [10¾:11¾:13]in from beg, ending with a Ws row.

Shape armholes

Cast off 4 sts at beg of next 2 rows. Dec one st at each end of next and every row until 47 [51:55:59] sts rem. Cont in st st without shaping until armholes measure 12 [12:14:15]cm/ 4¾ [4¾:5½:6]in from beg, ending with a Ws row.

Shape shoulders

Cast off at the beg of next and every row 6 [6:7:7] sts twice, 6 [7:7:8] sts twice, and 23 [25:27:29] sts once.

Front

Work as given for back to armhole shaping, ending with a Ws row.

Shape armholes and divide for neck opening

Cast off 4 sts at beg of next 2 rows.
Next row Sl 1, K1, psso, K24 [27:30:33], cast off 5 sts, K to last 2 sts, K2 tog.
Complete right shoulder first. Dec one st at armhole edge on next 4 [5:6:7] rows. 21 [23:25:27] sts.
Cont without shaping until work measures 8cm/3¼in from 5 cast-off

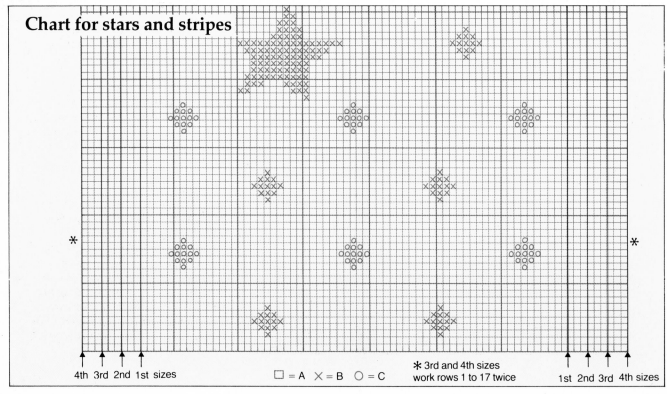

Chart for stars and stripes

4th 3rd 2nd 1st sizes   □ = A ✕ = B ○ = C   ✱ 3rd and 4th sizes work rows 1 to 17 twice   1st 2nd 3rd 4th sizes

sts ending at centre front.

Shape neck
Dec one st at neck edge on next and every row until 12 [13:14:15] sts rem. Cont in st st without shaping until work measures same as back to shoulder, ending with a Rs row.

Shape shoulder
Cast off 6 [6:7:7] sts at beg of next row. Work one row. Cast off rem sts. Rejoin yarn to rem sts for left shoulder.
Complete to match first side reversing all shapings.

Sleeves
With 3¼mm/No 10 needles and B cast on 35 [37:39:41] sts. Work 5cm/2in K1, P1 rib as given for back. Change to 4mm/No 8 needles. Beg with a K row work in st st and striped patt of 6 rows A, 2 rows C, 2 rows A, 2 rows C, 6 rows A, 4 rows B, *at the same time* inc one st each end of the 3rd and every foll 6th row until there are 49 [53:57:61] sts. Cont in stripes without shaping until work measures 22 [27:32:37]cm/8¾ [10¾:12½:14½] in from beg, or required length to underarm, ending with a Ws row.

Shape top
Keeping striped patt correct, cast off 4 sts at beg of next 2 rows. Dec one st at each end of next and every foll alt row until 27 sts rem. Dec one st at each end of every row until 15 sts rem. Cast off.

Neckband
With 3¼mm/No 10 needles and B cast on 7 sts.

Above: All set to join the big parade in this smart little jersey in red, white and blue. To make it for a boy, sew on the neckband so that the button-holes are on the left front.

Work 4 rows in K1, P1 rib as given on back, ending with a Ws row.
Next row (buttonhole row) Rib 3, yfwd, K2 tog, rib to end.
Cont in rib, working 2 more buttonholes on Rs rows 2.5cm/1in apart, then cont in rib until band is long enough to reach all round neck edge and back down left front to centre cast off sts. Cast off.

To make up
Join shoulder seams. Join side and sleeve seams. Set in sleeves. Sew neckband neatly into position, placing buttonholes on right front for a girl or left front for a boy. Overlap right over left or left over right and stitch to cast off 5 sts of centre front. Sew on buttons to correspond with buttonholes. Press lightly under a damp cloth with a warm iron.

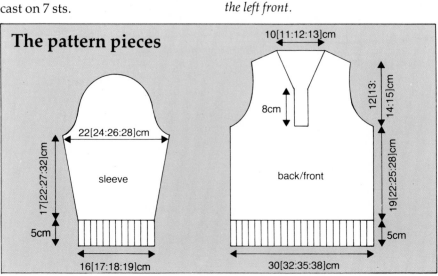

The pattern pieces

sleeve

22[24:26:28]cm

17[22:27:32]cm

5cm

16[17:18:19]cm

10[11:12:13]cm

8cm

back/front

12[13:14:15]cm

19[22:25:28]cm

5cm

30[32:35:38]cm

Left: To knit the dress and frill in one colour, add quantities together for the total amount of yarn needed.

Next row (dec row) K19 [21], (K2 tog) 42 times, K20 [21]. 81 [84] sts.
Next row P.
Next row (eyelet hole row) K1 [2], *yfwd, K2 tog, rep from * to last 0 [2] sts, K0 [2].
Next row P.**
Cont in st st without shaping until work measures 25 [28]cm/9¾ [11]in from beg, ending with a P row.

Shape armholes

Cast off at the beg of next and every row 3 sts twice and 2 sts twice. 71 [74] sts.
Dec one st at each end of next and every foll alt row until 61 [64] sts rem, ending with a P row.
Cont without shaping until armholes measure 7.5cm/3in from beg ending with a P row.

Shape neck

Next row K24 [25], sl next 13 [14] sts on to holder, K to end.
Cont on last set of sts for right shoulder.
Next row P to end.
Cast off 3 sts at beg of next row for neck edge and 2 sts at beg of foll alt row.
P one row.
Dec one st at neck edge on next and every foll alt row until 17 [18] sts rem.
Cont in st st, without shaping, until armhole measures 10.5cm/4in from beg, ending at armhole edge.

Shape shoulder

Cast off at beg of next and every foll alt row 4 sts twice, 3 [4] sts once, and 3 sts twice.
With Ws facing, rejoin yarn to sts for left shoulder and complete to match right shoulder, reversing all shapings.

Back

Work as for front from ** to **. Cont in st st without shaping until work measures 24 [27]cm/9½ [10¾]in from beg, ending with a P row.

Divide for back opening

Next row K38 [39], cast off next 5 [6] sts, K to end.
Cont on last set of sts for left shoulder. Work in st st without

Toddler's dress with frills

This attractive dress has contrasting frills and ribbons – just right for a baby's first party.

Sizes

To fit 46-51 [56]cm/18-20 [22]in chest (9 [12] months)
Length to shoulder, 41.5 [44.5]cm/16¼ [17½]in
Sleeve seam, 4cm/1½in
The figures in [] refer to the 56cm/22in size only

You will need

5 [6]×20g balls Emu Treasure 3 ply (60% Courtelle, 40% Bri-nylon) in main colour A
4 [5]×20g balls Emu Treasure Baby Spot Print (60% Courtelle, 40% Bri-nylon) in contrast colour B
One pair 2¾mm/No 12 needles
One pair 3mm/No 11 needles
Five small buttons
2m/2yd narrow ribbon

Tension

30 sts and 46 rows to 10cm/4in over st st worked on 3mm/No 11 needles

Front

**With 3mm/No 11 needles and A cast on 123 [126] sts. Beg with a K row work 23 [26]cm/9 [10¼]in st st, ending with a P row.

shaping until back measures 25 [28]cm/9¾ [11]in from beg, ending at armhole edge.

Shape armhole
Cast off 3 sts at beg of next and 2 sts at beg of foll alt row.
Dec one st at armhole edge on next and every foll alt row until 28 [29] sts rem.
Cont in st st without shaping until armhole measures 10.5cm/4in, ending at neck edge.

Shape shoulder and back neck
Next row S1 first 3 sts on to a holder, K to end.
Next row Cast off 4 sts at beg of next row, P to end.
Next row S1 first 2 sts on to the holder with the first 3, K to end.
Cast off at beg of next and every foll alt row 4 sts once, 3[4] sts once, and 3 sts twice, *at the same time* dec one st at neck edge on next and every foll alt row 6 times in all.
With Ws facing, rejoin yarn to sts for right shoulder and complete to match left shoulder, reversing all shapings.

Sleeves
With 3mm/No 11 needles and A cast on 57 [60] sts. K one row.
Next row (eyelet hole row) P1 [2], *yrn, P2 tog, rep from * to end.
Beg with a K row, work in st st inc one st at each end of next and every foll 4th row 3 times in all. 63 [66] sts.
Cont in st st without shaping until sleeve measures 4cm/1½in from beg, ending with a P row.

Shape top
Cast off at beg of next and every row 3 sts twice and 2 sts twice.
Dec one st at each end of next row, work one row without shaping.
Dec one st at each end of next row, work 2 rows without shaping.
Rep the last 5 rows 5 [6] more times. 29 [28] sts.
Dec 1 [0] st at each end of next row. P one row.
Cast off at beg of next and every row 2 sts twice, 3 sts twice and 17 [18] sts once.

Neckband
Join shoulder seams.
With Rs of work facing, 2¾mm/No 12 needles and A, pick up and K11 sts from back neck edge, 15 sts

down left front neck, 13 [14] sts from holder at front neck, 15 [16] sts up right front neck, then 11 sts from right back neck. 65 [67] sts.
Beg with a P row, work 3 rows st st.
Next row (eyelet hole row) K1, *yrn, K2 tog, rep from * to end.
Beg with a P row, work 3 rows st st.
Cast off.

Back button band
With Rs of work facing, 2¾mm/No 12 needles and A, pick up and K39 sts down left back opening.
Complete as for neckband.

Back buttonhole band
Work as for button band working buttonholes as foll:
1st row P.
2nd row K4, *cast off 3 sts, K4 sts, rep from * 4 times altogether, cast off 3 sts, K4.
3rd row P to end, casting on 3 sts above those cast off in previous row.
4th row Work eyelet hole row as given for neckband.
5th to 7th rows As 1st to 3rd.
Cast off.

Sleeve frill
With 2¾mm/No 12 needles and B, cast on 143 [153] sts. Commence rib patt.
1st row P3, *K7, P3, rep from * to end.
2nd row K3, *P7, K3, rep from * to end.
3rd to 8th rows As 1st and 2nd.
9th row (dec row) P3, *sl 1, K1, psso, K3, K2 tog, P3, rep from * to end. 115 [123] sts.
10th row K3, *P5, K3, rep from * to end.

11th row (dec row) P3, *sl 1, K1, psso, K1, K2 tog, P3, rep from * to end. 87 [93] sts.
12th row K3, *P3, K3, rep from * to end.
13th row (dec row) P3, *sl 1, K2 tog, psso, P3, rep from * to end. 59 [63] sts.
14th row K3, *P1, K3, rep from * to end.
Cast off in rib.
Work 2nd sleeve frill in same way.

Yoke frill
With 2¾mm/No 12 needles and B, cast on 283 sts. Work in rib patt as given for sleeve frill. 115 sts. Cast off.
Work another piece in the same way.

Hem frill
With 2¾mm/No 12 needles and B, cast on 303 [313] sts. Commence rib patt.
1st row As 1st row sleeve frill.
2nd row As 2nd row sleeve frill.
3rd to 22nd rows As 1st and 2nd.
23rd to 28th rows As 9th to 14th row of sleeve frill. 123 [127] sts. Cast off.
Work another piece in same way.

To make up
Fold back and neck edgings in half to Ws and slip st into place. Sew round edges of buttonholes to neaten. Sew on buttons. Sew in sleeves gathering at shoulder to fit. Join side and sleeve seams. Join seams on frills and sew to lower edges of sleeves, skirt and on to yoke. Thread ribbon through eyelet holes to tie at front and on top of sleeves. Catch down short ends of back edgings.

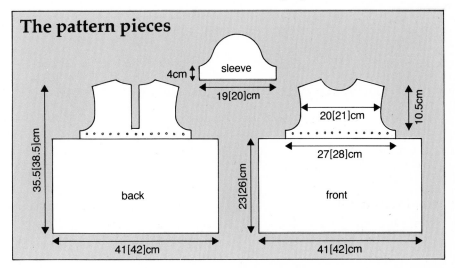

The pattern pieces

4cm — sleeve — 19[20]cm

35.5[38.5]cm — back — 41[42]cm

10.5cm — 20[21]cm — 23[26]cm — front — 27[28]cm — 41[42]cm

Party-time slipover

This neat little slipover is just right to wear over a blouse or dress for a party – or any other special occasion. The sides are prettily edged with a lacy frill and joined only at the waist, so there is plenty of room for the fullest sleeve.

There is also a small, back neck opening that fastens with two buttons to ensure a snug fit combined with ease of putting on and removing.

It is so quick and easy to knit – and so pretty – that you may well find yourself cajoled into making several in different colours.

Sizes

To fit 61 [66:71]cm/24 [26:28]in chest
Length to shoulder
33.5 [37:40.5]cm/13[14½:16]in
The figures in [] refer to the 66/26 and the 71cm/28in sizes respectively

You will need

6 [7:8]×20g balls Robin Bunny Brushed Double Knitting (60% Courtelle, 40% Bri-nylon)
One pair 3mm/No 11 needles
One pair 3¾mm/No 9 needles
Two small buttons

Tension

24 sts and 28 rows to 10cm/4in over patt worked on 3¾mm/No 9 needles

Back

With 3mm/No 11 needles cast on 79 [85:91] sts.
1st row (Rs) K1, *P1, K1, rep from * to end.
2nd row P1, *K1, P1, rep from * to end.

Rep these 2 rows 7 times more, then the first row again.
Next row Cast off 8 sts, rib 63 [69:75], cast off rem 8 sts.
Change to 3¾mm/No 9 needles.
With Rs facing rejoin yarn to right-hand side of work.
Commence patt.
1st row K1 [4:1], *yfwd, K2 tog, K10, rep from * until 2 [5:2] sts rem, yfwd, K2 tog, [yfwd, K2 tog, K3: yfwd, K2 tog].
2nd and every alt row P1 [4:1], *yrn, P2 tog, P10, rep from * until 2 [5:2] sts rem, yrn, P2 tog, [yrn, P2 tog, P3: yrn, P2 tog].
3rd row K1 [4:1], *yfwd, K2 tog, K2, K2 tog, yfwd, K1, yfwd, sl 1, K1, psso, K3, rep from * until 2 [5:2] sts rem, yfwd, K2 tog, [yfwd, K2 tog, K3: yfwd, K2 tog].
5th row K1 [4:1], *yfwd, K2 tog, K1, K2 tog, yfwd, K3, yfwd, sl 1, K1, psso, K2, rep from * until 2 [5:2] sts rem, yfwd, K2 tog, [yfwd, K2 tog, K3: yfwd, K2 tog].
7th row As 5th.
9th row K1 [4:1], *yfwd, K2 tog, K3, yfwd, sl 1, K2 tog, psso, yfwd, K4, rep from * until 2 [5:2] sts rem, yfwd, K2 tog, [yfwd, K2 tog, K3: yfwd, K2 tog].
10th row As 2nd.
These 10 rows form the pattern.
Cont in patt for a further 59 [69:79] rows.**

Divide for back neck opening

Next row (Ws) Patt across 29 [32:35] sts and leave these sts on a holder for left shoulder, patt across the next 5 sts and leave these on a safety pin for border, patt to end.

Complete right shoulder on last 29 [32:35] sts.
Cont in patt for 10 rows.

Shape shoulder

Cast off at the beg of next and every alt row 6 [6:8] sts once and 6 [7:7] sts twice.
Work 1 row. Leave rem 11 [12:13] sts on holder for back neck.
With Rs facing, rejoin yarn to 29 [32:35] sts on holder.
Work 11 rows in patt.

Shape shoulder

Cast off at the beg of next and every alt row 6 [6:8] sts once and 6 [7:7] sts twice.
Leave rem 11 [12:13] sts on holder for back neck.

Front

Work as given for back to **.

Divide for neck

Next row (Ws) Patt 26 [28:30] sts and leave these sts on a holder for right shoulder, patt the next 11 [13:15] sts and leave these on holder for front neck, patt to end.

Shape neck

Complete left shoulder on last 26 [28:30] sts.
Cont in patt, dec one st at neck edge on the next 8 rows. Work 2 rows without shaping.

Shape shoulder

Cast off at the beg of next and every alt row 6 [6:8] sts once and 6 [7:7] sts twice.
With Rs facing rejoin yarn to 26 [28:30] sts on holder. Complete to match first side reversing shapings.

Right back buttonhole border

With Rs facing and 3mm/No 11 needles pick up the 5 sts for the back border left on a safety pin. Rejoin yarn and work 8 rows in g st.
Next row (buttonhole row) K1, K2 tog, yfwd, K2.
Work a further 11 rows g st. Break yarn. Place sts back on safety pin. Sew border in place to opening edge.

Left back button border

With 3mm/No 11 needles cast on 5 sts. Work 21 rows in g st. Do not break yarn. Sew border in place to opening edge.

The pattern pieces

11[12:13]cm

back

26[28.5:31]cm

28.5[31:35.5]cm

5cm

front

25[28.5:32]cm

33.5[37:40.5]cm

Neckband

Join shoulder seams.
With Rs facing and using needle with 5 sts from left back border, K across 11 [12:13] sts from left back, pick up and K12 sts down left front neck, K across 11 [13:15] sts from centre front neck, pick up and K12 sts from right front neck, K across 11 [12:13] sts of right back, K5 sts from right back border. 67 [71:75] sts.
K one row.
Next row (buttonhole row) K1, K2 tog, yfwd, K to end.

Work 3 more rows g st. Cast off loosely.

Armhole frills

With Rs facing and 3¾mm/No 9 needles beg at cast off sts at top of welt and pick up and K161 [181:201] sts along row ends to cast off sts at top of other welt.
1st row K.
2nd row K1, *yfwd, K3, sl 1, K2 tog, psso, K3, yfwd, K1, rep from * to end.
3rd row P.
4th row As 2nd.

Rep these 4 rows once more. Cast off K-wise very loosely.

To make up

Press each piece under a dry cloth with a cool iron omitting ribbing. Join ribbed welts.
Catch down cast-on edge of left back border behind right. Sew on 2 buttons. Sew row ends of armhole frills to sts cast off at top of ribbing.

Child's pelican motif jersey

This jersey, with its delightful pelican motif, can be made in three sizes and is knitted in a light supersoft yarn. The motif on the front can be omitted and the jersey worked entirely in stocking stitch, if preferred.

Sizes

To fit 51 [56:61]cm/20 [22:24]in chest
Length to back neck, 34 [39:43]cm/ 13½ [15¼:17]in
Sleeve seam, 21 [23:27]cm/ 8¼ [9:10¾]in, adjustable
The figures in [] refer to the 56/22 and 61cm/24in sizes respectively

You will need

3 [4:4]×40g balls of Patons Promise (67% acrylic, 33% nylon) in main colour A
1 ball each or oddments of same in contrast colours B, C and D
One pair of 4mm/No 8 needles
One pair of 5mm/No 6 needles

Tension

19 sts and 25 rows to 10cm/4in over st st worked on 5mm/No 6 needles

Note

When working from chart do not carry colours across Ws of work but use separate balls as required, twisting yarns at back of work when changing colours to avoid a hole. Read odd numbered K rows from right to left and even numbered P rows from left to right.

Front

**With 4mm/No 8 needles and A, cast on 48 [52:58] sts. Work 5cm/2in K1, P1 rib.
Next row (inc row) Rib 6 [6:8], M1, * rib 12 [8:14], M1, rep from * to last 6 [6:8] sts, rib to end. 52 [58:62] sts. **
Change to 5mm/No 6 needles. Beg with a K row work 4 rows st st. Cont in patt from 5th row of chart joining in and breaking off contrast colours as required, until 42nd [52nd:58th] row has been completed.

***Shape armholes
1st and 3rd sizes only
Cast off 4 sts at beg of next 2 rows. Dec one st at each end of next and foll 4th row. Work 3 rows without shaping.
2nd size only
Cast off 4 sts at beg next 2 rows. ***
All sizes
Dec one st at each end of next and every alt row until 30 [30:32] sts rem, ending with a Ws row.

Shape neck

Next row Dec one st, K9 sts, turn and leave rem sts on holder. Complete left shoulder first. Cont to dec at armhole edge as before, dec one st at neck edge on every row 4 times in all. Cont dec at armhole edge until 2 sts rem, ending with a Ws row. K2 tog. Fasten off.
With Rs of work facing sl first 8 [8:10] sts on to holder for centre front neck. Rejoin yarn to rem sts and complete to match left side, reversing shaping.

Back

Work as given for front from ** to **
Change to 5mm/No 6 needles. Beg

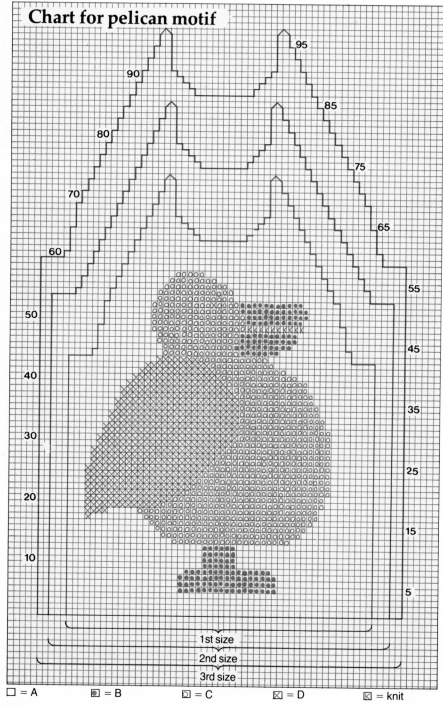

Chart for pelican motif

95 90 85 80 75 70 65 60 55 50 45 40 35 30 25 20 15 10 5

1st size
2nd size
3rd size

□ = A   ▣ = B   ◩ = C   ⊠ = D   ☒ = knit

110

with a K row cont in st st until back measures same as front to underarms, ending with a P row.

Shape armholes
Work as given for front from *** to ***.
All sizes
Dec one st at each end of next and every alt row until 20 [20:22] sts rem, ending with a P row. Leave sts on holder for centre back neck.

Sleeves
With 4mm/No 8 needles and A, cast on 26 [28:30] sts. Work 5cm/2in K1, P1, rib.
Next row (inc row) Rib 3 [4:2], M1, (rib 4 [4:5], M1) 5 times, rib to end. 32 [34:36] sts.
Change to 5mm/No 6 needles. Beg with a K row cont in st st, inc one st at each end of 11th [13th:15th] and every foll 10th [12th:15th] row until there are 38 [40:42] sts. Cont without shaping until sleeve measures 21 [23:27]cm/ 8¼ [9:10¾]in, or required length to underarm, ending with a P row.

Shape top
Cast off 4 sts at beg of next 2 rows. Dec one st at each end of next and every foll 4th row until 26 [28:26] sts rem. Work 3 rows. Dec one st at each end of next and every alt row until 6 sts rem ending with a P row. Leave sts on a holder.

Neckband
Join raglan seams leaving left back raglan open. With Rs facing, 4mm/ No 8 needles and A, K6 sts from left sleeve top, pick up and K8 sts down left side of neck, K8 [8:10] sts from centre front neck, pick up and K8 sts up right side of neck, K6 sts from right sleeve top then K20 [20:22] sts from centre back neck. 56 [56:60] sts. Work 6cm/2¼in K1, P1 rib. Cast off loosely in rib.

To make up
Do not press. Join left back raglan and neckband seam. Fold neckband in half to Ws and slip st down. Join side and sleeve seams. Using D embroider eye as chart.

Right: The simple shape of this stocking stitch jersey makes it easy to adapt if you want to include your own motif or a child's name.

Cardigan with cat pocket

Knit this enchanting cardigan for your favourite little girl. It has an unusual crocheted cat's head motif sewn on to the pocket to make it even more appealing.

Sizes

To fit 56 [61:66]cm/22 [24:26]in chest
Length to shoulder, 31 [35:39] cm/ 12¼ [13¾:15¼]in
Sleeve seam, 22 [25:28]cm/ 8¾ [9¾:11]in
The figures in [] refer to the 61/24 and the 66cm/26in sizes respectively

You will need

Cardigan 3 [3:4]×50g balls of Anny Blatt Soft'Anny Mohair Kid (80% mohair kid, 20% chlorofibres) in main colour A
1 [1:1] ball of same in contrast colour B
One pair 3mm/No 11 needles
One pair 3¾mm/No 9 needles
One 5.00mm/No 6 crochet hook
Six buttons
Two sew-on eyes or buttons for cat's face
Oddment of cotton yarn for whiskers

Tension

Cardigan 20 sts and 30 rows to 10cm/4in over patt worked on 3¾mm/No 9 needles using single yarn

Cardigan back

With 3mm/No 11 needles and one strand of A cast on 61 [67:73] sts.
1st row K1, *P1, K1, rep from * to end.
2nd row P1, *K1, P1, rep from * to end. Rep these 2 rows for 4cm/ 1½in, ending with a 2nd row and inc one st at end of last row. 62 [68:74] sts.
Change to 3¾mm/No 9 needles. Commence patt.
1st row K.
2nd row P.
3rd row K2, *P4, K2, rep from * to end.
4th row P2, *K4, P2, rep from * to end.
5th and 6th rows As 3rd and 4th.
7th and 8th rows As 1st and 2nd.
9th row P3, *K2, P4, rep from * to last 5 sts, K2, P3.
10th row K3, *P2, K4, rep from * to last 5 sts, P2, K3.
11th and 12th rows As 9th and 10th. These 12 rows form patt. Cont in patt until work measures 30 [34:38]cm/11¾ [13½:15]in from beg, ending with a Ws row.

Shape neck

Next row Patt 25 [27:29] sts, turn and leave rem sts on holder. Complete right shoulder first. Cast off at beg of next and every alt row 2 sts twice and 21 [23:25] sts once.
With Rs of work facing leave first 12 [14:16] sts on holder for back neck, join yarn to rem sts for left shoulder.
Complete to match right shoulder, reversing shaping.

Left front

Pocket lining With 3¾mm/No 9 needles and one strand of A cast on 18 sts. Beg with a K row work in st st for 36 rows. Break off yarn and leave sts on holder.
With 3mm/No 11 needles and one strand of A cast on 33 [37:39] sts and work 4cm/1½in in rib as given for back, ending with a 2nd row and inc one st at end of last row on 1st and 3rd sizes only. 34 [37:40] sts.
Change to 3¾mm/No 9 needles.

Commence patt.
1st row K to last 8 sts, rib 8.
2nd row Rib 8, P to end.
3rd row K2, *P4, K2, rep from * to last 8 [11:8] sts, P0 [3:0], rib 8.
4th row Rib 8, K0 [3:0], *P2, K4, rep from * to last 2 sts, P2.
5th and 6th rows As 3rd and 4th.
7th and 8th rows As 1st and 2nd.
9th row P3, *K2, P4, rep from * to last 13 [10:13] sts, K2, P3 [0:3], rib 8.
10th row Rib 8, K3 [0:3], P2, *K4, P2, rep from * to last 3 sts, K3.
11th and 12th rows As 9th and 10th. Rep these 12 rows once more, then first 7 rows again.**

Place pocket

Next row Rib 8, P4 [6:7], cast off 18 sts for pocket, P4 [5:7].
Next row Patt 4 [5:7], patt across sts of pocket lining, patt to last 8 sts, rib 8.
Cont in patt until work measures 25 [29:33]cm/9¾ [11½:13]in from beg, ending with a Ws row.

Shape neck

Next row Patt 26 [29:32], turn and leave rem sts on holder for neckband.
Cast off 2 sts at beg of next row, then dec one st at neck edge on every alt row until 21 [23:25] sts rem. Cont without shaping until work measures same as back to shoulder, ending with a Ws row. Cast off.
Mark the position of 6 buttons on front edge, the first to come in centre of welt, the last just below neck edge, with 4 more evenly spaced between.

Right front

Work pocket lining as for left front.
With 3mm/No 11 needles and one strand of A, cast on 33 [37:39] sts and work 2cm/¾in in rib as given for back, ending with a 2nd row.
Next row (buttonhole row) K1, P1, K1, P2 tog, yrn, rib to end.
Cont in rib until work measures 4cm/1½in from beg, ending with a 2nd row and inc one st at beg of last row on 1st and 3rd sizes only. 34 [37:40] sts.
Change to 3¾mm/No 9 needles. Commence patt.
1st row Rib 8, K to end.
2nd row P to last 8 sts, rib 8.
3rd row Rib 8, P0 [3:0], *K2, P4, rep from * to last 2 sts, K2.

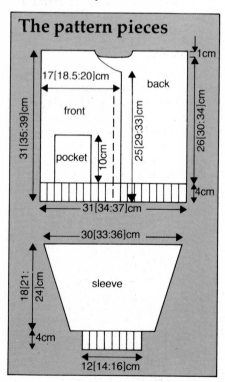

The pattern pieces

17[18.5:20]cm

back

front

1cm

31[35:39]cm

26[30:34]cm

25[29:33]cm

pocket

10cm

4cm

31[34:37]cm

30[33:36]cm

18[21:24]cm

sleeve

4cm

12[14:16]cm

Right: Knitted in soft mohair this well-shaped cardigan is light and warm. The pockets can be left plain or decorated with the crochet motif as you prefer.

4th row P2, *K4, P2, rep from * to last 8 [11:8] sts, K0 [3:0], rib 8.
5th and 6th rows As 3rd and 4th.
7th and 8th rows As 1st and 2nd.
9th row Rib 8, P3 [0:3], K2, *P4, K2, rep from * to last 3 sts, P3.
10th row K3, *P2, K4, rep from * to last 13 [10:13] sts, P2, K3 [0:3], rib 8.
11th and 12th rows As 9th and 10th.
Cont in patt as given for left front to **

Place pocket
Next row P4 [5:7], cast off 18 sts for pocket, P4 [6:7], rib 8.
Next row Rib 8, patt 4 [6:7], patt across sts of pocket lining, patt 4 [5:7].
Complete to match left front, making buttonholes as before as markers are reached and reversing all shapings.

Sleeves
With 3mm/No 11 needles and one strand of A cast on 23 [27:31] sts. Work in rib as given for back for 4cm/1½in, ending with a 1st row.
Next row (inc row) Rib 3, *inc in next st, K1, rep from * to last 2 sts, rib 2. 32 [38:44] sts.
Change to 3¾mm/No 9 needles and cont in patt as given for back, inc one st at each end of 3rd and every foll 4th row until there are 56 [54:52] sts, then each end of every 6th row until there are 60 [66:72] sts. Cont without shaping until sleeve measures 22 [25:28]cm/ 8¾ [9¾:11]in from beg, ending with a Ws row. Cast off loosely.

Neckband
Join shoulder seams.
With Rs of work facing, 3mm/No 11 needles and one strand of A, sl the first 8 sts from right front holder on to needle, rejoin yarn and pick up and K19 [20:21] sts up right front neck, then 5 sts down right back neck, K across back neck sts inc one st in centre, pick up and K5 sts up left back neck and 19 [20:21] sts down left front neck, then rib 8 sts from holder for left front band. 77 [81:85] sts.
Work 2cm/¾in in rib as given for back. Cast off in rib.

Cat's face
With 5.00mm/No 6 crochet hook and 2 strands of B, make 4ch. Join with a ss to first ch to form ring.
1st round 2ch, work 6dc into ring. Join with a ss to 2nd of 2ch. 7dc.
2nd round 2ch, 1dc into st at base of 2ch, 2dc into each dc to end. Join with a ss to 2nd of 2ch. 14dc.
3rd round 2ch to count as first dc, 2dc into next dc, *1dc into next dc, 2dc into next dc, rep from * to end. Join with a ss to 2nd of 2ch. 21dc.
4th round 2ch to count as first dc, 1dc into next dc, 2dc into next dc, *1dc into each of next 2dc, 2dc into next dc, rep from * to end. Join with a ss to 2nd of 2ch. 28dc.
Cont to inc 7dc in every round in this way, working one more dc between each inc for a further 4 rounds. 56dc. Fasten off.

Ears
With 5.00mm/No 6 hook and 2 strands of B, make 10ch.
1st row Work 1dc into 3rd ch from hook, 1dc into each ch to end. 9dc

Work in rows of dc for about 7cm/2¾in or until the work forms a square. Fasten off.
Make second ear in the same way.

To make up
Sew in sleeves. Join side and sleeve seams. Stitch down pocket linings. Sew on buttons. Fold ears as shown in diagram and join the two corners. Stitch into place as shown. Make whiskers from length of contrast yarn, about 14cm/5½in long, and stitch to face with the same yarn to make nose. Attach eyes. Stitch face to left pocket.

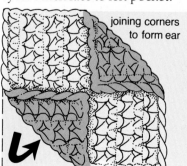

joining corners to form ear

Children's jerseys with animal motifs

The elephant and bear motifs are seen from the front on the fronts of the jerseys and from the back on the backs – complete with elephant's tail. The teddy is knitted in a fluffy yarn to make him appear furry and details such as the rain, trees and birds are added in Swiss darning.

Sizes

To fit 61 [66:71]cm/24 [26:28]in chest
Length to shoulder, 42 [45:48]cm/ 16½ [17¾:19]in
Sleeve seam, 30 [33:36]cm/ 11¾ [13:14¼]in
The figures in [] refer to the 66/26 and 71cm/28in sizes respectively

You will need

Elephant motif jersey 3[4:4]×50g balls of Hayfield Grampian DK (45% acrylic, 40% super crimp Bri-nylon, 15% wool) in main colour A
1 [1:2] balls of same in contrast colour B
1 ball of same in contrast colour C for elephant
Teddy motif jersey 2 [3:3]×50g balls of Hayfield Grampian DK in main colour A
1 [2:2] balls of same in contrast colour B
Oddments of yarn to embroider details, if required

1×50g ball Hayfield Encore (80% acrylic, 15% nylon, 5% wool) in contrast colour C for teddy
One pair 3mm/No 11 needles
One pair 3¾mm/No 9 needles

Tension

24 sts and 32 rows to 10cm/4in over st st worked on 3¾mm/No 9 needles

Note

Use small separate balls of yarn for each part of the motifs, twisting each colour round the next to avoid leaving a hole between the blocks of colour.

Left: The teddy bear and elephant motifs are knitted into these simple round-necked jerseys. To add to their appeal, you can embroider extra details on afterwards.

Elephant jersey back

With 3mm/No 11 needles and A cast on 78 [86:90] sts.

1st row (Rs) K2, *P2, K2, rep from * to end.

2nd row P2, *K2, P2, rep from * to end.

Rep these 2 rows for 5cm/2in, ending with a 2nd row and inc one st at each end of last row on 1st and 3rd sizes only. 80 [86:92] sts.
Change to 3¾mm/No 9 needles.
Break off A. Join in B.
Beg with a K row work in st st for 3 [5:7]cm/1¼ [2:2¾]in, ending with a P row.**

Next row (position elephant) K26 [29:32] B, 6 C, 4 B, 6 C, 38 [41:44] B.
Next row P38 [41:44] B, 6 C, 4 B, 6 C, 26 [29:32] B.

Cont in patt from chart as now set, beginning with 3rd row and noting that the chart shows the front view so to reverse it for the back, read K rows from left to right and P rows from right to left, omitting the end of the trunk.
When the 57 rows of the chart have been completed, cont in A only until work measures 33 [35:37]cm/13 [13¾:14½]in from beg, ending with a P row.

Next row (position cloud) K57 [60:63] A, 6 B, 17 [20:23] A.
Next row P15 [18:21] A, 10 B, 55 [58:61] A.

Cont working cloud from chart as now set for another 10 rows.
Next row (position 2nd cloud) K16 [19:22] A, 6 B, 34 A, 4 B, 1 A, 7 B, 12 [15:18] A.
Cont as now set until both clouds have been completed.
Cont in A until work measures 42 [45:48]cm/16½ [17¾:19]in from beg, ending with a P row.

Shape shoulders

Next row Cast off 25 [27:29] sts for shoulder, K30 [32:34] sts for back neck, cast off rem 25 [27:29] sts for 2nd shoulder.
Sl rem sts on holder.

Elephant jersey front

Work as given for back to **.
Next row (position elephant) K38

[41:44] A, 6 C, 4 B, 6 C, 26 [29:32] B.
Cont in patt from chart as now set, reading K rows from right to left and P rows from left to right, then cont in A only until work measures 33 [35:37]cm/13 [13¾:14½]in from beg, ending with a P row.
Next row (position cloud) K17 [20:23] A, 6 B, 57 [60:63] A.
Work a further 11 rows as now set for first cloud.
Next row (position 2nd cloud) K16 [19:22] A, 4 B, 1 A, 7 B, 34 A, 6 B, 12 [15:18] A.
Cont in patt as now set until work measures 12 [14:16] rows less than back to shoulders, ending with a P row.

Shape neck

Next row K34 [36:38] sts, turn and leave rem sts on holder.
Complete left shoulder first.
Cast off at neck edge on next and every foll alt row 3 sts once, 2 sts

twice and one st twice. 25 [27:29] sts.
Work 2 [4:6] rows without shaping.
Cast off.
With Rs of work facing, leave first 12 [14:16] sts on holder for centre front neck, rejoin yarn to rem sts for right shoulder, cast off 3 sts at neck edge, then complete to match left shoulder, reversing all shapings and keeping patt correct.

Elephant jersey sleeves

With 3mm/No 11 needles and A cast on 34 [34:38] sts. Work 5cm/2in in rib as given for back, ending with a 2nd row and inc one st at each end of last row on 2nd size only. 34 [36:38] sts.
Change to 3¾mm/No 9 needles.
Beg with a K row cont in st st inc one st at each end of first and every foll 4th row until there are 72 [76:80] sts, then cont without shaping until sleeve measures 30 [33:36]cm/11¾ [13:14¼]in from

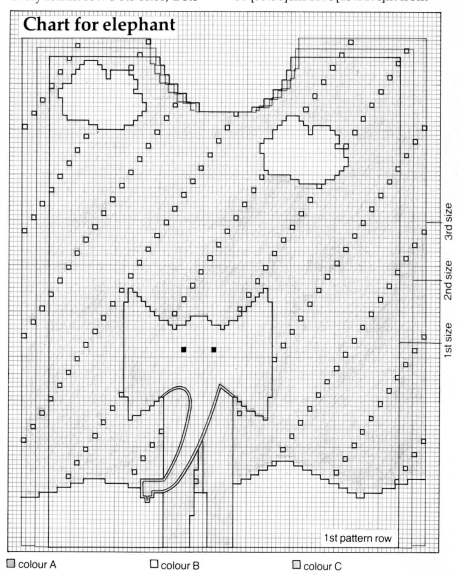

Chart for elephant

3rd size

2nd size

1st size

1st pattern row

☐ colour A   ☐ colour B   ☐ colour C

115

Chart for sleeve

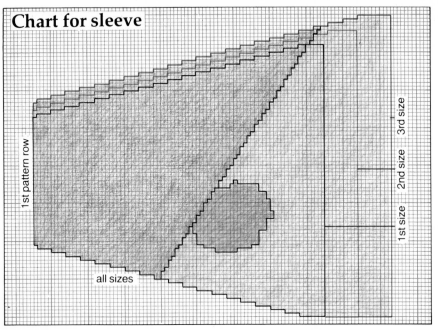

1st pattern row

3rd size

2nd size

1st size

all sizes

Chart for bear

3rd size

2nd size

1st size

1st pattern row

Note: Trees, sun, birds and bear's face are Swiss darning.

◼ colour A   ◻ colour B   ◻ colour C   ◼ colour D   ◼ colour E   ◼ colour F

The pattern pieces

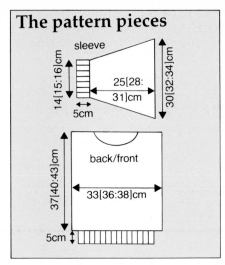

sleeve

14[15:16]cm

25[28:31]cm

30[32:34]cm

5cm

back/front

37[40:43]cm

33[36:38]cm

5cm

beg, or required length to underarm, ending with a P row. Cast off loosely.

Elephant jersey neckband

Join right shoulder seam. With Rs of work facing, 3mm/No 11 needles and A, pick up and K16 [18:20] sts down left front neck, K front neck sts on holder, pick up and K16 [18:20] sts up right front neck and K back neck sts on holder. 74 [82:90] sts. Beg with a 2nd row work 2cm/¾in rib as given for back. Cast off loosely.

Teddy bear jersey back

With 3mm/No 11 needles and A cast on 78 [86:90] sts.
1st row (Rs) K2, *P2, K2, rep from * to end.
2nd row P2, *K2, P2, rep from * to end.
Rep these 2 rows for 5cm/2in, ending with a 2nd row and inc one st at each end of last row on 1st and 3rd sizes only. 80 [86:92] sts.
Change to 3¾mm/No 9 needles.
Beg with a K row work in st st for 0 [2:4]cm/0 [¾:1½]in, ending with a P row.**
Next row (position teddy) K28 [31:34] A, 9 C, 5 A, 9 C, 29 [32:35] A.
Next row P29 [32:35] A, 9 C, 5 A, 9 C, 28 [31:34] A.
Cont in patt from chart as now set, beg with a 3rd row and noting that the chart shows the front view so to reverse it for the back read K rows from left to right and P rows from right to left. When the chart has been completed, cont in B until work measures 42 [45:48]cm/ 16½ [17¾:19]in from beg, ending with a P row.

Shape shoulders
Next row Cast off 25 [27:29] sts for shoulder, K30 [32:34] sts for back neck, cast off rem 25 [27:29] sts for 2nd shoulder.
Sl rem sts on holder.

Teddy bear jersey front
Work as given for back to **
Next row (position teddy) K29 [32:35] A, 9 C, 5 A, 9 C, 28 [31:34] A.
Cont in patt from chart as now set, reading K rows from right to left and P rows from left to right until patt is completed.
Cont in B only until work measures 12 [14:16] rows less than back to shoulders, ending with a P row.

Shape neck
Next row K34 [36:38] sts, turn and leave rem sts on holder.
Complete left shoulder first.
Cast off at neck edge on next and every foll alt row 3 sts once, 2 sts twice and one st twice. 25 [27:29] sts.
Work 2 [4:6] rows without shaping.
Cast off.
With Rs of work facing, leave first 12 [14:16] sts on holder for centre front neck, rejoin yarn to rem sts for right shoulder, cast off 3 sts at neck edge, then complete to match left shoulder, reversing all shapings.

Right: Back view of elephant jersey showing elephant's tail and embroidery detail. Below: Back of teddy jersey.

Teddy bear jersey sleeves
With 3mm/No 11 needles and A cast on 34 [34:38] sts. Work 5cm/2in rib as given for back, ending with a 2nd row and inc one st at each end of last row on 2nd size only.
34 [36:38] sts.
Change to 3¾mm/No 9 needles.
Beg with a K row, work 34 rows in st st, inc one st at each end of first and every foll 4th row.
Cont working in patt from chart until all sts are being worked in B, *at the same time* cont inc one st at each end of every 4th row as before until there are 72 [76:80] sts, then cont without shaping until sleeve measures 30 [33:36]cm/11¾ [13:14¼]in from beg, or required length to underarm, ending with a P row.
Cast off loosely.

Teddy bear jersey neckband
Work as given for elephant jersey neckband.

To make up
Elephant jersey Embroider diagonal lines in B in Swiss darning, spacing the lines 14 sts apart, on back, front and sleeves. Embroider eyes and outline trunk.
Make short length of twisted cord in C for tail and sew on back as in picture.
Teddy bear jersey Embroider trees, sun and birds with Swiss darning as shown. Embroider eyes, nose and mouth.
Both jerseys Press lightly under a dry cloth with a warm iron.
Join left shoulder and neckband.
Sew in sleeves. Join side and sleeve seams.

Chunky jersey and cardigan for children

This thick jersey and cardigan are just right to keep a child warm on a cold winter's day. The jersey has a ribbed polo neck and the cardigan buttons up to a neat shawl collar.
Simple twisted stitches and cable panels are worked on the back and front, with the cable stitch repeated up the sleeves.

Sizes

To fit 56 [61:66:71]cm/22 [24:26:28]in chest
Length to shoulder, 36.5 [39:42.5:47]cm/14½ [15¼:16½:18½]in, adjustable
Sleeve seam, 23 [26.5:30.5:33]cm/9 [10½:12:13]in, adjustable
The figures in [] refer to the 61/24, 66/26 and 71cm/28in sizes respectively

You will need

9 [9:10:11]×50g balls of Wendy Shetland Chunky (100% wool)
One pair 5½mm/No 5 needles
One pair 6½mm/No 3 needles
Cable needle
Five buttons for cardigan

Tension

15 sts and 24 rows to 10cm/4in over st st worked on 6½mm/No 3 needles

Jersey back

With 5½mm/No 5 needles cast on 42 [46:50:54] sts. Work 8 [8:10:10] rows K1, P1 rib.
Next row (inc row) Rib 4 [6:8:10] sts, (inc in next st) twice, rib 8, (inc in next st) twice, rib 10, (inc in next st) twice, rib 8, (inc in next st) twice, rib 4 [6:8:10] sts. 50 [54:58:62] sts.
Change to 6½mm/No 3 needles. Commence patt.
1st row (Ws) P4 [6:8:10] sts, (K1, P4) twice, (K1, P6) 3 times, (K1, P4) twice, K1, P4 [6:8:10] sts.
2nd row K4 [6:8:10] sts, P1, K into front of 2nd st on left-hand needle then into front of first st and sl both sts off needle tog – **called T2F**, K into back of 2nd st on left-hand needle then into front of first st and sl both sts off needle tog – **called T2B**, P1, K4, P1, keep yarn at back and sl next st P-wise – **called sl 1 wyb**, K4, sl 1 wyb, P1, K6, P1, sl 1 wyb, K4, sl 1 wyb, P1, K4, P1, T2F, T2B, P1, K4 [6:8:10] sts.
3rd row K5 [7:9:11] sts, P4, K6, keep yarn at front and sl next st P-wise – **called sl 1 wyf**, P4, sl 1 wyf, K8, sl 1 wyf, P4, sl 1 wyf, K6, P4, K5 [7:9:11] sts.
4th row K4 [6:8:10] sts, P1, T2B, T2F, P1, K4, *P1, keep yarn at back and put next sl st on to cable needle and hold at front of work, K2 from left-hand needle, K1 from cable needle – **called C3F**, keep yarn at back and put next 2 sts on to cable needle and hold at back of work, K next sl st from left-hand needle, K2 from cable needle – **called C3B**, P1*, K6, rep from * to * once more, K4, P1, T2B, T2F, P1, K4 [6:8:10] sts.
These 4 rows form the patt. Cont in patt until work measures 22 [24:26.5:29]cm/8¾ [9½:10½:11½]in, or required length to underarm, ending with a Ws row.

Shape armholes

Cast off 2 sts at beg of next 2 rows. Dec one st at each end of next and foll 0 [1:2:2] alt rows. 44 [46:48:52] sts.
Cont without shaping until armholes measure 14.5 [15:16:18]cm/5¾ [6:6¼:7]in, ending with a Ws row.

Shape shoulders

Cast off at beg of next and every row 5 [6:6:6] sts twice, 6 [6:6:7] sts twice and 22 [22:24:26] sts once.

Jersey front

Work as given for back until armholes measure 8 [9:9.5:9.5]cm/3¼ [3½:3¾:3¾]in from beg, ending with a Ws row.

Shape neck

Next row Patt 17 [18:18:19] sts, turn. Complete left shoulder first. Dec one st beg of next and at same edge on every row until 11 [12:12:13] sts rem. Cont without shaping until armhole measures same as back to shoulder, ending at armhole edge.

Shape shoulder

Cast off at beg of next and foll alt row 5 [6:6:6] sts once and 6 [6:6:7] sts once.
With Rs of work facing, sl first 10 [10:12:14] sts on to holder and leave for centre front neck, rejoin yarn to rem sts and complete to match first side, reversing shapings.

Jersey sleeves

With 5½mm/No 5 needles cast on 28 [30:32:32] sts. Work 10 rows K1, P1 rib.
Next row (inc row) Rib 13 [14:15:15] sts, (inc in next st) twice,

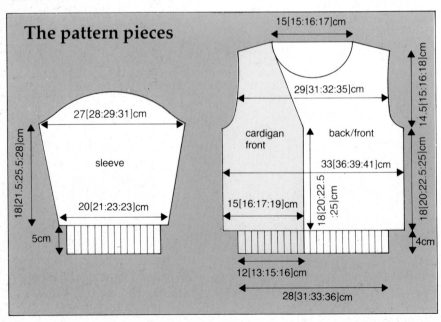

The pattern pieces

27[28:29:31]cm
sleeve
18[21.5:25.5:28]cm
20[21:23:23]cm
5cm

15[15:16:17]cm
29[31:32:35]cm
cardigan front
back/front
14.5[15:16:18]cm
33[36:39:41]cm
18[20:22.5:25]cm
18[20:22.5:25]cm
15[16:17:19]cm
4cm
12[13:15:16]cm
28[31:33:36]cm

Right: Choose either the cardigan or the jersey to make in this quick knitting Shetland chunky wool.

rib to end. 30 [32:34:34] sts.
Change to 6½mm/No 3 needles.
Commence patt.
1st row (Ws) P11 [12:13:13] sts, K1,
P6, K1, P11 [12:13:13] sts.
2nd row K11 [12:13:13] sts, P1, sl 1
wyb, K4, sl 1 wyb, P1, K11
[12:13:13] sts.
3rd row K12 [13:14:14] sts, sl 1 wyf,
P4, sl 1 wyf, K12 [13:14:14] sts.
4th row K11 [12:13:13] sts, P1, C3F,
C3B, P1, K11 [12:13:13] sts.
Cont in patt as now set, inc one st at
each end of next and every foll 6th
row until there are 40 [42:44:46] sts.
Cont without shaping until sleeve
measures 23 [26.5:30.5:33]cm/9
[10½:12:13]in from beg, or required
length to underarm, ending with a
Ws row.

Shape top
Cast off 2 sts at beg of next 2 rows.
Dec one st at each end of next and
foll 0 [1:2:2] alt rows. Work one row.
Cast off 2 sts at beg of next 10
[10:12:12] rows. Cast off rem 14
[14:10:10] sts.

Jersey neckband or polo collar
Join right shoulder seam. With Rs of
work facing and 5½mm/No 5
needles, pick up and K66
[68:72:78] sts evenly round neck
including sts on holder.
Work 7.5cm/3in K1, P1 rib for crew
neck or 9.5 [10:10:11.5]cm/3¾
[4:4:4½]in for polo neck.
Cast off loosely in rib.

Cardigan back
Work as given for jersey back.

Cardigan right front
With 5½mm/No 5 needles cast on
18 [20:22:24] sts. Work 8 [8:10:10]
rows K1, P1 rib.**
Next row (inc row) Rib 2 sts, (inc in
next st) twice, rib 8, (inc in next st)
twice, rib 4 [6:8:10] sts. 22
[24:26:28] sts.
Change to 6½mm/No 3 needles.
Commence patt.
1st row (Ws) P4 [6:8:10] sts, (K1, P4)
twice, K1, P6, K1.
2nd row P1, sl 1 wyb, K4, sl 1 wyb,
P1, K4, P1, T2F, T2B, P1, K4
[6:8:10] sts.
3rd row K5 [7:9:11] sts, P4, K6, sl 1
wyf, P4, sl 1 wyf, K1.
4th row P1, C3F, C3B, P1, K4, P1,
T2B, T2F, P1, K4 [6:8:10] sts.
These 4 rows form the patt. Cont in

Detail of shawl collar showing shaping worked on edge stitched to neck.

patt until work measures same as
back to underarm, ending at side edge.

Shape armhole and front edge
Next row Cast off 2 sts for armhole,
patt to last 2 sts, dec one st for neck
edge.
Cont dec one st at armhole edge on
next and foll 0 [1:2:2] alt rows, *at the
same time* dec one st at front edge on
every 4th row until 11 [12:13:13] sts
rem. Cont without shaping until
armhole measures same as back to
shoulder, ending at armhole edge.

Shape shoulder
Cast off at beg of next and foll alt
row 5 [6:6:6] sts once and 6
[6:6:7] sts once.

Cardigan left front
Work as given for right front to **.
Next row (inc row) Rib 4 [6:8:10] sts,
(inc in next st) twice, rib 8, (inc in
next st) twice, rib 2 sts.
Change to 6½mm/No 3 needles.
Commence patt.
1st row (Ws) K1, P6, K1, (P4, K1)
twice, P4 [6:8:10] sts.
2nd row K4 [6:8:10] sts, P1, T2F,
T2B, P1, K4, P1, sl 1 wyb, K4, sl 1
wyb, P1.
Cont in patt as now set and
complete as given for right front,
reversing all shapings.

Cardigan sleeves
Work as given for jersey sleeves.

Cardigan front band and collar
With 5½mm/No 5 needles cast on
7 sts. Work in g st until band
measures 22 [24:26.5:29]cm/8¾
[9½:10½:11½]in from beg.

Shape collar
Inc one st at beg of next and every
foll 4th row until collar, when
slightly stretched, fits along front
neck shaping edge to shoulder seam.
Cont without shaping for a further
12 [12.5:12.5:13.5)cm/4¾ [5:5:5¼]in
to fit across back neck.
Dec one st at inside edge of collar on
next and every foll 4th row until
7 sts rem, ending at outer edge.
Next row (buttonhole row) K2, cast
off 2 sts, K3.
Next row K to end, casting on 2 sts
above those cast off in previous row.
Cont in g st until band reaches
along other front edge, making 4
more buttonholes at intervals of 4.5
[5:5.5:6]cm/1¾ [2:2¼:2½]in. Cast off.

To make up
Do not press.
Jersey Join left shoulder seam. Join
side and sleeve seams. Set in
sleeves. For crew neck, fold ribbing
to Ws and sl st down. Fold polo
neck to Rs.
Cardigan Sew bands and collar to
front edges with buttonholes on
right front for a girl, or left front for
a boy. Join side and sleeve seams.
Set in sleeves. Sew on buttons.

Zip-up knitted suits

Knit this warm fun suit to keep your toddler warm on cold winter days. The simple zip-up style is perfect for country walks in blustery winds. Children love dressing up so add ears and paws to make a polar bear, or a mane and tail to turn it into a lion. Change of colour and the appropriate features will make other animals.

Sizes
To fit 56 [61]cm/22 [24]in chest
Length to shoulder, 70 [80]cm/
27½ [31½]in
Sleeve seam, 25 [30]cm/9¾ [11¾]in
Inside leg length, 32 [40]cm/
12½ [15¾]in
The figures in [] refer to the 61cm/
24in size only

You will need
Lion suit 18 [19]×50g balls of
  Poppleton's Emmerdale Chunky
  Knitting (45% acrylic, 40% nylon,
  15% wool)
Polar bear suit 16 [17] balls of same
One pair 4½mm/No 7 needles
One pair 5½mm/No 5 needles
30cm/12in zip fastener
Synthetic stuffing for tail
Oddment of felt for ears of lion suit
Teazle brush for polar bear suit
Oddments of felt for paw prints on

Tension
14 sts and 28 rows to 10cm/4in over

121

g st worked on 5½mm/No 5 needles

Body left side
With 4½mm/No 7 needles cast on 19 [21] sts.
1st row (Rs) K1, *P1, K1, rep from * to end.
2nd row P1, *K1, P1, rep from * to end.
Rep these 2 rows for 4cm/1½in, ending with a 1st row.
1st size only
Next row (inc) Working in rib, inc one st in every st. 38 sts.
2nd size only
Next row (inc) Working in rib (inc one st in every st 7 times, pick up loop to M1) twice, (inc one st in every st) 7 times. 44 sts.
Change to 5½mm/No 5 needles.
Cont in g st, shaping sides by inc one st at each end of every 8th [12th] row until there are 54 [58] sts.
Work without shaping until leg measures 32 [40]cm/12½ [15¾]in from beg.

Shape crutch
Cast off 2 sts at beg of next 2 rows.
Dec one st at each end of next 2 rows, then at each end of every alt row until 42 [46] sts rem. Cont without shaping until work measures 60 [69]cm/23½ [27¼]in from beg, ending with a Ws row.

Divide for armhole
Next row K21 [23] sts, turn and leave rem sts on holder.
Cont without shaping until armhole measures 10 [11]cm/4[4¼]in from beg, ending with a Rs row.
Next row Cast off 14 [16] sts, K to end. Leave rem 7 sts on holder.
With Rs of work facing, rejoin yarn to rem 21 [23] sts. Cont without shaping until armhole measures 5 [6]cm/2 [2¼]in from beg, ending with a Rs row.

Shape neck
Next row Cast off 3 sts, K to end.
Keeping armhole edge straight, dec one st at neck edge on every alt row until 14 [16] sts rem.
Cont without shaping until armhole measures 10 [11]cm/4 [4¼]in from beg. Cast off.

Body right side
Work as given for left side, reversing all shaping.

Sleeves
With 4½mm/No 7 needles cast on 15 [17] sts. Work 4cm/1½in rib as given for body, ending with a 1st row.
Next row (inc) (Rib 2 [3] sts, M1) twice, (rib 3 sts, M1) twice, rib 2 [3] sts, M1, rib to end. 20 [22] sts.
Change to 5½mm/No 5 needles.
Cont in g st, inc one st at each end of every 10th row until there are 28 [32] sts.
Cont without shaping until sleeve measures 25 [30]cm/9¾ [11¾]in from beg. Cast off.

Lion hood and ears
**Join centre back seam of body and shoulders.
With Rs of work facing and 4½mm/No 7 needles, pick up and K14 sts up right front neck to shoulder, K across back neck sts on holders inc one st in centre, pick up and K14 sts down left side of neck. 43 sts.
Work 6 rows rib as given for body. **
Next row (inc) Rib 4 [5] sts, (M1, rib 5 [3] sts) 7 [11] times, M1, rib 4 [5] sts. 51 [55] sts.
Change to 5½mm/No 5 needles.
Commence loop patt.
1st row (Rs) *K1, make loop by K next st but do not drop off needle, yfwd and make loop round thumb approx 6cm/2¼in long, ybk, K same st again, slip these 2 sts back on to left-hand needle and K2 tog tbl – **called ML** –, rep from * to last st, K1.
2nd and 4th rows K to end.
3rd row K2, *ML, K1, rep from * to last st, K1.
These 4 rows form loop patt. Rep 1st and 2nd rows once more.

Shape front
Keeping patt correct, cast off 6 sts at beg of next 2 rows. 39 [43] sts.
Cont in patt without shaping, gradually dec length of loops, until work measures 12 [14]cm/4¾ [5½]in from cast off edge.

Shape top
Cast off 13 [14] sts at beg of next 2 rows. 13 [15] sts rem.
Cont without shaping until strip reaches across cast off edge to front edge, ending with a Ws row.

Break off yarn, leave rem sts on holder. Join top seams.

Front border
With Rs facing and 4½mm/No 7 needles, beg with 6 cast off sts pick up and K28 [30] sts up right side of hood, K across sts on holder, pick up and K28 [30] sts down left side of hood, ending with 6 cast off sts. 69 [75] sts.
Work 5 rows K1, P1 rib as given for body. Cast off in rib.
Cut ears from felt and sew to hood as illustrated.

Lion tail
With 5½mm/No 5 needles cast on 15 sts. Work 46 [56]cm/18 [22]in g st.
Next row (inc) K1, *M1, K1, rep from * to end. 29 sts.
Work 13 rows loop patt as given for lion hood.

Shape end
Next row K1, *K2 tog, rep from * to end. 15 sts.
Next row K to end.
Next row K1, *K2 tog, rep from * to end. 8 sts.
Break off yarn, thread through rem sts, draw up and fasten off.
Join seam. Stuff lightly.

Polar bear hood and ears
Work as given for lion hood from ** to **.
Next row (inc) Rib 3, (M1, rib 2 [1] sts) 8 times, (M1, rib 1 [2] sts) 8 [12] times, (M1, rib 2 [1] sts) 8 times. 67 [71] sts.
Change to 5½mm/No 5 needles.
Work 8 rows g st.

Below: Back view of animal suits.

Shape front

Cast off 8 sts at beg of next 2 rows. 51 [55] sts.
Cont without shaping until work measures 12 [14]cm/4¾ [5½]in from cast off edge.

Shape top

Cast off 17 [18] sts at beg of next 2 rows. 17 [19] sts rem.
Cont without shaping until strip reaches across cast off edge to front edge. Complete as given for lion hood noting that there are 4 more sts on holder.

Ears

With 5½mm/No 5 needles cast on 8 sts.
Work 6 rows g st.

Shape top

Next row Sl 1, K1, psso, K to last 2 sts, K2 tog.
Next row K to end.
Rep last 2 rows once more.
Next row Sl 1, K1, psso, K2 tog.
Next row P2 tog. Fasten off.
Sew ears to hood as illustrated,

Trace patterns

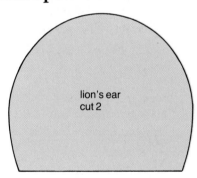

lion's ear
cut 2

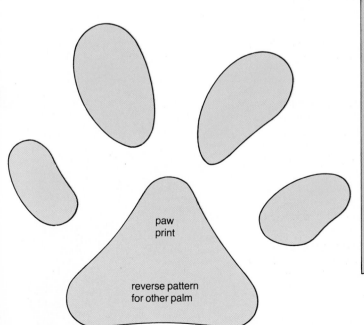

paw
print

reverse pattern
for other palm

pleating at centre and gathering outside edge slightly to form a curve.

Polar bear tail

With 5½mm/No 5 needles cast on 15 sts.
Work 6 rows g st. Inc one st at each end of next and foll 6th rows twice. 21 sts. Cont without shaping until tail measures 9cm/3½in from beg.

Shape end

Next row K1, *sl 1, K1, psso, K5, K2 tog, K1, rep from * once more.
Next row K to end.
Next row K1, *sl 1, K1, psso, K3, K2 tog, K1, rep from * once more.
Next row K to end.
Next row K1, *sl 1, K1, psso, K1, K2 tog, K1, rep from * once more.
Cast off rem sts. Join seams. Stuff lightly.

Right mitten

**With 4½mm/No 7 needles cast on 19 [21] sts. Work 5cm/2in rib as given for body, ending with a 1st row.
Next row (inc) Rib 3 [4] sts, (M1, rib 2) 7 times, M1, rib to end. 27 [29] sts. Change to 5½mm/No 5 needles. **

Lion mitten

1st row (K1, ML) 6 [7] times, K to end.
2nd and 4th rows K to end.
3rd row K2, (ML, K1) 6 [7] times, K to end.
Rep these 4 rows until work measures 11 [12]cm/4¼ [4¾]in from beg, ending with a Ws row.

Polar bear mitten

Cont in g st until work measures 11 [12]cm/4¼ [4¾]in from beg, ending with a Ws row.

Shape top (both versions)

Next row K1, (sl 1, K1, psso, patt 8 [9] sts, K2 tog, K1) twice.
Next and every alt row K to end.
Next row K1, (sl 1, K1, psso, patt 6 [7] sts, K2 tog, K1) twice.
Next row K1, (sl 1, K1, psso, patt 4 [5] sts, K2 tog, K1) twice.
Cast off.

Left mitten

Work as given for right mitten from ** to **.

Lion mitten

1st row K15, *ML, K1, rep from * to end.
2nd and 4th rows K to end.
3rd row K14, *ML, K1, rep from * to last st, K1.
Complete as given for right mitten.

Polar bear mitten

Complete as given for right mitten.

To make up

Do not press.
Lion and polar bear suits Join front seam leaving 30cm/11¾in open for zip. Sew in zip to come to top of front border on hood. Join inside leg seams. Set in sleeves. Join sleeve seams. Sew in tail.
Brush polar bear suit lightly with teazle.
Mittens Join side seam. Cut paw prints from felt, see diagram, and sew to palm of mitten.

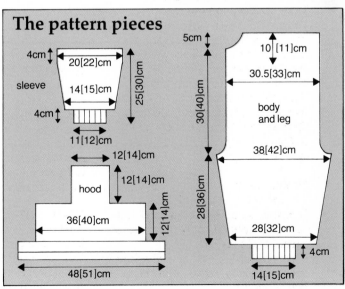

The pattern pieces

sleeve
4cm
20[22]cm
14[15]cm
25[30]cm
4cm
11[12]cm

hood
12[14]cm
12[14]cm
36[40]cm
12[14]cm
48[51]cm

5cm
10 [11]cm
30.5[33]cm
body and leg
38[42]cm
30[40]cm
28[36]cm
28[32]cm
14[15]cm
4cm

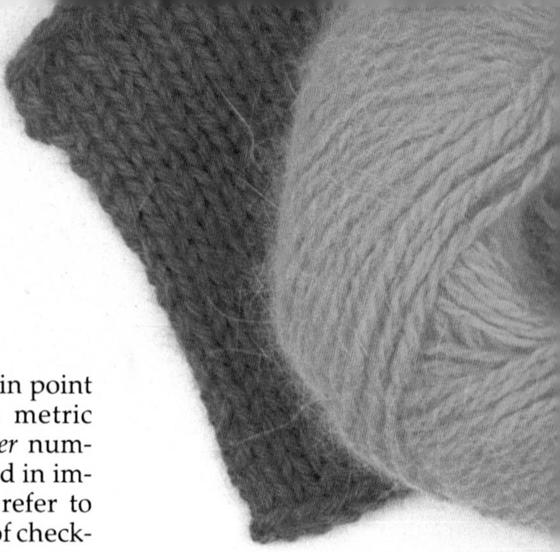

Metric and imperial measurements

You may have an old pattern which you would like to knit up but are unsure how much yarn or what needle size you should use. The yarn conversion chart below shows the number of 25g balls you should buy in place of ounces. (Note that many yarns are also packed in 50g balls.)

Knitting needles and crochet hooks are now sold in millimetre widths, see the chart below. The main point to remember is that with metric hooks and needles the *higher* numbers refer to coarser sizes and in imperial sizes *lower* numbers refer to coarser sizes. A handy way of checking the size of old needles is to use a needle gauge – an inexpensive gadget particularly useful for double-pointed needles that don't have the size stamped on them.

Converting needle sizes

Metric	Imperial
2mm	14
2¼mm	13
2½mm	—
2¾mm	12
3mm	11
3¼mm	10
3½mm	—
3¾mm	9
4mm	8
4½mm	7
5mm	6
5½mm	5
6mm	4
6½mm	3
7mm	2
7½mm	1
8mm	0
9mm	00
10mm	000

Converting ounces to grammes

oz balls	25g balls
1	1
2	3
3	4
4	5
5	6
6	7
7	8
8	9
9	10
10	12
11	13
12	14
13	15
14	16
15	17
16	18
17	19
18	21
19	22
20	23

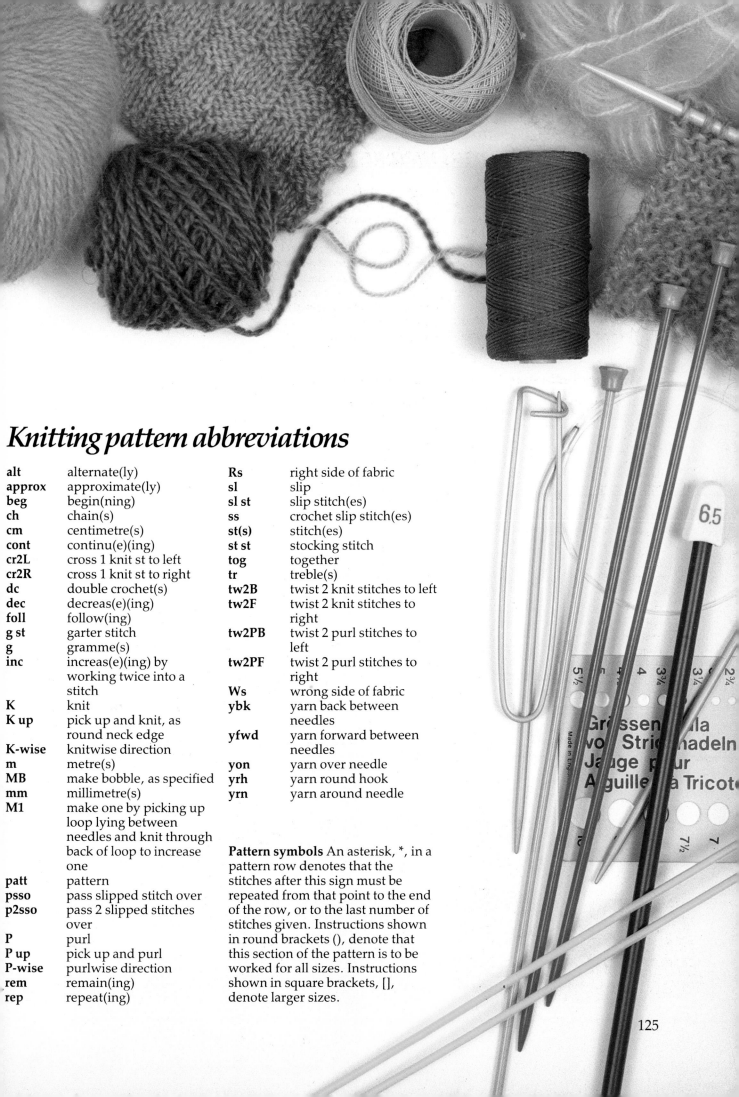

Knitting pattern abbreviations

alt	alternate(ly)		**Rs**	right side of fabric
approx	approximate(ly)		**sl**	slip
beg	begin(ning)		**sl st**	slip stitch(es)
ch	chain(s)		**ss**	crochet slip stitch(es)
cm	centimetre(s)		**st(s)**	stitch(es)
cont	continu(e)(ing)		**st st**	stocking stitch
cr2L	cross 1 knit st to left		**tog**	together
cr2R	cross 1 knit st to right		**tr**	treble(s)
dc	double crochet(s)		**tw2B**	twist 2 knit stitches to left
dec	decreas(e)(ing)		**tw2F**	twist 2 knit stitches to right
foll	follow(ing)			
g st	garter stitch		**tw2PB**	twist 2 purl stitches to left
g	gramme(s)			
inc	increas(e)(ing) by working twice into a stitch		**tw2PF**	twist 2 purl stitches to right
			Ws	wrong side of fabric
K	knit		**ybk**	yarn back between needles
K up	pick up and knit, as round neck edge			
			yfwd	yarn forward between needles
K-wise	knitwise direction			
m	metre(s)		**yon**	yarn over needle
MB	make bobble, as specified		**yrh**	yarn round hook
mm	millimetre(s)		**yrn**	yarn around needle
M1	make one by picking up loop lying between needles and knit through back of loop to increase one			
patt	pattern			
psso	pass slipped stitch over			
p2sso	pass 2 slipped stitches over			
P	purl			
P up	pick up and purl			
P-wise	purlwise direction			
rem	remain(ing)			
rep	repeat(ing)			

Pattern symbols An asterisk, *, in a pattern row denotes that the stitches after this sign must be repeated from that point to the end of the row, or to the last number of stitches given. Instructions shown in round brackets (), denote that this section of the pattern is to be worked for all sizes. Instructions shown in square brackets, [], denote larger sizes.

125

Choosing the right yarn

Every effort has been made to ensure that the colours and qualities shown in the knitting patterns are available at the time of publication. However, the spinners (yarn manufacturers) introduce new ranges each year and reserve the right to withdraw colours in each range, or a complete range, at any time entirely at their discretion. They assess each range at regular intervals and change the yarns according to fashions and sales.

When possible, it is wise to use the yarn recommended for each design featured in this book but do remember that many of the yarns are probably unique and will not be interchangeable without adjusting the pattern.

If you have difficulty in obtaining the correct yarn, contact the spinner at the address shown below or use the mail order address if there is one given. The yarns used in this book are given alphabetically under each spinner together with the manufacturer's recommended tension and aftercare advice. If the recommended yarn is unobtainable, make a note of the number of stitches and rows to a 10cm/4in square and look for another yarn with the same tension. If a yarn is near to this size, you could use a coarser or finer needle to achieve the required tension, check by knitting a tension square. Remember also, that if you substitute one yarn for another, the texture may not be the same as the original and the quantities and aftercare may vary.

Yarn data

Anny Blatt (UK) Ltd
UK: 1-3 Mortimer Street, London W1.
Angor'Anny (p 55)
Recommended tension 28 sts and 42 rows to 10cm/4in over st st worked on 3¾mm/No 9 needles.
Aftercare Hand or machine wash (30°C), do not iron, dry clean Ⓐ.

Kid Anny (p 55)
Recommended tension 16 sts and 20 rows to 10cm/4in over st st worked on 5mm/No 6 needles.
Aftercare Hand or machine wash (30°C), do not iron, dry clean Ⓕ.

Soft 'Anny Mohair Kid (p 112)
Recommended tension 20 sts and 30 rows to 10cm/4in over st st worked on 3¾mm/No 9 needles.
Aftercare Hand or machine wash (30°C), dry clean Ⓕ, do not bleach or press.

Argyll Wools Ltd
UK: PO Box 15, Priestley Mills, Pudsey, West Yorkshire LS28 9LT.

Ferndale Chunky (p 23)
Recommended tension 15 sts and 22 rows to 10cm/4in over st st worked on 5½mm/No 5 needles.
Aftercare Hand or machine wash (6), do not iron.

Starlite Double Knitting (p 19)
Recommended tension 22 sts and 30 rows to 10cm/4in over st st worked on 4mm/No 8 needles.
Aftercare Machine wash (6), do not iron or bleach.

Chat Botte
UK: Groves of Thame Ltd., Lupton Road, Industrial Estate, Thame, Oxfordshire, OX9 3PR.

Kid Mohair (p 69)
Recommended tension 24 sts and 34 rows to 10cm/4in over st st worked on 3mm/No 11 needles.
Aftercare Hand or machine wash (35°C), dry clean Ⓕ, do not iron or bleach.

D.M.C.
UK: Dunlicraft Ltd., Pullman Road, Wigston, Leicestershire LE8 2DY.
Mail order: The Needlewoman of Chingford, 15 Station Road, London E4.
Australia: Olivier (Australia) PTY Ltd., 47-57 Collins Street, Alexandria, New South Wales 2015, Australia.

Pearl Coton No 4 (p 8)
Recommended tension 26 sts and 34 rows to 10cm/4in over st st worked on 3¼mm/No 10 needles.
Aftercare Warm hand wash, cold rinse, dry flat, dry clean Ⓐ, warm iron under a damp cloth.

Emu Wools
UK: Leeds Road, Greengate, Bradford, West Yorkshire.

Treasure 3 ply (p 106)
Recommended tension 30 sts and 46 rows to 10cm/4in over st st worked on 3mm/No 11 needles.
Aftercare Hand or machine wash (40°C), dry clean Ⓟ, cool iron.

Hayfield
UK: Hayfield Textiles Ltd., Hayfield Mills, Glusburn, Keighley, West Yorkshire BD20 8QP.
Australia: Mr J Birch, E C Birch PTY Ltd., 153 Bridge Road, Richmond 3121, Victoria, Australia.

Grampian Double Knitting (p 114)
Recommended tension 24 sts and 32 rows to 10cm/4in over st st worked on 3¾mm/No 9 needles.

Aftercare Hand or machine wash (40°C), cool iron.

Jaeger
UK: Jaeger Hand Knitting Ltd., Alloa FK10 1EG, Clackmannanshire, Scotland.
Mail order: Woolfayre, 120 High Street, Northallerton, Yorkshire.
Australia: Coats Patons (Australia) Ltd., 321-355 Ferntree Gulley Road, PO Box 110, Mount Waverley, Victoria 3149, Australia.

Alpaca (p 66)
Recommended tension 28 sts and 36 rows to 10cm/4in over st st worked on 3mm/No 11 needles.
Aftercare Hand wash, dry clean Ⓐ, warm iron, do not bleach.

Mohair Spun (p 25)
Recommended tension 16 sts and 21 rows to 10cm/4in over st st worked on 5½mm/No 5 needles.
Aftercare Hand wash only, dry clean Ⓐ, do not iron or bleach.

Lister-Lee
UK: George Lee & Sons Ltd., Whiteoak Mills, PO Box 37, Wakefield WF2 9SF, Yorkshire.
Australia: M J Shaw & Co, 248 la Perouse 3, Red Hill, ACP 2603, Australia.

Nursery Time Double Knitting (p 102)
Recommended tension 22 sts and 28 rows to 10cm/4in st st worked on 4mm/No 8 needles.
Aftercare Dry clean, hand wash or machine wash (40°C), medium iron, do not bleach.

Thermoknit for Aran (p 39)
Recommended tension 18 sts and 22 rows to 10cm/4in over st st worked on 5mm/No 6 needles.

Aftercare Hand wash (40°C) or machine wash (6), do not dry clean, bleach or iron.

Neveda Hand Knitting Yarns

UK: Smallwares Ltd., 17 Galena Road, King Street, Hammersmith, London W6 0LU.
Mail order: The Yarn Barn, 144A King Street, Hammersmith, London W6 0QU.

Bistro (p80)
Recommended tension 15 sts to 10cm/4in over st st worked on 4½mm/No 7 needles.
Aftercare Hand wash only, dry clean Ⓟ, do not iron.

Patons and Baldwins Ltd

UK: Alloa FK10 1EG, Clackmannanshire, Scotland.
Mail order: Woolfayre, 120 High Street, Northallerton, Yorkshire.
Australia: Coats Patons (Australia) Ltd., 321-355 Ferntree Gulley Road, PO Box 110, Mount Waverley, Victoria, 3149, Australia.

Clansman 4 ply (p77)
Recommended tension 28 sts and 36 rows to 10cm/4in over st st worked on 3¼mm/No 10 needles.
Aftercare Hand wash (40°C), machine wash (5), dry clean Ⓐ, warm iron, do not bleach.

Fairytale with Lambswool 4 ply (p98)
Fairytale 4 ply Courtelle/Bri-nylon (p98)

Recommended tension 28 sts and 36 rows to 10cm/4in over st st worked on 3¼mm/No 10 needles.
Aftercare Hand wash (40°C), machine wash (7), dry clean Ⓐ.

Fairytale 3 ply Courtelle/Bri-nylon (p98)
Recommended tension 32 sts and 40 rows to 10cm/4in over st st worked on 3mm/No 11 needles.
Aftercare Hand wash (40°C), machine wash (7), dry clean Ⓐ.

Promise (p110)
Recommended tension 19 sts and 25 rows to 10cm/4in over st st worked on 5mm/No 6 needles.
Aftercare Hand wash only, dry clean Ⓐ, do not iron or bleach.

Shetland Chunky (p79)
Recommended tension 15 sts and 20 rows to 10cm/4in over st st worked on 6mm/No 4 needles.
Aftercare Handwash (40°C), machine wash (7), dry clean Ⓐ, do not bleach or iron.

Phildar (UK) Ltd

UK: 4 Gambrel Road, Westgate Industrial Estate, Northamptonshire.
Mail order: Ries Wools, 243 High Holborn, London WC1.

Anouchka (p100)
Recommended tension 27 sts and 38 rows to 10cm/4in over st st worked on 2¼mm/No 13 needles.
Aftercare Hand or machine wash (30°C) dry clean Ⓐ, cool iron, do not bleach.

Kadischa (p36)
Recommended tension 13 sts and 19 rows to 10cm/4in over st st worked on 6mm/No 4 needles.
Aftercare Hand and machine wash (30°C), dry clean Ⓐ, warm iron, do not bleach.

Luxe (p53)
Recommended tension 30 sts and 40 rows to 10cm/4in over st st worked on 2¼mm/No 13 needles.
Aftercare Hand or machine wash (40°C), dry clean Ⓐ, do not bleach.

Pingouin

UK: French Wools (Pingouin) Ltd., 7-11 Lexington Street, London W1R 4BU.

Confort (p104)
Recommended tension 23 sts and 28 rows to 10cm/4in over st st worked on 3¾mm/No 9 needles.
Aftercare Hand or machine wash (40°C), dry clean Ⓐ, warm iron, do not bleach.

Corrida No 3 (p82)
Recommended tension 28 sts and 36 rows to 10cm/4in over st st worked on 3mm/No 11 needles.
Aftercare Hand or machine wash (30°C), cool iron.

Poudreuse (p31)
Recommended tension 21 sts and 27 rows to 10cm/4in over st st worked on 4mm/No 8 needles.
Aftercare Hand or machine wash (40°C), dry clean Ⓐ, do not iron or bleach.

Standard aftercare symbols

A tub indicates that the yarn can be hand or machine washed.

A hand in the tub means hand wash only.

A figure in the water shows the correct water temperature.
Numbers 1 to 9 above the water line denote washing machine programmes.

Where the tub is crossed through, dry-clean only.

An iron means the yarn can be pressed – one dot means cool; two dots medium and three dots hot.

Where the iron is crossed through do not attempt to press the yarn or you may ruin the fabric.

An empty circle means the yarn can be dry-cleaned.

An A inside the circle means dry-cleaning in all solvents.

The letter P means dry-cleaning only in certain solvents.

The letter F means dry-cleaning only in certain solvents.

Where the circle is crossed through do *not* dry-clean.

A triangle means that the yarn can be bleached.

Where the triangle is crossed through do not bleach.

Square signs denote drying instructions.

Three vertical lines in a square means drip dry.

One horizontal line in a square means dry flat.

A circle in a square means tumble dry.

A loop at the top of a square means dry on a line.

Poppleton

UK: Richard Poppleton and Sons Ltd., Albert Mills, Horbury, Wakefield, West Yorkshire WF4 5NJ.

Emmerdale Chunky Knitting (p121)
Recommended tension 17 sts and 20 rows to 10cm/4in over st st worked on 5½mm/No 5 needles.
Aftercare Hand or machine wash, dry cool press.

Robin Wools Ltd

UK: Robin Mills, Idle, Bradford, West Yorkshire.
Australia: Mrs Rosemary Mallet, The Needlewoman, Karingal, Grove, Huon, Tasmania 3066, Australia.

Bunny Brushed Double Knitting (p108)
Recommended tension 24 sts and 28 rows to 10cm/4in over st st worked on 4mm/No 8 needles.
Aftercare Hand or machine wash.

Reward Double Knitting (p59)
Recommended tension 22 sts and 30 rows to 10cm/4in over st st worked on 4mm/No 8 needles.
Aftercare Hand or machine wash (40°C), dry clean Ⓟ, cool iron.

Scheepjeswol

UK: Aero Needles Group Plc (Scheepjeswol), Box 2, Edward Street, Redditch, Worcestershire.

Voluma (p61)
Recommended tension 22 sts and 29 rows to 10cm/4in over st st worked on 4mm/No 8 needles.
Aftercare Hand or machine wash (30°C), dry clean Ⓐ, do not iron.

Sirdar Ltd

UK: Flanshaw Lane, Alverthorpe, Wakefield, Yorkshire WF2 9ND.
Mail order: The Best Woolshop, 26-28 Frenchgate, Doncaster, South Yorkshire.

Country Style Double Knitting (p71)
Recommended tension 24 sts and 30 rows to 10cm/4in over st st worked on 3¾mm/No 9 needles.
Aftercare Hand wash (40°C), dry clean, medium iron.

Majestic 4 ply (p17)
Recommended tension 28 sts and 36 rows to 10cm/4in over st st worked on 3¼mm/No 10 needles.

Aftercare Handwash (40°C), machine wash (7), dry clean Ⓐ, hot iron, do not bleach.

Nocturn (p26)
Recommended tension 16 sts and 22 rows to 10cm/4in over st st worked on 5½mm/No 5 needles.
Aftercare Hand wash only, dry clean Ⓐ, warm iron under a damp cloth, do not bleach.

Pullman Chunky (p11)
Recommended tension 14 sts and 19 rows to 10cm/4in over st st worked on 6½mm/No 3 needles.
Aftercare Hand wash or dry clean, hot iron.

Wash 'n' Wear Double Crêpe (p29)
Recommended tension 24 sts and 30 rows to 10cm/4in over st st worked on 4mm/No 8 needles.
Aftercare Hand or machine wash (40°C), dry clean Ⓐ, warm iron under a dry cloth.

3 Suisses

UK: Filature de l'Espierres, Marlborough House, 38 Welford Road, Leicester LE2 7AA.

Suizetta 4 ply (p45)
Recommended tension 26 sts and 40 rows to 10cm/4in over st st worked on 2¾mm/No 12 needles.
Aftercare Hand wash (40°C), machine wash (7), dry clean Ⓟ, do not iron or bleach.

Sunbeam

UK: Richard Ingham & Co. Ltd., Crawshaw Mills, Pudsey, Yorkshire.
Mail order: Woolfayre, 120 High Street, Northallerton, Yorkshire.

Aran Knit and Aran Tweed (p73)
Recommended tension 20 sts and 28 rows to 10cm/4in over st st worked on 4½mm/No 7 needles.
Aftercare Hand wash (30°C).

Mohair (p51)
Recommended tension 16 sts and 21 rows to 10cm/4in over st st worked on 5½mm/No 5 needles.
Aftercare Hand wash, dry clean Ⓐ, cool iron, do not bleach.

Sceptre Double Double Knitting (p35)
Recommended tension 16 sts and 20 rows to 10cm/4in over st st worked on 5½mm/No 5 needles.
Aftercare Hand or machine wash (40°C), cold rinse, short spin, dry flat. Dry clean Ⓟ, cool iron, do not bleach.

Twilleys

UK: H G Twilley Ltd., Roman Mill, Stamford, Lincoln PE9 1BG.
Mail order: Ries Wools, 243 High Holborn, London WC1.
Australia: Panda Yarn, 17-27 Brunswick Road, East Brunswick, 3057 Victoria.

Capricorn (p42)
Recommended tension 14 sts and 17 rows to 10cm/4in over st st worked on 6mm/No 4 needles.
Aftercare Hand wash only, dry clean Ⓟ.

Minx (p42)
Recommended tension 10 sts to 10cm/4in over st st worked on 9mm/No 00 needles.
Aftercare Hand wash only, dry clean Ⓟ.

Stalite (p13)
Recommended tension 28 sts and 36 rows to 10cm/4in over st st worked on 3¼mm/No 10 needles.
Aftercare Warm hand wash, cold rinse, dry flat away from sun, dry clean Ⓐ, warm iron under a damp cloth.

Wendy

UK: Carter and Parker Ltd., Gordon Mills, Guiseley, West Yorkshire.
Australia: Cruft Warehouse, 30 Guess Avenue, Arncliff, New South Wales, 2205, Australia.

Capri (p64)
Recommended tension 20 sts and 29 rows to 10cm/4in over st st worked on 4½mm/No 7 needles.
Aftercare Hand or machine wash (40°C), can be dry cleaned, dry press.

Peter Pan Darling 3 ply (pp85-97)
Recommended tension 34 sts and 42 rows to 10cm/4in over st st worked on 3mm/No 11 needles.
Aftercare Hand wash (40°C), machine wash (6), cool iron under a dry cloth.

Shetland 4 ply (p47)
Recommended tension 28 sts and 36 rows to 10cm/4in over st st worked on 3¼mm/No 10 needles.
Aftercare Hand wash (30°C), dry clean Ⓟ, warm iron.

Shetland Chunky (p118)
Recommended tension 14 sts and 20 rows to 10cm/4in over st st worked on 6½mm/No 3 needles.
Aftercare Hand wash (40°C), machine wash (7), dry clean Ⓟ, warm iron.